Early Hispanic Colorado
1678-1900

by Joseph P. Sánchez

Published by Río Grande Books
925 Salamanca NW, Los Ranchos, NM 87107-5647
505-344-9382 www.LPDPress.com

Printed in the United States of America
Book Design: Paul Rhetts

Library of Congress Cataloging-in-Publication Data

Sánchez, Joseph P., author.
 Early Hispanic Colorado, 1678-1900 / by Joseph P. Sánchez.
   pages cm
 Includes bibliographical references and index.
 ISBN 978-1-943681-00-6 (pbk. : alk. paper)
  1. Hispanic Americans--Colorado--History. 2. Colorado--
History--To 1876. 3. Hispanic American pioneers--Colorado--
History. I. Title.
 F785.S75S63 2015
 305.868'0730788--dc23
                                   2015023568

Cover: Facsimile of Map of New Mexico drawn by Bernardo Miera y
Pacheco 1778. Yale Collection of Western Americana, Beinecke Rare Book
and Manuscript Library

Table of Contents

For
Moises and Bernilda Sandoval
of Pueblo, Colorado

Introduction

> The Hispano land nurtures *La Gente*, a lesson we
> ignore at our peril....Hispanos make no excuses for
> being here; they earned the right to live in their
> homeland.
>
> — Vincent C. de Baca, 1999

When, in 1846, Brigadier General Stephen Watts Kearney led the Army of the West into the Plaza de Santa Fe during the U.S.-Mexico War, a new era began in the Greater Southwest, once governed by Spain (1540-1821) and later by Mexico (1821-1848). At that time, New Mexico did not conform to the present cartographical configuration of today. Instead, it included Colorado, Utah, northern Arizona, and parts of western Texas. Indeed, New Mexico was a cultural heartland for Hispanos who had settled the land in 1598 and established towns, governance, language, religion, traditions, and other cultural amenities. Suddenly they found themselves as "foreigners in their own land." Land grant issues proliferated as did questions regarding citizenship rights granted by the United States under the provisions of the Treaty of Guadalupe Hidalgo. The history of the settlement of Hispanic Colorado, which is a part of our national story, begins, not necessarily with sixteenth century explorers into New Mexico, but

1

with seventeenth century Hispanic New Mexican traders who, with certainty, ventured into the land of the Yutas, and learned about the tribes, the pathways, the rivers and the terrain. Between them and later explorers in the eighteenth century, knowledge of Colorado and names of rivers and places were added to the heritage of our national story, which is shared with Spain, Mexico and Native American tribes in the region.

In the background of a fast-changing world, Hispanics in the New Mexico-Colorado region adapted to a dynamic historical process[1] that evolved quickly before them. History had taught them well, for under Spain, they had protected their lands under the contractual land grant system governed by the Laws of the Indies, *Las Siete Leyes*, and other compilations of Spanish laws. Litigation for the use of water, common lands, sales and transfers of land was carried out before the world and documented. Regarding Spanish period land grants under Mexico, the legal system changed but little in terms of legal practices and interpretation of the law governing those earlier concessions. Under Mexico, land grants held under Spain were basically left alone and acknowledged as legal entities. Meanwhile, the Mexican government did issue new land grant ordinances that followed revised provisions. A synopsis of the history of some of those grants narrated in this study presents a snapshot historical perspective in regard to how the grants were created and their final disposition as they are generally perceived by the descendants of those who pioneered the settlement of Hispanic southern Colorado.

---

1 I define the historical process an an occurrence, a state of or phenomenon that has to do with the evolution of an idea or concept that ties to an event or a series of events. The historical process is a function of the interactions of the affairs of humankind with time, events, the sequence and continuities of events, causes, effects and the change or changes that develop as a consequence. The historical process may provide directionality. In summary, the historical process is evident in the questions, who are we, where do we come from, and where are we going? In the historical dialectic, the historical process is best defined as an unanswerable paradox that can never be completed because it is something that is in a perpetual state of becoming.

The actions of the U.S. government in the Southwest had other consequences. In 1861, when the Territory of Colorado was created, Hispanics in southern Colorado suddenly found themselves further isolated, and to an extent, abandoned. Its southern boundary line separated over 7,000 Hispanics from their New Mexico homeland, which shared a common language, culture, traditions, heritage and religion. Even more significantly, their political ties and destiny had been tied to Santa Fe, where their culture, ethnicity, and heritage were better understood. Denver was too far away to understand their situations, especially in regard to their property rights and land grants.

At the time of the United States' annexation of New Mexico, following the U.S.-Mexico War of 1846, over 300 land grants existed in New Mexico and hundreds of others from California to Texas. Under Spain, the majority of them were granted by the governor in the name of the Spanish king. Under Mexico, the grantor, whether it be the governor, a prefect, or an *alcalde mayor*, did so in the name of Mexico, as a sovereign nation. The land grants were tracts of land granted under contract for the purpose of settlement and development of the land in settled areas within a specified time period. In New Mexico, as elsewhere, the grants were made to individuals or communities of people or families who, under terms of their contracts, were obligated to use the land for the purpose intended. Land grants were primarily given for farming and raising small herds of livestock. Sometimes they were given as *estancias* — solely for ranching or raising cattle, horses or mules. In all cases the Laws of the Indies, and later those of Mexico, required that land be settled where water, pasturage, and wooded areas were located. The people were charged with caring for the land as stewards, thus inaugurating a responsibility to care for the environment and its sustainability for future generations.

In many ways, Spanish land grants, in particular, preserved a way of life and in so doing became cultural enclaves. The legacy of the land grants, particularly those granted under Spain as early as 1640 in New Mexico, is that they preserved through practice and tradition Spanish colonial period linguistics, religion, law, literature, governance, local political organization, agriculture, and, equally important, Spanish lore of seventeenth century Spain. *Dichos* (proverbs), folktales, medicinal cures, husbandry, dances and songs or ballads — among other cultural activities — were preserved by the people and modified in the evolution of an historical process that passed through Spanish colonial, Mexican Territorial and Anglo-American periods.

Sustainability of the land is a part of that legacy, for the many miles of *acequias* (irrigation ditches) that exist today to bring water to farmlands are from that period. The organization of acequia administration still exists, as do many of the Spanish colonial period land grants in New Mexico that today form farming communities. The lasting genealogies of land grant families and descendants continue to preserve the values born in Spain and modified in the theater of the Spanish Colonial and Mexican Territorial periods in the Greater Southwest as well as throughout Latin America and the Caribbean. Land grants given in the Mexican Territorial Period continued to exhibit the cultural traits that hark back to the culture of the mother country. Today, despite the passage of time, that tie is relatively unbroken. In many ways, centuries-old Hispanic cultural traditions, language, lore and customs, introduced in 1598, when New Mexico was settled, have survived to modern times.

The recent and growing literature about the history of southern Colorado that has emanated from the pens of Colorado-based Hispanos explains their desire to understand and tell their own history, not from textbooks, but from their own family experiences as well as from historical, regional and cultural perspectives. They are the descendants of the early settlers who established towns, farms, ranches and land grants in southern Colorado that stretched from the Arkansas River to the La Plata Mountains, inclusive of the rich San Luis Valley. While a few of their writings, and those of others, are presented herein, there are many more accounts that have and will be written by southern Coloradans, who know that their heritage is a part of our national story.

In 1974, ethnologist Frances Leon Swadesh published *Los Primeros Pobladores: Hispanic Americans of the Ute Frontier*. Her book was one of the first modern-day anthropological studies to explore the history, settlement patterns and culture of Hispanic pioneers who pushed the frontier northward from New Mexico. While Swadesh focused on early settlers who daringly moved northward to settle the Chama River Valley in far northern New Mexico during the eighteenth century, her study also included facets of the economic activities, settlement patterns, social relationships, and cultural and political institutions practiced in the expanding Hispanic communities, particularly those in the San Luis Valley. She used archival documents and oral histories that she had gathered from over 200 interviews. Her landmark study revealed much about the history and culture of Hispanic Colorado. Frances Leon Swadesh was a staunch defender of Hispanics and Native Americans. Her writings focused on rural Hispanic poverty, discrimination, and land grant grievances as well as the plight of farm workers.

Originally published in 1975 and updated in 1992, Olibama López Tushar's *The People of El Valle* is a classic mix of both historical writings and the oral traditions. López Tushar examined the life and times of early settlers of south central Colorado. She not only wrote about early explorers in the region of southern Colorado, but also focused on settlers, their homes, their folklore, religion, education, occupations and their genealogies. López Tushar's book is one of the earliest examples of modern scholarship about *The People of El Valle* by a Hispanic Coloradan writer and educator focused on the San Luis Valley with expanded vistas of southern Colorado.

A new generation of Hispanic authors has emerged to tell the story of Hispanic Colorado. Among them, Vincent C. de Baca, editor of *La Gente: Hispano History and Life in Colorado* (1998), an anthology of essays written by thirteen authors who chronicle Colorado's Hispanic life and history. Topics range from the history of the settlement of the area to displacement and adaptation issues, and a dialog on the cultural landscape. The authors explore their historical environment as well as the place of southwestern Hispanics in our national story. To that end, C. de Baca writes,

> The tremendous growth of the Hispano population in Colorado and throughout the nation has provoked controversy and, in some cases, measures designed to curtail the full expression and diversity of *La Gente*—demands for immigration restriction, English-only laws, an end to bilingual eduction, abolition of Cinco de Mayo[2] festivities, and strict policing of Chicano youth. Yet in the face of what seems to be a degenerating national *Independence* promises all Americans the same right to 'life liberty, and the pursuit of happiness and that the most important issue for discussion is whether or not this nation will pursue its commitment to civil, political, and social justice for all.[3]

C. de Baca's book is much more than a plea for social justice, because his collection of essays serves as "a major step toward explaining the dynamic historical experience of *La Gente* in Colorado."

Life in Los Sauces (2005), a memoir by Olivama Salazar de Valdez and her daughter Dolores Valdez de Pong, is another example of a study that tells about Hispanic life in southern Colorado. Like many Hispanos, they seek to understand the origins of a people that are culturally tied to New Mexico and its history, but who have been cut off, administratively and politically, by a border line that has isolated them from their New Mexican homeland for generations. Rich in genealogical information, *Life in Los Sauces* details the lives of people

---

2 It should be noted that General Ignacio Zaragosa, who led the victorious Mexican army against French invaders at the Battle of Puebla on May 5, 1862, was born in Goliad, Texas in 1828. He and his family are from the same frontier stock that settled the Greater Southwest. Therefore, the Mexican national celebration of Cinco de Mayo is appropriately part of the Hispanic tradition of celebrating one of their own in the Greater Southwest.

3 C. de Baca, Vincent, ed. *La Gente: Hispanio History and Life in Colorado*. Niwot: The University Press of Colorado and Colorado Historical Society, 1998, p. vii.

6

who once lived within the isolated village of Los Sauces in the San Luis Valley. The historical settlement of Los Sauces lies between two rivers, the Río Grande and the Río de los Conejos. The book, about farming and ranching practices, daily life inclusive of spiritual and cultural matters, is a collection of vignettes that reflect on the early twentieth century.

Perhaps one of the most telling historical narratives to come out of southern Colorado is the biography of José Francisco Torres from Trinidad as told by Lois Gerber Franke. In her book *J. Frank Torres, Crusader and Judge: An Oral History* (2007), Franke presents an excellent biographical account that covers the life and times of an individual in his own words. Torres saw the social injustices as a child and, as an adult, acted to assure that his people deserved better treatment and respect. Despite being rejected in his first attempts to enter law school, he persisted and became a prominent figure in southern Colorado. Of the character of Judge Torres, renowned historian, Marc Simmons, who knew him, wrote, "Viewing the life long struggles of Frank Torres, we are reminded that courage and talent, combined with effort, truly can make a difference...that individual character is what counts. As his story unfolds, the reader increasingly gains respect and liking for the idealistic young man with an iron will who obtains his law degree against all odds, battles back from a near-fatal illness, and faces down the Ku Klux Klan, just for starters."[4] This book offers not only the biography of an individual, but the history of a people, for the historical process has indelibly marked the trials and tribulations, the life-long struggles for survival and cultural sustainability as well as the retention of the Coloradans' ethnic identity.

Each generation, it is often said, writes its own history, and the Hispanics of Colorado are poised to do just that. One of the most prolific research-focused groups in Colorado is the Colorado Society for

---

4 Marc Simmons, "Foreword," in Lois Gerber Franke, *J. Franke Torres, Crusader and Judge: An Oral History* (Santa Fe: Sunstone Press, 2007), p. 7.

Hispanic Genealogy. In its mission statement, the Colorado Society for Hispanic Genealogy proclaims that it seeks to "promote the sharing and dissemination of genealogical research and information" for the purpose of genealogical study. Its association with the Genealogical Society of Hispanic America (GSHA) has broadened its vistas in tying together the role of Hispanics in Colorado as participants in the historical process that links to our national story. Of significant importance is GSHA's *Nuestas Raíces Journal*, which includes not only articles about historic and modern Hispanic families throughout the nation, but also many articles and genealogical studies about New Mexico and Colorado. Their publication is dedicated to presenting authoritative genealogical information about Hispanic families that have participated in the early settlement of America, particularly, today's Greater Southwest. Both the Colorado Society for Hispanic Genealogy and GSHA, through its members, have compiled an outstanding collection of genealogies of the early settlers of southern Colorado and their descendants.

The present volume, *Early Hispanic Colorado 1678-1900*, adds to the telling of early Hispanic Colorado as a part of our national story that is shared with both Mexico and Spain as well as with regional Native American tribes. *Early Hispanic Colorado 1678-1900* is about a people who have heroically survived nearly two hundred years of cultural change, beginning in 1848. It is about a people who learned to navigate the legal systems of Spain, Mexico, and the United States in order to keep their lands and their values alive. It is about a people who have defended their lands against all comers, insiders and outsiders. It is about an intelligent and robust people who learned to adapt, for they are still here. While not every Hispanic settlement is specifically mentioned in this study, they are all a part of the same historical processes that shaped Colorado. This book is more than a success story; it is about a people who have participated in American history.

A word about the use of the word Yuta. Its historical spelling, found in Spanish colonial and Mexican period documents, is usually "Yuta." The modern spelling, "Ute," for the general tribal affiliation, and "Utah" for the state, emerged from the Spanish derivation. Early Spanish colonials tended to spell words as they heard them. Usually the phonetic spellings they gave to indigenous words are what have emerged in modern vocabularies throughout the Americas. This work favors "Yuta" for its historical value, and uses "Ute" and "Yuta" interchangeably. The same is true for the spellings of modern Albuquerque and colonial Alburquerque. In time, the extra "r" was lost in its pronunciation.

This book owes many debts of gratitude to numerous people from the staffs in the archives of Spain and Mexico: the Archivo Historico Nacional, Archivo del Servicio Historico Militar, and Real Academia de la Historia in Madrid, the Archivo General de Indias in Sevilla, and the Archivo General de Simancas in Simancas, Spain, as well as the staff at the Archivo General de la Nación in Mexico City. I also wish to thank the staffs at the Bancroft Library, University of California Berkeley, Center for Southwest Studies, Zimmerman Library at the University of New Mexico in Albuquerque, Archives of the Archdiocese of Santa Fe and the New Mexico State Record Center and Archives Santa Fe. Special thanks to my wife Loretta Sánchez for patiently reading through the manuscript and making valuable suggestions in the early drafts of this study. I also thank Julianne Burton-Carvajal for assistance in the proofing of the book and a special thanks to Paul Rhetts, co-owner of Río Grande Books, whose dedication to publishing works dealing with the regional history of the Greater Southwest is highly commendable and greatly appreciated.

Chapter I
Colorado and the Road to Mythical Teguayo

> Beyond the pueblos of Moqui (Hopi), looking westerly at a distance of 26 leagues, one arrives at the nation which are called Yutas, which is the one formerly called Teguayo, it is one nation of the Yutas which reaches close to the South Sea.
> — Fray Alonso Posada, 1686

The history of Hispanic Colorado is as much linked to the national story of the United States as it is to the history of New Mexico, the expansion of the Spanish Empire and the early development of Mexico as a nation-state. Similarly, like almost every colonial region of exploration and settlement, the pathways to Colorado are part of the prehistory and history of the various Indian tribes that inhabited the area since time immemorial. In many ways, imaginary cartography emanating from both European and Indian lore led to Spanish interests in lands north, northwest, and northeast of New Mexico. In the end, one of the most historical of trails in North America, the Old Spanish Trail, leading from New Mexico to California via southern Colorado and Utah, with all of its variations, was forged from Indian pathways similar to those that crisscrossed other areas of the Western

Hemisphere. Archaeological sites bear out the location of many Indian pathways through mountains, canyons, and valleys, and over ridges and rivers. Those trails were used and new ones blazed by Hispanic New Mexican traders who dared trade with the Yutas (Ute tribes) as early as the seventeenth century. Slowly, Colorado emerged from the mists of pre-history, first coming into the historical limelight when Spanish colonial frontiersmen from New Mexico recorded their whereabouts as they went northwestward to trade with tribes who lived along rivers that ran through the mountains and forests of that region.

Sometime in the mid-seventeenth century, New Mexican frontiersmen had ventured northward to the headwaters of the Río Grande to trade with Ute or Comanche warriors. Certainly by 1678, New Mexicans had learned about a place far to the northwest near a great salt lake called "Teguayo." Before long, New Mexicans, in search of Teguayo, had dared go north beyond the Río Dolores and beyond to trading sites near present Montrose, thence westward to the La Sal Mountains as far as a place they called Timpanogos on the edge of a large salt lake. To get there, New Mexicans, now following Indian trails, now blazing new routes, discovered western Colorado and learned of its valuable resources. In time, their descendants would return to settle the area. As early as the seventeenth century, Spanish explorers and traders had expanded, however tentatively, the Spanish claim northward to Colorado and Utah.

The Spanish claim to New Mexico in the sixteenth century became the first step toward the eventual settlement of Colorado. Significantly, not quite forty-eight years had passed since Christopher Columbus's first voyage, when, in 1540, Spanish explorers under Francisco Vázquez de Coronado visited Taos Pueblo, which they called Braba, along the upper Río Grande. Peering northward they could see a rim of snow-covered mountain tops that tiered their way southward from a land New Mexican frontiersmen would later call Colorado, after a long, colorful river that flowed through it. Thus, Coronado's men were the first Europeans to penetrate that far north before returning to their camp on the west side of present-day Albuquerque.[5] From there, they went eastward into the interior of the continent until they reached the Great Plains of present-day central Kansas. They had, indeed, taken a major step north from Mexico.

Spain's fascination with North America grew throughout the colonial period thanks to maps drawn between 1500, when Juan de la Cosa, having sailed with Columbus, printed his chart featuring the Caribbean Islands, and 1819, when Facundo Melgares, governor of New Mexico, sent a map to the viceroy in Mexico City showing Santa Fe in relation to the southern Rockies as far north as South Pass, in present-day Wyoming. The latter map presented new perspectives regarding the Spanish claim to the far northern reaches of the Americas. Among other natural landmarks, the 1819 map featured Colorado's southern Rocky Mountains, then called the "Sierra de las Grullas" (Mountain of the Cranes), and several rivers inclusive of the Yellowstone River in relation to the wild, meandering Missouri River. The map was produced during a flurry of activity in which Spanish officials in New Mexico were concerned that a possible invasion was being planned by the United States via Yellowstone. In his communications with the viceroy, Melgares promised to send an expedition to the *Río Piedra Amarilla* (Yellowstone River) "against the Anglo-americanos" as soon as the weather warmed.[6]

One of the earliest views of New Mexico appeared in 1577,

---

5 For an explanation of the possible location of the Coronado campsite see Stanley M. Hordes "A Sixteenth-century Spanish Campsite in the Tiguex Province: A Historian's Perspective," pp. 155-164 in Bradley J. Vierra, General Editor, *Current Research on the Late Prehistory and Early History of New Mexico* (Albuquerque: New Mexico Archaeological Council, July 1992); and Bradley J. Vierra, "A Sixteenth-century Spanish Campsite in the Tiguex Province: An Archaeologist's Perspective," pp. 165-174, in Bradley J. Vierra, General Editor, *Current Research on the Late Prehistory and Early History of New Mexico* (Albuquerque: New Mexico Archaeological Council, July 1992).

6 *El Virey de Nueva España Conde del Venadito continua dando cuenta de las novedades ocurridas en las costas y Provincias internas de aquel Reyno, 30 de Noviembre de 1818,* Archivo General de Indias (herinafter AGI) Sección Estado, Legajo 33, Numero 24.

when Abraham Ortelius, a Dutch cartographer, having gathered as much hearsay information about Spanish exploration of the Western Hemisphere as he could, published his hemispheric map of the Americas. Ortelius' map showed a distorted placement of New Mexico and the surrounding region was filled with geographic inaccuracies. Ortelius' map, for example, misplaced the Río Grande and had it flowing southwestward from its far northern reaches to the Pacific Ocean. Other places in New Mexico, known to Coronado and his men in 1540, such as the mythical Quivira and other large Indian districts like Cicuic (Pecos) and Tiguex (a large area of Indian pueblos in the valley of present Albuquerque) were placed along the Pacific coast. While many of these places did, in fact, exist, others such as Quivira, Sierra Azul, Siete Cuevas, and Copala, as shown on his map, were part of the lore known to many tribes in northern Mexico as well as the Aztecs, further south.

Soon after New Mexican frontiersmen first learned of Teguayo, it appeared on a Spanish map in 1678. Teguayo, a large area near a great salt lake, was quickly associated with the mythical origins of the Aztecs. In 1778, New Mexican cartographer Bernardo Miera y Pacheco, having sketched out the configuration of the lakes, associated that place with Utah's Great Salt Lake. In North America, early Spanish writers believed that American Indians came from seven caves near the Lake of Copala, which was later associated with Gran Teguayo, northwest of New Mexico.[7] By the 1700s, Hispanic traders from New

---

7 Fascination with Teguayo transcended the Spanish colonial period. In the late nineteenth century scholars such as Cesáro Fernandez Duro, John Gilmary Shea, Adolph F. Bandelier, and Oscar W. Collet renewed the search for mythical Teguayo by sifting through historical documents, maps and archaeological reports. Viz., Ernest J. Burrus, S.J., "Quivira and Teguayo in the Correspondence of Bandelier and Shea with Collet 1882-1889," *Manuscripta*, Vol. XI, No. 2 (July 1967), pp. 67-83. Regarding the relationship of Teguayo to the Great Salt Lake, Burrus writes, "Teguayo, just as unstable cartographically as Quivira, had been variously identified with Salt Lake, Utah, and the regions from which the Pueblo Indians originally came," p. 69.

Mexico had gone as far northwest as a place called Timpanogos in the area of the Great Salt Lakes in present-day Utah. These expeditions were illegal throughout the Spanish colonial period in New Mexico as trade with Utes and Plains tribes had, since 1599, been prohibited by Spanish officials. Fear of antagonizing Plains or mountain tribes like the Apache, Comanche or Utes who could overrun settlements caused Spanish officials to prohibit trade except by license. By the 1770s, Spanish maps pointed to both the salt lakes and Timpanogos. Thus, Timpanogos and Teguayo would almost become synonymous.

Other illegal expeditions, which, in the sixteenth century, had crossed the Río Grande near present-day El Paso without permission from the Viceroy in Mexico City, had alerted Spanish officials to the possibility of an uncontrolled rush to Nuevo México in search of trade or mineral wealth. At least one illegal expedition treaded onto southeastern Colorado. In 1693, Francisco Leyva de Bonilla led an ill-fated expedition northeast of Taos, beyond the Arkansas River. While officials in Mexico had learned about the illegal expedition from some of Leyba y Bonilla's men, who had refused to go with him, they did not know of its fate for five years. As part of his contract to settle New Mexico in 1598, Governor Juan Pérez de Oñate had been ordered by the viceroy to investigate the whereabouts of Leyva de Bonilla and his men and to arrest them for illegal entry into New Mexico. Governor Oñate learned of Leyva de Bonilla's fate from an informant named Jusepe, a Nahua-speaking Mexican Indian, who was the sole survivor of the expedition.

In 1593, as Jusepe revealed, Captain Leyva de Bonilla led a company of soldiers out of southern Chihuahua on a punitive expedition against marauding Indians who had fled northward. Somewhere in the northern Chihuahua desert, after the soldiers had completed their mission, Leyva de Bonilla told his men of his desire to penetrate the *tierra adentro* (interior). Six soldiers refused to join the party, but the rest of them were intrigued about what lay ahead. The horsemen led by Leyva de Bonilla and his second-in-command officer,

Antonio Gutiérrez de Humaña, crossed the Río Grande and followed it northward for days to the pueblos along it banks. After having spent some months among the pueblos, they traveled to the northernmost Indian village, probably Taos, and made another decision.

Perhaps it was the Taoseños who told them about the plains, or maybe the Spaniards had arrived at the northern pueblo in time for the annual trade fair which was attended by Plains Indians. In any event, Leyva and Gutiérrez learned about the plains and were determined to go there in the hope that some great civilization similar to the Aztec kingdom existed. After all, they may have reasoned, other officially-sanctioned explorers such as Francisco Vázquez de Coronado (1540), Francisco Sánchez Chamuscado (1580) and Antonio de Espejo (1581) had not gone far enough in the correct direction to find it. Leyva and Gutiérrez headed northeastward into southeastern Colorado probably reaching as far as what is now Kansas. They may have gone as far as the Nebraska plains—farther than any European had heretofore gone into the North American heartland. Somewhere in the lonely *llano* (plain) of that region, Leyva and Gutiérrez had a falling-out and, in the fight which followed, Gutiérrez killed his captain. Antonio Gutiérrez de Humaña now found himself in command of the expedition in hostile territory.

Not long after the death of Leyva de Bonilla, presumably in Kansas, Gutiérrez de Humaña and his men were ambushed by Plains Indians. The attack began at daybreak under cover of a grass fire. All the Spaniards and their Indian allies were slain except for Jusepe, who somehow managed to escape. Five years later, in 1598, Juan de Oñate found Jusepe living at San Juan Pueblo. Oñate at last learned the sad fate of those Spaniards who had dared to defy the Crown and venture beyond the authorized frontier.[8] Still others for whom no record

8 Herbert E. Bolton, ed., *Spanish Exploration in the Southwest, 1542-1706*, New York, Charles Scribner's Sons, 1908), p. 224. Also see, Alfred Barnaby Thomas, *After Coronado, Spanish Exploration Northeast of New Mexico, 1696-1727* (Norman: University of Oklahoma Press, 1935).

exists, save for a vague reference, had ventured into the *tierra adentro* (interior) and had returned to spin a tale or two about what they had seen beyond the Río Grande. Despite royal orders which prohibited exploration, conquest and colonization without official sanction, Spanish frontiersmen often ventured beyond the limits without authorization.

By the end of the sixteenth-century, Spanish officials approved New Mexico for settlement. In 1598, Governor Juan de Oñate led nearly 600 settlers including Nahua-speaking Mexican Indian allies to northern New Mexico near the confluence of the Río Grande and Río Chama. Opening a new stretch of the Camino Real from Santa Barbara, in present Chihuahua, to New Mexico, the settlers, after a six month trek, reached what they called San Juan de los Caballeros near present-day San Juan Pueblo in July. San Juan de los Caballeros was, at once, New Mexico's first capital and the northernmost Spanish outpost on the Mexican frontier. Once established, the settlers explored New Mexico in all directions visiting every Indian pueblo and the Great Plains several times over the next few years.

In 1601, based on Oñate's explorations of New Mexico and beyond, the Royal Cartographer Enrico Martínez produced a map of New Mexico that included Texas and southern Oklahoma to the Great Bend of the Arkansas. Martínez' map depicted all of the Indian pueblos along the Río Grande and the route from Mexico City, known as the *Camino Real de Tierra Adentro* (Royal Road of the Interior), northward to the Río Conchos and beyond to the area of present-day El Paso, Texas.

Significantly, as Martínez's map demonstrated, Oñate's settlers knew that the Río Grande emanated from the north far above Taos Pueblo. It is probable that New Mexican frontiersmen had wandered beyond Taos into present-day Colorado prior to 1601. Later, by the middle seventeenth century, New Mexicans would learn that the *nacimiento* (headwaters) of the Río Grande began as a stream in the

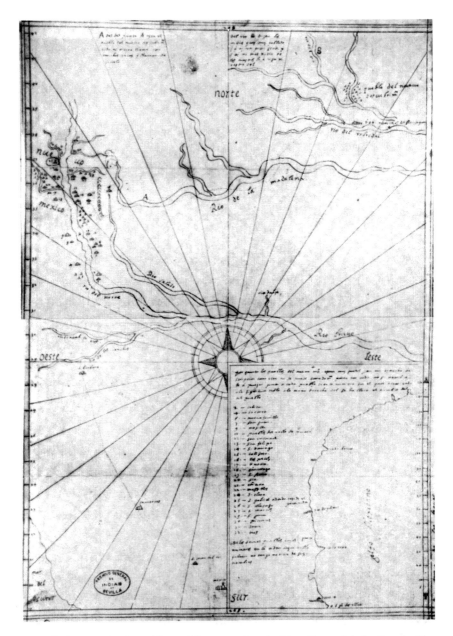

Mapa de Enrico Martínez, Nuevo Mexico, 1601, Archivo General de Indias, Sevilla, España, Archivo General de Indias: Estante 1. Cajón 1. Legajo 3 / 22. Ramo 12. Cf. As listed in P. Torres Lanzas, *Relación descriptiva de los mapas, planos, &, de México y Floridas existentes en el Archivo General de Indias* (1900) p. 44 no. 49.

18

San Juan Mountains of southern Colorado.[9] Indeed, Martínez' map pointed the way to the San Luis Valley.

Throughout the early seventeenth century, New Mexicans busied themselves in establishing farms, ranches, and missions. Under Governor Oñate, a system of governance was established in la Provincia de Nuevo México. The *cabildo* (town council) comprised of elected and appointed councilmen who made decisions within the colony as guided by viceregal policies and the Laws of the Indies. They reported to the governor, who answered to the viceroy of New Spain in Mexico City. By 1599, Oñate had moved his capital from San Juan de los Caballeros to San Gabriel at the confluence of the Río Grande and Río Chama, probably in early 1599. San Gabriel became New Mexico's second capital. Ten years later, in 1610, Santa Fe was established under the direction of Governor Pedro de Peralta. The *cabildo*, under Peralta, was moved from San Gabriel to Santa Fe, which became the capital of New Mexico and the jumping off point to southern Colorado and western Utah via Abiquiú or Taos Pueblo.

By then, New Mexicans had been visiting and trading with tribes in Utah since the mid-1600s. Similarly, they had been trading with tribes on the Great Plains since 1599. Fear that such tribes, which greatly outnumbered the Spanish settlers, could overrun New Mexico if they were antagonized caused Governor Oñate to decree that henceforth it was illegal for any New Mexican frontiersman to trade without license with any of the mountain or plains tribes surrounding the Provincia de Nuevo México. That included Apaches, Comanches, Navajos, and Utes. Throughout the entire Spanish Colonial period, all governors of New Mexico honored that policy. Violation of the policy was punishable by fine, confiscation of goods, and imprisonment. Still, New Mexicans carried on a clandestine trade with those tribes. As a result, much geographical knowledge was gained about the lands

---

9 The headwaters of the Río Grande begin in a spring that flows from the San Juan Mountains of southern Colorado and is today a part of the Río Grande National Forest in San Juan County Colorado.

that came to be known as Utah, Colorado, northern Arizona, and the region of the Great Plains. All of those areas were, during the Spanish colonial period, part of New Mexico.

Although intrepid New Mexican frontiersmen who had ventured into southern Colorado and Utah had offered descriptive glimpses of the land, the region north of New Mexico was little known to Spanish officials. In 1678, Governor Diego de Peñalosa proposed to explore the area.[10] A sketchy field map was offered to show its location northwest of the upper Río Grande. The map is the earliest known depiction of the location of Teguayo or Tatago. Over a century later, in his report of 1686, Fray Alonso de Posada, who had served as the Franciscan Custodian of the New Mexico missions during the period 1661-1665, wrote about the relationship between Teguayo and the Utes, whom New Mexicans originally called Yutas:

> Beyond the pueblos of Moqui (Hopi), looking westerly at a distance of 26 leagues, one arrives at the nation which are called Yutas, which is the one formerly called Teguayo; it is one nation of the Yutas which reaches close to the South Sea (the Pacific Ocean).[11]

Historically, New Mexicans appear to have learned about the Yutas much earlier than heretofore believed. From the oral tradition, Fray Geronimo de Zarate Salmerón in 1626 wrote his *Relaciones*[12] that in 1601, after Oñate had returned from his exploration of the Great Plains, he had met with a delegation from Quivira. The Quivirans hoped to get the Spaniards to ally themselves against the Escanjaques,

---

10 Dictamen del Padre [Alonso de] Posada, Año de 1686, *Colección Muñoz, Real Academia de la Historia* (Hereinafter cited as RAH), Madrid, Spain. Also see Alfred Barnaby Thomas, *After Coronado: Spanish Exploration Northeast of New Mexico, 1696-1727* (Norman: University of Oklahoma Press, 1935), p. 9.
11 Posada, Dictamen, 1686, Colección Muñoz, RAH.
12 See Alicia Ronstadt Milich, trans., *Relaciones by Zarate Salmerón* (Albuquerque: Horn & Wallace Publishers, Inc., 1966)

a Plains tribe with whom they were at war. Oñate thought better of that entangling alliance. His goal was to explore as far northeastward as possible in search of the legendary *Estrecho de Anián* (the Strait of Anian or Northwest Passage). One of the Quivirans told him that the "Spaniards had traveled a great deal out of their way on the route that they took, that if they had gone directly north, they would have arrived quickly, and so according to what they said, one should go by way of Taos and through the lands of the great Captain Quima."[13] The Quiviran even offered to take Oñate there but, after planning to send twelve soldiers, the governor changed his mind and missed making the first documented contact with the Utes.

New Mexicans, however, would be drawn in a different direction, that is, northwest of the New Mexico settlements to the lands of the Yutas. In his account, Friar Salmerón wrote about the route to the northwest stating, "If one goes from New Mexico on this exploration, one ought to go by way of the Río Zama (Chama) traveling to the northwest. That is what the Indians of New Mexico told me when I questioned them."[14]

Just as Quivira had drawn Spanish explorers to the Great Plains, mythical Teguayo marked the way through southwestern Colorado to the Yuta country far to the northwest. In his report of 1686, Alonso de Posada, offered a first view of Teguayo to Spanish officials when he wrote:

> Many cosmographers and astrologers confuse this kingdom of Teguayo with that of Gran Quivira, but the facts are that Gran Quivira is to the east and borders on the North Sea [Atlantic Ocean], while Teguayo is north and borders on the Sea of the West [Pacific Ocean]. The many islands, gulfs and bays which are in the direction of the south they say belong to La Quivira. It is not surprising that they do so because these lands are unknown.[15]

13 Zarate Salmerón, *Relaciones*, p. 62.
14 Zarate Salmerón, *Relaciones*, p. 91.
15 Alfred Barnaby Thomas, *Alonso de Posada Report, 1686: A Description of the Area of the Present Southern United States in the Seventeenth Century* (Pensacola: Perdido

The myth of Teguayo served only to create more interest in the lands northwest of New Mexico among Hispanic frontiersmen who wished to trade in the area.

By the middle of the century, Yuta tribesmen had ventured south to trade openly with Puebloans and Spaniards alike. By the end of the century, Friar Posada had placed the Yuta country in geographic perspective from Santa Fe when he wrote:

> It remains only for us to tell of the location and direction of the kingdom and provinces which they call Teguayo. To provide some understanding of this land, let us recall again the location of the villa of Santa Fe, the capital of New Mexico, which is as stated at thirty-seven degrees. Taking from this villa a straight line to the northwest between north and south and crossing the sierras called Casafuerte or Nabajo, one reaches the large river which runs directly west for a distance of sixty leagues which are possessed by the Apacha nation. Crossing this river, one enters the nation called the Yuta, a warlike people. Beyond this nation some seventy leagues in the same northwest direction one enters afterwards between some hills at a distance of fifty leagues more or less, the land which the Indians of the North call Teguayo, and the Mexican Indians by an old tradition call Copala.[16]

Posada's description seemed to refer to the present Four Corners area. The large river was probably the San Juan. To New Mexicans, Nabajo was a geographic area inhabited by the Diné — a place clearly identified as *el centro de Nabajo* located south and east of present Flagstaff,

---

Bay Press, 1982), p. 43. Also see footnote 147, p. 43, in which Thomas explains that the word "astrologist" is derived from "astronomis" which appears in other copyist versions of Posada's Report. Also see Posada, Dictamen, 1686, *Colección Muñoz, Real Academia de Historia* (RAH) Madrid, Spain.

16 Thomas, *Posada Report*, 1686, p. 42.

Arizona. The "centro de Nabajo" likely extended northeastward as well as eastward toward the Río Grande. In 1765, when Juan María Antonio Rivera explored north of the Four Corners area, he reported seeing Navajo hogans along the Sierra de la Plata Mountains near present Dolores.

By the middle 1600s, contact between New Mexican frontiersmen and Utes had been established. Somewhere in the wilderness south of the Río San Juan Ute warriors met with Hispanic New Mexicans for trade. It is also likely that early Spanish contact with them occurred uneventfully at some of the northern Río Grande pueblos north of Santa Fe such as Taos, San Juan, Santa Clara, San Ildefonso, and Pojoaque.

The location of the pueblos north of Santa Fe that participated in trade with Utes lined up with a route leading to present-day southern Colorado. Of Santa Fe's strategic position, Posada wrote:

> Looking from the said villa [Santa Fe] to the northwest, we will have at seventy leagues the Yuta nation. Beyond at a distance of some one hundred and eighty leagues from the villa are the kingdom and provinces of Teguayo. Looking directly west are the South Sea [Pacific Ocean] and California at two hundred leagues. Looking to the southwest at a hundred leagues we find El Cuartelejo of the Apacha nation and Sierra Azul. At seventy leagues from there are the provinces of Sonora and Sinaloa.[17]

Posada, who probably meant that El Cuartelejo was about 100 leagues from Teguayo, likely referred to the edge of the Great Plains in present-day Kansas some distance east of today's Trinidad, Colorado. Even though New Mexicans knew about El Cuartelejo as an Apache stronghold, it would not be until the first decade of the eighteenth century that a "rescue" expedition from New Mexico would negotiate

---

17 Thomas, *Posada Report*, 1686, p. 45, item 44.

with the Apache for the safe return of Pueblo Indians from Picuris. The Picuris had fled there in fear of a returning Spanish army under Governor Diego de Vargas, who reconquered New Mexico in 1692 after the Pueblo Revolt of 1680. In 1706. Juan de Ulibarrí and 60 men found them in their elusive campsites at El Cuartelejo. To get to El Cuartelejo, Ulibarrí left Taos Pueblo headed in an easterly direction, veering slightly north into a corner of southeastern Colorado. It is believed he passed by Capulin Mountain, headed toward the Cimmaron River where he camped. From there, he veered slightly north toward Two Buttes, Colorado and then to a point along the Arkansas River. From there he treaded onto the Kansas plains reaching El Cuartelejo.[18]

During this period, the Utes had been going eastward onto the Great Plains to wage war against the Apache and Comanche warriors who had been raiding into their territory. The warfare between them endangered Spanish settlements in northern New Mexico as these tribes also turned on them for foodstuffs and booty. In 1719, Governor Antonio Velarde led a punitive expedition into southern Colorado against them. Having crossed eastward into the Sangre de Cristo Mountains from Taos, Velarde encountered several Apache settlements and left them in peace. Zigzagging through the Sangre de Cristo Mountains, Velarde and his men crossed into Colorado through Raton Pass and the area of Trinidad, Huerfano, Pueblo until they reached the vicinity of Colorado Springs. The expedition is believed to have reached as far as present-day Limon, Colorado, before heading southward to the Arkansas River. Without having contacted hostiles, Velarde and his men returned to Santa Fe, but not before having made an important

---

18 James and Dolores Gunnerson, *Ethnohistory of the High Plains* (Bureau of Land Management Cultural Resources Studies No. 26. pp. 4-5). Based on the historic literature, the Gunnersons trace the route of Ulibarrí and Velarde. However, Alfred Barnaby Thomas wrote that El Cuartelejo was in "eastern Colorado." See Alfred Barnaby Thomas, *Forgotten Frontiers: A Study of the Spanish Indian Policy of Don Juan Bautista de Anza, Governor of New Mexico 1777-1787* (Norman: University of Oklahoma Press, 1932), p. 58.

reconnaissance of the region.[19] Although the two expeditions did not result in the settlement of southern Colorado, they not only added to the historical narrative of Hispanic Colorado, but to the expansive geographic knowledge of southern Colorado leading to the eventual settlement of the area from New Mexico. The area of settlement would be to the west of the trajectories of these two expeditions.

Meanwhile, New Mexicans carried out trade with Utes, largely clandestine, over a vast area covering much of present-day Utah and southern Colorado as far west as the Great Salt Lake and the Great Basin and as far east as Walsenburg. Throughout a larger area as far as the Platte River, New Mexicans formed varied relationships with the many tribes within it. The more important tribes between Utah and the southeastern edge of present-day Colorado included Comanches, Apaches, Cuartelejos, Faraones, Jicarillas, Pananas (Pawnees), Yutas (Utes), and the Kansa. They ranged within an area covered by many river valleys with names such as the Arkansas (Río Napestle), the Colorado (Río Colorado), the Red (Río Rojo), the North Platte (the Río San Lorenzo), the South Platte (Río de Jesús María), the Platte (Río Chato), the Purgatoire (Río de las Animas), and as well as many lesser streams throughout the area.[20]

Wrought by trial and error, friendships, animosities and hostilities, a long history of relationships, inclusive of extend families, between New Mexican frontiersmen and various tribes played out on a broad geographic stage from the headwaters of the Canadian River to the Colorado. Although relationships among them were forged by many years of illegal trade, the complexities involving the many cultures that lived within that broad geographic area made it virtually impossible for Spanish policy to be administered with any degree of consistency.

Throughout the seventeenth century, New Mexicans petitioned

19 Gunnerson, *Ethnohistory* pp. 5- 6.

20 Alfred Barnaby Thomas, translator and editor, *After Coronado: Spanish Exploration Northeast of New Mexico, 1696-1727* (Norman: University of Oklahoma Press, 1935), p. 1.

their governors for licenses to trade with the Utes, but officials in Santa Fe continued to deny licenses for trade with any of the tribes to the north and northwest. Father Posada recounted the story of one such petition that was made and denied. In recounting Captain Francisco Luján's petition to go north, Posada included much information about the land of the Yutas. He wrote that an Indian from the Pueblo of Jemez called don Juanillo told him of the many people and different nations in that kingdom of Teguayo. Don Juanillo had been a captive for two years in the provinces of Teguayo and described the area for Posada. Don Juanillo said:

> ...they have in them a very large number of people of different languages some of which were spoken in New Mexico and also a large lake with its entire circumference populated. On different occasions he [Luján] told the governors of New Mexico they should make a journey to those provinces and that he would go as a guide for the Spaniards. Although Captain Francisco Luján petitioned once and again a second time for this journey, he was unable to secure permission. This is the most that can be said and is known at present of the river and provinces of Teguayo.[21]

Don Juanillo's brief description, confirmed to Posada that Teguayo was a real place. After all, don Juanillo, who had been the victim of a longstanding indigenous slave trade, had been held there against his will.

Despite the dangers of proceeding northward, intrepid frontiersmen continued to expand the New Mexican frontier by establishing new settlements in out-of-the-way areas frequented by war-like tribes. Expansion into river valleys that offered fertile soils and a new start at a livelihood motivated Hispanic settlers to establish towns north and northwest of Santa Fe, beyond the Española Valley.

---

21 RAH, 6-3-1. Also see Thomas, *Posada Report*, 1686, p. 44.

In the 1730s two towns were settled northwest of Santa Fe that would become significant outposts in trade with the Yutas. Abiquiú was settled by 1734, although settlers had begun to move into the area as early as the 1720s. Similarly, Ojo Caliente was established by 1735.[22] By 1830, a century later, Tierra Amarilla, with its large land grant stretching northward to Chama and into parts of southern Colorado, became the sequential offshoot of the settlement pattern started by the establishment of Abiquiú. The route from Abiquiú to the Yuta country crossed through the heart of present-day Tierra Amarilla near Los Ojos and the escarpments of Tecolote Mesa.

While the settlement pattern expanded northward from Abiquiú, the Franciscans did not expand the missionary field in that direction. Although in the 1740s Franciscans did propose that a mission field be established among the Utes, that idea came to naught. Relationships between Utes and Spanish settlers hampered the possibility of a mission field in the Yuta country. Official Spanish Indian policies regarding semi-sedentary tribes evolved in New Mexico from 1599 with the administration of Governor Juan de Oñate. Because Oñate considered Apache, Comanche, and Utes, among other semi-sedentary tribes, to be warlike, he outlawed trade with them. Oñate, dealt with the fragile relationships with Plains Indians because he knew that New Mexico could easily be overrun in an extended war with the Plains tribes to east. On the other hand, trade with the Pueblos, who were often targets by raiding tribes since prehistoric times, was allowed. Besides, New Mexican frontiersmen often allied with the Pueblos on campaigns against Plains tribes that raided their towns, farms and ranches. Such a dual Indian policy influenced the nature of trade with the tribes.[23] Still, peace with

---

22 Malcolm Ebright, *Land Grant and Lawsuits in Northern New Mexico* (Albuquerque: University of New Mexico, 1994), p. 26.

23 See Cyclone Covey, trans., *Cabeza de Vaca's Adventures in the Unknown Interior of America* (Albuquerque: University of New Mexico Press, 1961); Cleve Hallenbeck, *Alvar Nuñez Cabeza de Vaca: The Journey of the First European to Cross the Continent of North America, 1534-1536* (Glendale, 1939), Also see George P. Hammond and Agapito Rey, *The Rediscovery of New Mexico, 1580-1594* (Albuquerque: University of

the Pueblos was tentative. Spanish officials knew that the administration of the dual Indian policies would never be a simple matter.

Oñate's fears were realized — not in his time, but later. Longstanding grievances among the pueblos regarding Spanish colonial policies, attitudes and abuses, however, exploded in the Pueblo Revolt of 1680; and, the widespread rebellion interrupted Spanish occupation of New Mexico for twelve years.[24] Utes and Apache warriors had allied with the pueblos to drive out the Spaniards. Twelve years later, with the Reconquest of New Mexico in 1692 by Governor Diego de Vargas, Spanish officials admitted that Spain's hold on New Mexico was tenuous at best. Following Oñate's decree, subsequent governors prohibited New Mexicans from trading with those tribes without special permission.[25] After the Pueblo Revolt, New Mexicans were even more concerned about the Utes, Comanches, Navajos and Apaches.[26]

Eighteenth century colonial governors in New Mexico continued to prohibit trade with Plains Indians and limited trading activities to fairs at designated pueblos. Anyone wishing to trade with those tribes were required to petition the governor for a license to do so. If granted, licensing offered the advantage of trading legally. In general, every applicant was scrutinized with reference to his character, and controlled by officials who could recommend or deny the license.[27] Yet, despite licensing, unlawful trading continued to plague trade fairs. Often, bad trading deals led to increased warfare between Plains Indians

---

New Mexico Press, 1966).

24 Joseph P. Sánchez, "Twelve Days in August: The Pueblo Revolt in Santa Fe," in David Grant Noble, ed., *Santa Fe: History of an Ancient City* (Santa Fe, School of American Research Press, 1989), pp. 40-44.

25 See Joseph P. Sánchez, *The Río Abajo Frontier, 1540-1692: A History of Early New Mexico.* (Albuquerque: Albuquerque Museum History Monograph Series, 1987, Revised Second Edition, 1996).

26 Patente de Custos Zavaleta, Santa Fe, 2 July 1700, Archives of the Archdiocese of Santa Fe (Hereinafter cited as AASF), Santa Fe, New Mexico, General List of Patentes, Patentes 1.

27 Marc Simmons, *Spanish Government in New Mexico* (Albuquerque: University of New Mexico Press, 1968), p. 185.

and Spanish settlers as well as Pueblo Indians, who just as frequently suffered attacks from Plains tribes.

Regulation, control and restraint of trade was a sound policy preferable to military intervention. In his *bando* (edict) of August 25, 1705, Governor Francisco Cuervo y Valdes[28] decreed that no one could trade without a license from the governor under penalty of forfeiture of goods to be traded or received in trade. Additionally, the *bando* prohibiting such trade provided that a fine, half of which would be paid to the local war fund and the rest to the Real Hacienda (Treasury), would be levied against all violators. Furthermore, Cuervo y Valdes prohibited any acts of deception at trade fairs particularly at Taos, Pecos and Picuris.[29]

Seven years later, on December 16, 1712, Governor Juan Ignacio Flores Mogollón published a similar *bando*.[30] His restraining orders specifically directed Spanish settlers and Pueblo Indians to cease trade with the Jicarilla and Cuartelejo Apaches in northern New Mexico as well as the Utes in southern Colorado and western Utah. Citing fraudulent trading practices by Pueblo Indians and Spanish colonists, he explained that such activities had placed the Province in harm's way. Along with the usual fines and penalties for unauthorized and unlicensed trading, the governor added a jail term of several months for those violating his proclamation.[31] To Governor Flores Mogollón, control of trade and trading practices, not military intimidation, were solutions practiced by previous Spanish officials, who believed that a lasting peace with Utes, Comanches, Apaches and Navajos could never be achieved solely through military force.

---

28 Francisco Cuervo y Valdés, *Bando*, Santa Fe, 5 August 1705, Spanish Archives of New Mexico, Santa Fe Archives (Hereinafter cited as SANM), #118.
29 *Ibid.*
30 Juan Ignacio Flores Mogollon, *Bando*, Santa Fe, 16 December 1712, SANM #185.
31 *Ibid.* For similar Bandos issued by other Spanish officials, see, Alcalde mayor of Taos, Bando, 9 September 1725, SANM #339, and Juan Domingo Bustamante, Bando, Santa Fe, 17 September 1725, SANM #340.

Barter was the mode of trade, but the process was not always peaceful. The primary rule of the marketplace, "let the buyer beware," seemed to soothe the bitter-sweet aspect of trade, but when touched by buyer's or seller's regret or tainted with the feeling that one was cheated, resentment followed. Bartering for things was one thing. Bartering or ransoming for kidnapped kin, women and children was another. Trading activities with Plains Indians were known as *rescates*, trade fairs in which captives were traded or rescued by barter. During Spanish colonial times, rescates were held throughout New Mexico in such places as Taos, Picuris, Pecos, San Juan, Santa Clara, Abiquiú, Tierra Amarilla, and Santa Cruz de la Cañada. There, Spanish or Indian captives taken in war or merely kidnapped and eslaved were ransomed by kinsmen.

Sometimes Royal funds were expended for ransom, or alms collected in the churches were allocated to buy freedom for captives who were in life threatening situations by their captors. Hispanics sometimes ransomed native captives, referred to as *"piezas de indios,"* who were baptized and reared as Catholic Christians. Commonly, they were treated as domestic servants by their Spanish liberators, some of whom were Franciscan missionaries.[32] Similarly, Plains Indians tended to keep non-tribal captives as their slaves. Spanish women and children who had been held captive for years, some of them from Texas, New Mexico, Coahuila, Chihuahua and Sonora, were often rescued at the *rescates*. Like the Spaniards, Plains Indians returned their own kind to their kinsmen after ransoming them at the *rescates*.

Throughout the 1740s, Comanche raiders increased their raiding activities in New Mexico. During his first term as governor (1749-1754), Governor Tomás Vélez Cachupín established a peaceful trading arrangement with the Utes and Comanches. In 1749, hoping to achieve peace and stability in New Mexico, Governor Vélez permitted trade

---

32 Patente de Custos Zavaleta, Santa Fe, 2 July 1799, AASF, General List of Patentes, Patentes 1.

with Comanches who ventured into the Province. Sternly, he warned the Comanche leaders that trading privileges would be curtailed if the raiding continued.[33] His policy of peace by negotiation to control the Comanches, seemed to work. Hoping to cultivate peaceful relations with the Yutas, Vélez attempted to form an alliance with the Utes in case hostilities with the Comanches resumed.[34]

Monitoring trade in the forests, mountains, and villages of northwestern New Mexico proved difficult in any case. Trade between Utes and settlers in the Española Valley, inclusive of those at Abiquiú, Santa Cruz de la Cañada and other nearby villages, was common. Tribal relationships between Pueblos and raiding Ute and Comanche bands were a constant problem. Too, the Utes and Comanches were traditional enemies. During his first term in office, Vélez's efforts suffered setbacks. After he had encouraged peace and alliances with the Utes against the Comanche, there occurred a major breach between them. Over time, the Ute retaliation against the Spaniards had devastated much of the frontier in New Mexico. New Mexicans were forced to seek a peace with them. As certain Utes had raided southward toward Santa Fe in 1750, New Mexican frontiersmen organized a force and moved against Ute camps. In one incident, Vélez and his men attacked a camp of a hundred tepees, capturing or killing many Utes. After that, the Utes, upon learning of his efforts to talk peace with them, met with him on one of their trading trips to San Juan Pueblo.[35] Soon after, Vélez visited their rancherias a day's ride from San Juan and negotiated a self-monitoring plan whereby the Yuta chiefs, not the Spaniards, would punish warriors who stole Spanish livestock. The policy seemed to work well, because the Yutas, who resented Spanish authority, preferred

33 For a detailed treatment of the period 1751-1778, see Alfred B. Thomas, *The Plains Indians and New Mexico 1751-1778* (Albuquerque: University of New Mexico Press, 1940).
34 Governor Tomás Vélez Cachupín to Viceroy Revillagigedo, Santa Fe, 29 September 1752, in Thomas, *The Plains Indians*, p. 123.
35 *Ibid.*

that the tribe punish individuals for their crimes rather than let the Spaniards find the entire tribe culpable for the acts of a few warriors.[36] Vélez had managed to pacify them by promising to treat them fairly. If Utes raided New Mexico, Vélez, instead of carrying out a punitive expedition against them, notified their leaders who would return stolen property and punish the raiders themselves.[37] Still, Vélez maintained that the *bandos*, which prohibited Hispanic New Mexicans from trade with those tribes were in effect. Vélez' trade arrangement with the Utes and Comanches did not supersede, unlicensed trading activities between New Mexicans and Apaches, Navajos, Comanches and Utes.

Between 1754, when Vélez' term ended, and 1762, succeeding governors weakened much of what he had accomplished.[38] During those years, the Comanche reverted to raiding and taking Spanish property and trading it openly at local fairs. When Vélez returned for a second term in 1762, he immediately worked to restore peace with the Comanche. Turning his attention to the Utes, Vélez assured them that they could count on fairness from the Spaniards. To prove his point, Vélez took an interest in a case involving a *genízaro* (detribalized Indian) named Juan de la Cruz Valdéz who was charged with stealing a horse from a Ute who had been trading at San Juan and sold the horse to a settler of the area. Knowing the eyes of the Yutas were upon him, Vélez ordered that Cruz Váldez receive fifty lashes in the presence of Utes and sentenced him to four years at the *obraje* (prison work farms) at Encinillas, in Chihuahua.[39]

36 Thomas, *The Plains Indians*, p. 32.
37 Elizabeth A.H. John, *Storms Brewed in Other Men's Worlds* (College Station: Texas A & M Press, 1975), p. 327.
38 Francisco Marín del Valle, *Bando*, 26 November 1754, SANM, #530. Hubert H. Bancroft, *Arizona and New Mexico, 1530-1888* (San Francisco:1889). Eleanor B. Adams, ed., *Bishop Tamaron's Visitation to New Mexico, 1760* (Albuquerque: Historical Society of New Mexico, 1954), p. 103; Thomas, *The Plains Indians*, pp. 33-34. Oakah L. Jones, Jr., *Pueblo Warriors & Spanish Conquest* (Norman: University of Oklahoma Press, 1966), p. 136.
39 Proceso contra Juan Baldés, Genízaro, May 1762, SANM #548.

The succeeding governor, Pedro Fermín de Mendinueta, virtually dismantled Vélez' Indian policy. Taking office in 1767, Mendinueta encouraged open warfare against the raiding tribes, especially the Comanche. In retaliation against Mendinueta's repressive military actions, the Comanche, from their camps in southeastern Colorado, penetrated the Sangre de Cristo Mountains north of Taos Pueblo and directed their attacks westward toward their Ute enemies in the San Luis Valley and southward toward Hispanic settlements and Pueblo villages as far as Santa Fe. The Utes, who had earlier expanded into New Mexico, were pushed westward by the Comanches from the San Luis Valley to the San Juan Mountains along the present New Mexico-Colorado border.[40] To combat Comanche depredations, Mendinueta enlisted the aid of Pueblo, Apache and Ute warriors as auxiliaries in 1768,[41] without apparent success.

Between 1598 and 1821, Hispanic New Mexicans had established governance within the Provincia de Nuevo México and had extended Spain's claim over a wider region. Yet, relationships between them and the various tribes plagued the settlement for decades at a time. Relationships with the Pueblos had settled after 1680, particularly as they had common cause against enemy raiders that continued to prey upon them and their farms. In the next decade, the tempo and rhythm of New Mexico, in general, would change to a more peaceful time. Yet, the raiding would persist well into the nineteenth century, inclusive of the time after which, the United States occupied the area following the U.S.-Mexico War of 1846. Meanwhile, New Mexico in the waning years of the Spanish Colonial period continued to deal with trade, raiders, and renewed explorations of Colorado and Utah.

New Mexicans were not the only traders, legal or otherwise, who lived in the wilderness and traded with various tribes. For nearly two centuries French, English, Spanish and Anglo-American trappers had

---

40 Jones, *Pueblo Warriors*, p. 139.
41 *Ibid*, p. 144.

crossed the Mississippi River and had slowly moved westward. The French traders and trappers first moved up the St. Lawrence River, then along the Appalache Mountains, and finally westward until they reached the Mississippi and Missouri rivers. Others moved southward into Spanish governed Louisiana between 1762 and 1800. West of there, the Great Plains, virtually stretching from the Mississippi River to New Mexico, posed a barrier to them for several decades. After crossing the Plains, in 1739, French trappers reached Santa Fe and began trading in the area from varied directions. They too contributed knowledge and influenced the settlement of Colorado.

By the early nineteenth century, Anglo-American trappers had similarly reached Santa Fe from their rendezvous camps north of New Mexico. The way to the Great Plains from the Mississippi and Missouri River drainages had, before the Lewis and Clark Expedition of 1804-1806, been blazed by Spanish and French trappers from St. Louis. In time much knowledge about the Great Plains from St. Louis to Santa Fe had been gathered by French and Spanish traders. Pedro Vial and Francisco Fragoso explored routes from St. Louis and New Orleans to Santa Fe, respectively, in the 1780s and 1790s. By 1821, a route from Missouri to New Mexico, known as the Santa Fe Trail, had been developed. The Santa Fe Trail also linked up with another ancient road known as *El Camino Real de Tierra Adentro* (the Royal Road of the Interior) between Mexico City and Santa Fe. The Santa Fe-Chihuahua Trail, as it became known, resulted from the Spanish Colonial period trade between Alburquerque and Ciudad Chihuahua. It is important to note that, after months on the Great Plains, traders on the Santa Fe Trail entered New Mexico via southeastern Colorado as it passed near La Junta before turning south through present-day Trinidad and passing through Raton Pass as it meandered toward Santa Fe via Las Vegas.

Meanwhile, other traders arrived in the Plaza de Santa Fe through other trails. Such efforts triggered yet another impetus for reaching California via the Yuta country, springing from another unexpected

34

source. Following the Missouri River drainages, Anglo-American trappers known as mountain men pushed deeper into the North American wilderness until they reached the Yellowstone River. From there they moved southwestward toward the Yuta country in Colorado and Utah where they retraced lands already known to the New Mexico traders. Among the Anglo-American mountain men who influenced the history of Colorado include Louis Ambroise (1891-1842), William Bent (1809-1869), Charles Bent (1799-1847), William Becknell (1788-1856), Prewett Fuller Sinclair (1803-1882), John Simpson Smith (1812-1882), Richens Lacy Wootton (1816-1893). One overlooked mountain man who influenced the history of northern New Mexico and southern Colorado is the black trapper, James Pierson Beckwourth (1798-1860), one of founders of Pueblo, Colorado.

Hispanic frontiersmen who lived along the Mississippi and Missouri rivers have long been ignored in favor of the exploits of Anglo-American mountain men and fur traders. Among those who participated in Colorado's history were Manuel Alvarez (1794-1835), Pierre Louis (Luis) Vásquez (1798-1868), Marcelino Baca (1808-1862), Manuel Lisa (1772-1820), and Mariano Medina (1812-1878).

The two most notable Hispanic mountain men from Louisiana Territory were Manuel Lisa, who subsequently formed the Missouri Fur Company, and Luis Vásquez, who later with Jim Bridger founded Fort Bridger near the Green River in southwestern Wyoming. Their family ties lasted at least another generation. Vásquez' son, Hiram Vásquez, was best friends with Felix Bridger, son of Jim Bridger. "We were raised together," he would later write of their familial association.[42] There were many association among Hispanic trappers and traders with their Anglo-American counterparts. Vásquez was, indeed, well regarded among mountain men.

Unlike Lisa, however, Vásquez travelled farther west into the

---

42 Leroy Hafen, "Louis Vasquez," in Hafen, *Mountain Men and the Fur Trade of the Far West* (Glendale: The Arthur H. Clark Company, 1971), Vol. II:337.

Yuta country and eventually to California. Pierre Luis Vásquez was the son of Benito Vásquez and Julie Papin. Benito Vásquez, born in Galicia, Spain in 1750, arrived in present-day St. Louis, Missouri, with Governor Piernas in 1770, when the region was still Spanish. Benito, a farmer and trader, served as captain of militia. He married Julie Papin, a French Canadian, in 1774. Luis, born in 1798, was one of twelve children reared by Benito and Julie.[43] Luis' brother Antoine Francois "Baronet" Vásquez also became a trapper and, at one point, worked for Manuel Lisa. In 1806, he joined the expedition led by Zebulon Montgomery Pike, serving as an interpreter for Pike. Another member of the family, Auguste Pike Vásquez, was their nephew.[44]

In his early twenties, Luis Vásquez had joined an expedition involved in the fur trade along the Missouri River — probably the Ashley-Henry party. Sometime after 1822, he reached the region of the Great Salt Lake, which he claimed to have discovered. The claim has not been accepted by historians. Although a Salt Lake City correspondent of the *San Francisco Bulletin* (29 October 1858) interviewed Vásquez and supported his claim by calling him "the oldest mountaineer in this country and the discoverer of Great Salt Lake."[45] The correspondent recounted that Vásquez:

> ...first entered this valley [Salt Lake City] 36 years ago. In the fall of 1822, he, with a company of trappers, arrived in Cache Valley, where they determined to spend the winter, and trap in the numerous streams with which it abounds. The winter, however, became so severe--the snow falling to the depth of 8 feet-- that they found it necessary to hunt out a better valley, in order to save their animals. Accordingly, Major Vásquez, with one or two of his party, started out, and crossing the divide, entered this valley, and

43 *Ibid*,II:321.
44 See Lecompte, "Antoine Francois ("Baronet") Vasquez," and Lecompte, "Auguste Pike Vasquez," in Hafen, *Mountain Men*, VII:321-341.
45 Hafen, "Louis Vasques," in Hafen, *Mountain Men*, II:322, fn. 8.

discovered Great Salt Lake. This, they at first took to be an arm of the Pacific Ocean. They found the valley free from snow, and well filled with herds of buffalo. Returning to their party, they guided them over into this valley, when they divided--one party, under Weber, wintering on the river which now bears his name; the other wintering on Bear river, near its mouth. The following spring, Vásquez built a boat, and circumnavigated this sheet of brine, for the purpose of finding out definitely whether it was an arm of the sea or not, and thus discovered that it was in reality merely a large inland lake, without an outlet. Since that time, the lake has been gradually receding.[46]

In his writings, Leroy Hafen[47] credits the discovery to other mountain men or possibly Mormons who later occupied the area. It is more probable that the discovery was made much earlier by one of the many illegal traders from New Mexico who traded with the Timpanogos. That discovery, however, would have gone unrecorded; but it appears likely that the Great Salt Lake was known if one infers that kind of knowledge was held even as late as 1813 by the Mauricio Arze-García Lagos expedition of that year. Certainly, Domínguez and Escalante were at the salt lakes, indeed, among the Timpanogos, in 1776. They even described the lake's circumference. Their cartographer, Bernardo Miera y Pacheco, drew it in his maps of the region done in the late 1770s.

Another New Mexican mountain man was Mariano Medina. Because Medina was a part of the New Mexican trading and trapping tradition in the general region of the Yuta country, he deserves special

---

46 *Ibid*, II:336.

47 *Ibid*, II:322. Hafen writes, "Positive data on the activities of Vasquez in the middle and late twenties are lacking." In footnote 9, p. 322, Hafen cites Dale L. Morgan who "presents the various conflicting claims to discovery of this inland sea but without resolving the problem." Regarding the interview by the correspondent of the *San Francisco Bulletin*, Hafen critically states that the "story, although garbled in chronology and certain data, is an important item....", Hafen, op. cit., II:335-6.

mention herein. He was born in Taos sometime between 1808 and 1818. Little is known about his early life other than that he had run away from home and had joined a party of Anglo-American trappers who took him to the Snake River.[48] Small of built, Medina was a spry and active individual whose black hair showed no trace of greying even as he grew older. He generally dressed in the "Mexican fashion, with a scarf around his waist."[49] By the 1840s, Medina had lived as far away from New Mexico as Walla Walla before settling at Fort Bridger, where he prospered by trading with emigrant wagon trains going to California through Utah. After Bridger and Vásquez sold Fort Bridger, Medina owned a trading post on the Sweetwater River, where the Oregon Trail left it to go over South Pass, and operated a ferry on the Green River. Later he moved eastward along the Oregon Trail to trade cattle with emigrants.

Medina subsequently served as a scout for Captain Randolph B. Marcy. It is probable that he was the "Mexican trapper" who escorted Marcy across the Colorado by finding Cochetopa Pass during the winter of 1857-58.[50] In 1859, Medina lived by Big Thompson Creek near the stage road between Fort Collins and Denver, later claiming to have been the "first white man on the creek."[51] His establishment on the Big Thompson was west of present-day Loveland, Colorado, where he operated a trading post. The adobe structure with its two-foot thick walls served as a fort. The building also had a watch tower and its walls had loop holes for firing from the interior. He built a bridge across the creek and charged a toll of one dollar for crossing it.

In the 1860s, he had trouble with Utes and Arapahoes, who he claimed, stole horses from his corral. On one occasion he led three men in pursuit of a party of eleven Utes into present North Park, killing four Utes and recovering his horses. The Utes swore revenge

48 Harvey L. Carter, "Mariano Medina," in Hafen, *Mountain Men*, VIII:247.
49 *Ibid*, VIII: 250.
50 *Ibid*, VIII:247-48, fn. 4.
51 *Ibid*, VIII:248.

and threatened to kill him.[52] Medina spent his last days in the Denver-Fort Collins area. He married twice and fathered four children. In 1868, the Medinas were visited by Kit Carson, who had taken the stage from Cheyenne to Mariano's house, where he spent the night. Medina, who had known Carson in Taos in their younger years, was pleased about the visit. Of his life as a mountain man, his biographer Harvey L. Carter, wrote that he "is interesting because he is one of the few examples of a Mexican who became a successful free trapper and trader, and because he seems to have lived on terms with equality with Americans, whether they were trappers or settlers."[53] Medina died on June 25, 1878.

Marcelino Baca, another New Mexican who joined Anglo-American trappers at an early age, was born in Taos in 1808. A contemporary of Medina, it is not known whether they ever met. Tall, easily over six feet, Baca was romantically described by George F. Ruxton in his novel *Life in the Far West* (1849) as having the "form of a Hercules, he had the symmetry of an Apollo; with strikingly handsome features, and masses of long black hair hanging from his slouching beaver over the shoulders of his buckskin hunting shirt."[54] Baca joined Jim Bridger's American Fur Company on the Yellowstone River and generally ranged in his trapping activities between the South Platte River near present Denver and Fort Laramie. His westernmost activity may have been as far west as the Humboldt River.[55] As trapper and settler of northern Colorado, Baca had his share of trouble with Utes who killed his brother, Benito, near Pueblo in 1854. Soon after, Baca moved back to New Mexico. When the Civil War broke out, he joined the New Mexico Volunteers and was killed at the Battle of Valverde, in New Mexico on February 21, 1862.[56]

---

52 *Ibid*, VIII: 249.
53 *Ibid*, VIII: 250.
54 Janet Lecompte, "Marcelino Baca," Hafen, *Mountain Men*, III:21.
55 *Ibid*, III:22-24 passim.
56 *Ibid*, III:26.

While few Hispanic trappers seem to have thrived among mountain men, the opposite was true for New Mexican traders in Utah. The general anti-Mexican sentiment among Anglo-American settlers in Utah tended to drive New Mexican traders from the area. Throughout the 1840s and 1850s, New Mexicans found themselves unwelcome in Utah. Two events prompted the apparently inevitable end to New Mexican dominance of the Yuta trade: the settlement of Utah by the Mormons, and the U.S.-Mexico War of 1846. The latter resulted in the creation of territorial boundaries separating the jurisdictions between Utah and New Mexico. Within a decade of the Mexican War, Mormon officials in Utah made it clear that New Mexicans were no longer welcome in the area. Yet, as trail blazers into the the Yuta country during the Spanish Colonial and Mexican Territorial periods, New Mexicans had opened the way to Utah and southern Colorado and inspired the search for a route to California from the interior of North America. Indeed, the opening of a trail to California by Antonio Armijo inspired the development of Old Spanish Trail, which crisscrossed through southern Colorado and Utah. Californians referred to it as *El Camino de Nuevo México* (the Road to New Mexico). Variants of that route were used by Anglo-American immigrants to Utah and California. The Old Spanish Trail National Historic Trail was designated by Congress in 2001, recognizing it as a part of our national story and patrimony.[57]

The long history of the trails — one to southern Colorado and the other to California — is intricately tied to one another. That story began with the illegal traders from New Mexico in the seventeenth century and culminated with three significant "official" expeditions, the first two being unsuccessful. The first, a series of two expeditions, was led by Juan María Antonio Rivera in 1765; the second was led by friars Atanasio Domínguez and Silvestre Escalante in 1776; the third,

---

57 See *Old Spanish Historic Trail Feasibility Study and Environmental Assessment,* United States Department of the Interior, July 2001.

a successful effort, was led by Antonio Armijo in 1829. Certainly, pathways to California from New Mexico had been blazed in part by New Mexican traders between the period when illegal traders ventured to the land of the Yutas and 1829, when Antonio Armijo blazed a route to Los Angeles. Other parts of the routes were well-known to the various Native American tribes that guided Spanish traders and Anglo-American trappers alike across their lands. The historical New Mexican practice of going to the Yuta country had blossomed into a significant emigration trail which resulted in the development of the West. Indeed, the Hispanic development of the route to Colorado and California, traversing lands known to Rivera in 1765 and Domínguez and Escalante in 1776 — with all of its historical implications in the settlement of southern and western Colorado, northern Arizona, Utah, Nevada and parts of California — is a key part of our national story. As trailblazers on *el Camino Real de Tierra Adentro* and the Santa Fe-Chihuahua Trail as well as the Old Spanish Trail — all of them designated by the U.S. Congress as National Historic Trails in modern times — Hispanic frontiersmen have a special place in making New Mexico the heartland of the southwest. Indeed, once upon a time all roads led to Santa Fe.

Anglo-Americans began migrating into New Mexico soon after the Republic of Mexico gained independence from Spain in 1821. Almost immediately, a lively commerce between Missouri and New Mexico was established by William Becknell, historically known as the "Father of the Santa Fe Trail." Becknell began a commerce that depended upon pack mules and freight wagons. The Santa Fe-Chihuahua Trail trade ran its course from 1821 to the 1890s, when it was displaced by the railroad lines that ran along its corridor from Missouri to Santa Fe and then south to connections in Chihuahua. Trappers and traders entered Mexican territory along the corridor's various routes.

Before long, a connection was made between the Santa Fe Trail and the old Spanish plan to reach California. The Santa Fe Trail became a feeder route for one of the many California trails that were developing with the westward expansion of the United States. Santa Fe, Taos, Santa Cruz de la Cañada, Chama and Abiquiú were havens for Spanish traders and Anglo-American mountain men. From there, Hispanic and Anglo trappers and traders often elected to push northward toward southern Colorado, or westward to California.

Chapter II
The Search for the Río del Tizón: Renewed Spanish Colonial Interest in Colorado and Utah

> After we had discussed the new information among ourselves, all in agreement resolved that Gregorio de Sandoval, Antonio Martín, the interpreter, and I should go to the Payuchi settlement.
> — Juan María Antonio Rivera, 1765

The official exploration of southern Colorado and western Utah took place during the administrations of governors Vélez Capuchin and Mendinueta. Sanctioned by Governor Vélez Cachupín, the first two official expeditions to the Yuta country as far north as the Gunnison River and as far northwest as the Colorado River were led by Juan María Antonio Rivera in June and October of 1765. Eleven years later, in 1776, the first official Spanish expedition to reach modern day Utah Lake, near Provo, and the Great Salt Lake, occurred during the administration of Governor Mendinueta. That expedition was led by Friar Francisco Atanasio Domínguez and Friar Silvestre Vélez de Escalante. Between intervening years of war and peace, traders — most of them in violation of the *bandos* — set the stage for official Spanish exploration of the Yuta country. The expeditions led by Juan María

Antonio Rivera, Domínguez and Escalante, and Juan Bautista de Anza all left a written record as the first "official expeditions" to enter southern Colorado. However, they were not the first Hispanic New Mexicans to penetrate the mountains and forests of southern Colorado and Utah. Individuals who had been involved in the trade prohibited by the *bandos* served as scouts and guides for each of those subsequent officially authorized expeditions.

Since the seventeenth century, New Mexican traders had illegally carried on commerce with the Utes but had not left a record for fear of being detected by authorities, who had outlawed trade with the Utes and Plains tribes. Still, a written history can be pieced together from court cases that reveal that they had traded along the Arkansas, Gunnison, Colorado and Dolores Rivers or had passed through Utah's canyonlands, possibly as far as the Great Salt Lakes. Oddly, some of them served as guides for the aforementioned "official" expeditions.

By opening trade with the Yutas, Governor Tomás Vélez Cachupín's efforts may have led directly to the two official expeditions to the Yuta country led by Rivera he authorized in 1765. The immediate cause of the first Rivera expedition, however, was quickly justified when, sometime in 1765, a Ute warrior known as *Cuero de Lobo* (Wolfskin), stopped to trade in Abiquiú. When he traded a piece of silver ore to a blacksmith, the small village was abuzz with talk about a mountain of silver.[58] Reports of the silver ingot reached Santa Fe, and Governor Tomás Vélez Cachupín entertained a proposal to send an official expedition north to find both *Cuero de Lobo* and any evidence of a mountain of silver. That expedition, authorized by Vélez Cachupín, was led by Juan María Antonio Rivera with instructions to be undertaken as soon as possible.[59]

In the first expedition led by Rivera, efforts to determine the

---

58 Incomplete and untitled copy of Juan María Antonio Rivera's original Diary of the First Expedition, 23 de julio de 1765, in Diarios de reconocimientos de una parte de la América septentrional española, 176, Archivo del Servicio Histórico Militar, Madrid, hereinafter cited as ASHM. Translation by Joseph P. Sánchez.
59 *Ibid.*

source of the silver ore fell short, but, in terms of recording new geographic knowledge about the land and the people in western Colorado, the expedition reported new intelligence about the area. Indeed, Vélez Cachupín had instructed Rivera to describe the terrain. Still, it appears that Governor Vélez Cachupín hoped to keep the route a secret,[60] at least for the time being. Even so, Rivera's scouts and guides obviously knew the way to the Yuta country for they were traders who had carried on illegal trade with the Utes for a number of years. They seemed to know the area and Yuta settlements around the Dolores River and the terrain that surrounds present-day Durango as well as the La Plata Mountains.

The small party rendezvoused at Santo Tomás y Santa Rosa de Abiquiú, from which they departed in late June 1765. Rivera's guides and translators included, among others, Gregorio Sandoval, Antonio Martín, Joseph Martín, Andrés Sandoval, and Joaquín or Juachinillo, the interpreter, probably a genízaro of Ute origin.[61] In his diary entry for July 19, Rivera also mentioned Andrés Chama and Miguel Abeita. Some of the men spoke various Ute dialects.

Wending their way northward from Abiquiú along a route familiar to the guides, Rivera and his men reached the Chama River valley in the direction of *Piedra Parada* (literally Standing Rock, a well-known landmark known presently as Chimney Rock) in northwestern New Mexico. In the last days of June, the small party had traversed much rocky terrain to reach a small river called Las Cebollas. Rivera commented that

60 Donald C. Cutter, "Prelude to a Pageant in the Wilderness," *The Western Historical Quarterly* (Hereinafter cited as *WHQ*), January 1977, 8:14. An interpretation of the above cited Rivera journals found in the Servicio Histórico Militar in Madrid (see footnote 48) is offered by Cutter in his article. Cutter believed at the time of the publication of his essay that identification of these journals was hampered by the fact that the cover page is missing. However, the incomplete and untitled copy of the first diary is signed by Juan María Antonio Rivera on July 23, 1765, as is the complete second diary dated November 20, 1765.
61 Entry for June, 1765, Rivera, Diario, 23 de julio de 1765, ASHM. Also see Cutter, "Prelude," *WHQ*, 8:7

although it had excellent meadows, pasturage and wood, it was not a permanent river. "During dry years," he wrote "the river dries up, but it opens up near another river two leagues hence."[62] They pitched camp along its banks for the night. Leaving the Río de las Cebollas the next day, they came to the Río Chama some distance away. On June 28 on the occasion, Rivera wrote:

> We left the said place following the same direction bearing a little to the northwest. We traveled about five and a half to six leagues until we reached the Río Chama, leaving behind us another river which is permanent called Las Nutrias. The said route is along gentle land without any rock. It is somewhat uneven with some chamiso but well-provided with much pasturage as well as sufficient and good water. We rested along this river in a large meadow adjoining it. About three o'clock in the afternoon, we departed in the same direction.[63]

Once beyond the Río Chama, they proceeded through flat land passing by a large lake which Rivera described as "half a league long.... we named this place Laguna de San Pedro because it was his feast day. Along the way are many meadow lands, the principle one is called *El Coyote* by the Yutas...it has forty pools filled with water."[64]

On June 29, a short distance beyond the Río Chama, they passed through a small canyon and found a brackish spring the Yutas called *Agua del Berrendo* (Antelope Spring). Beyond, they came to another spring that they called *Tierra Amarilla* (Yellow Earth). Afterwards, having crossed through another small canyon, they camped near its exit for the night. Because it was so narrow, Rivera called it *Embudo* (Narrows). The next day, they continued their northwesterly march,

---

62 ASHM. Entry for June 27, 1765, Rivera, Diario, 23 de julio de 1765. Translation by Joseph P. Sánchez.
63 *Ibid.* Entry for June 28, 1765.
64 *Ibid.* Entry for June 29, 1765.

reaching the Río de Navajo where they stopped to rest. Resuming their march, they traveled in the same direction, passing a steep hill before reaching a river they named San Juan.[65]

For the next two days Rivera and his men continued northwesterly through a spring-filled canyon that the Yutas called *Lobo Amarillo* (Yellow Wolf). On July 1, 1765, Rivera noted:

> There, we stopped to rest for the afternoon. There must be from the said river [San Juan] to the *cienega* [in the small narrow canyon] five leagues. Afterwards we continued in the same direction traveling about two leagues through good land until arriving at the river the Yutas call Piedra Parada [Standing Rock] where we camped for the night. There is much pasturage, good meadowlands, and sufficient water.[66]

Rivera likely crossed the Río Navajó soon after, and two rivers they named the San Xavier and the Nuestra Señora de Guadalupe[67] before reaching another with pine trees along its banks, which they called Río Los Pinos.[68] Within the proximity of the river, they found some ruins of burnt adobe construction, and took samples to show Governor Vélez as evidence for future exploration.

Traveling west and slightly north on July 4, 1765, Rivera and his men came to present day Río Florido, smaller than Río de los Pinos, where they again discovered ruins of adobes and burned metals. Moving on, they reached another river that they named Río de las Animas,[69] a designation still used. The Animas River originates high in

---

65 *Ibid.* Entry for June 30, 1765.
66 *Ibid.* Entry for July 1, 1765.
67 Cutter, "Prelude," *WHQ* 8:8.
68 Entry for July 1, 1765, Rivera, Diario, 23 de julio de 1765, ASHM. In 1776, Domínguez and Escalante, using some of Rivera's men as guides, passed through this same territory. Chávez, trans., and Warner, ed., *The Domínguez-Escalante Journal*, 10.
69 ASHM. Entry for July 4, 1765.

the San Juan Mountains. In 1776, Domínguez and Escalante, relying on Rivera's guides, said that, at that point, they were near the western point of La Sierra de la Plata.[70]

Along the river, Rivera encountered a *ranchería* (Indian settlement) led by principal chief Coraque and his three subordinate Indian captains Joso, El Cabezón, and Picado.[71] Quickly distributing gifts of maize, pinole, and tobacco, Rivera hoped to get information about the whereabouts of Cuero de Lobo. Chief Coraque responded that he was not there as he had gone to a Payuchi settlement about five leagues distant to visit his mother-in-law.[72]

Rivera also learned about another Ute *ranchería* downstream on the Animas River led by a chief whose name in Spanish was Caballo Rosillo (Red Horse). There, they understood, lived an old woman who knew of another silver deposit. As the story went, her father had at one time taken silver ore to trade with a Spaniard named Joseph Manuel Trujillo Herrera in Abiquiú. Trujillo, had "made two rosaries and a cross from it."[73] On July 6, along with a translator, Rivera took a small party to find the woman while the rest of the expedition continued to the Río Dolores near present-day Dolores, Colorado. Of his encounter with the woman, Rivera wrote:

> After we had discussed the new information among ourselves, all in agreement resolved that Gregorio de Sandoval, Antonio Martín, the interpreter, and I should go to the Payuchi settlement. Having finished our business, we went to see whether the said Yuta woman would give us new information about the Yuta we sought. When we got there, we presented her with gifts as we did with other Yutas. We visited with her hoping to get a better

---

70 Chávez, trans., and Warner, ed., *The Domínguez-Escalante Journal*, 11.
71 ASHM. Entry for July 5, 1765, Rivera, Diario, 23 de julio de 1765, ASHM. Also see, Cutter, "Prelude," *WHQ* 8:8.
72 *Ibid.* Entry for July 5, 1765.
73 *Ibid.* Entry for July 6, 1765.

understanding from her. When we told her our business, she put on such a mean face that she had nothing over the devil.[74]

Disappointed and offended by her attitude, the Spaniards departed.

They rode back to the to the *ranchería*, where Rivera voiced his displeasure about the woman to Chief Asigare, a Payuchi war captain. Through Antonio Martín, his interpreter, Rivera complained about her treatment of them. Asigare then sent one of his men to get the old woman. Standing before them, she explained that she and others, had just come down with a load of red clay from the mountain that Rivera's translator called the Sierra del Datil. When Rivera asked her to take them to the mountain and show them the silver deposits, she had refused, explaining that she had become abusive after she had explained to them that she would not go back to show them the silver deposits. To make amends, she agreed to give them directions to the silver outcroppings, which were some distance away. Hoping to reach the mountain before the end of the day, Rivera, his small escort, and their Yuta guides left, in a hurry on July 8. Running their horses first at a quick trot, then at a full gallop, they briefly stopped along a stream to rest themselves and their jaded horses. Of the excursion, Rivera explained that

> We continued the route, and after traveling a little way we came upon the hogan of a Navajo and the dry arroyo which seemed to be what the Yuta woman had told us about. Leaving the route on the right side, we went up the arroyo to the part where a small hill begins which faces north. We climbed and moved from one to another part for about six leagues through forest and flat land. We surveyed different places trying to find the land the Yuta woman had told us about and as the Yuta chieftain had shown us. So angry were we at the

---

74 *Ibid.* Entry for July 6, 1765.

Yuta woman, that we returned where she was as thoughts to kill her for lying to us and costing us so much hardship crossed our minds. By the time we got to the settlement, however, we had calmed down. At a fast trot and gallop, we got to a camp where our men were taking their siesta along one of the rivers which we had crossed previously. We called it Río del Luzero....There, we encountered and rejoined our men after three days of absence without anything to eat....In the end, what mattered most was to find the said Yuta Cuero de Lobo.[75]

Rivera and his men returned to Asigare's rancheria where they left the Ute guide, and headed back to Chief Coraque's ranchería to reunite with the rest of his men, who had stayed behind.

Eight days later, Rivera and his men passed through another Ute ranchería. There, Andrés Sandoval and Rivera met with Payuchis Chief Chino. As usual, Rivera presented Chief Chino with gifts of tobacco, pinole, flour, and corn, hoping to win him over.[76] Chief Chino asked them what they were doing in such forbidding country so far from home? Rivera told him that they sought a Yuta called Cuero de Lobo who was said to be living among the Payuchi. Changing subjects, Rivera asked Chief Chino about the large river known to the Spaniards as the Río del Tizón (a Spanish name for the lower Colorado River since the 1540s).

In regard to Cuero de Lobo, Chief Chino said that he had been living among them but had returned to his land. Hoping to discourage the Spaniards from traveling any further, Chief Chino told them that the river they sought was too far away and that the only way there was through rough waterless country with little forage for their animals. The route was so treacherous and winding that their horses would quickly fatigue. He also told them that the sun's heat was so severe and

---

75 *Ibid.* Entry for July 8, 1765.
76 *Ibid.* Entry for July 16, 1765.

insufferable along that route that he and his men would get dizzy and sick from it.

Worse things would plague them on the journey, Chief Chino said because, as he cautioned, the Spaniards did not know the way, they would suffer many hardships or they would die from hunger, that is, if hostile tribes on either side of the river did not kill them first. He urged them to return to their own land. Then, Chief Chino confided to Rivera saying that if he really wanted to proceed, the best time to go would be "when the leaves of the trees start to fall," sometime around the month of October on the Spanish calendar.[77] He also told them the best way to get to the Río del Tizón, saying that "we could go along the entire river where we were presently, which flows into the Río del Tizón."[78] The travel time, however, was an exaggeration. He said that from where they were presently, it would take six days among numerous tribes along the way.

Chief Chino told them spellbinding stories of strange, wild people and creatures they would encounter along the river's path. Warning them of the perils beyond Payuchi territory, Chief Chino told them that before getting there, they would encounter a tribe called Orejas Agujeradas [Pierced Ears]. He told them, as did Chief Asigare, that there was one tribe that "kills people solely with the smoke that they make without one being aware that they had done so." He explained that once the smoke reached the olfactory senses, the victim died quickly. He told them about a particular animal who would tear apart anyone who passed his domain and did not pay him a pelt as homage. He also told Rivera that "on the other side of the river there is a large trench which is so broad that trade is made without crossing it. The people throw what they want to trade across it: bridles and knives which the Spaniards trade with the Yutas and other tribes. Those from the other side throw their chamois across in exchange."[79]

---

77 *Ibid.* Entry for July 16, 1765.
78 *Ibid.* Entry for July 16, 1765.
79 *Ibid.* Entry for July 15, 1765.

So foreign was the area to him and other Utes in the area, said Chief Chino, that the languages spoken along the river were so different that some tribes could not intelligently communicate with one another. Despite the depth of the river, Chief Chino said that, it could be crossed. There, they would meet the "bearded Indians" they sought. Chief Chino explained that

> The manner of crossing the river is on a vessel called a jícara which carries only two people. They sit back to back, with one facing where they have left, and the other where they are going. Those on this bank of the river cannot cross until the river is low as it is so big. On the other side are some bearded white men dressed in armor with metal hats. Even their women adorn both their arms with iron armlets called brazaletes. Their hair is styled with braids as do Spanish women. Among them is one they call Castira, which means Castilla. that is what is known about the said river.[80]

The two talked into the night. Whether Rivera believed all that was said to him is uncertain, but he did, of course, record the conversation in his account to Governor Vélez Cachupin. Perhaps the most interesting part of Chino's ruminations about the Colorado River and its tie to the Río del Tizón, was the part about the bearded Indians who lived along the river. That story would be worth verifying by later expeditions.

The next day, Rivera continued his search for Cuero de Lobo. Stopping at different rancherías along the way, the Spaniards traded with the Payuchis. At day's end, they camped along the Río del Luzero. Departing the river the next day, they went toward a large mountain which was, as Rivera noted,

> part of the Sierra de la Plata called La Grulla where there is a river with abundant water. We called it the

---

80 *Ibid.* Entry for July 16, 1765.

Río de San Joaquín. There we found about twenty Yuta camps. Among them was Cuero de Lobo. We gave gifts to everyone in a way that would be possible to have enough. Afterwards we began to communicate. Cuero de Lobo said that if we gave him a horse for the next day, we would go see the silver."[81] Rivera observed that they spent the rest of the day in conversation with the Yutas, but learned nothing new.

On July 19, they prepared to go see the mountain of silver. Of the event, Rivera wrote:

> We got the horses ready. One of the Yutas named Chief Largo seeing that we prepared to leave asked us for a horse so that he could accompany us. One was given to him. Then Cuero de Lobo said that not all of us should go, only Gregorio Sandoval, Joseph Martín, Miguel Abeita, Andrés Chama, the interpreter, and myself. That done, we traveled along the upper river through the water instead of the land route as both banks were formed by an escarpment which appeared eminent. We went about eight leagues until we arrived at a bend which the mountain makes. There is a short piece of flat terrain....There, we left the horses and we climbed to its summit where we say a great variety of veins of various colors which are countless. It can be said without exaggeration that the entire mountain is made of pure metal. All around could be seen pamino which is red and yellow; in other parts there is caliche of small white gravel. The stone throughout manifested great richness of metals. We particularly found some veins of black lead [atescatetado] and others of red lead. Punta de Ahuja [needle point] and other dark or light metals

---

81 *Ibid.* Entry for July 17-18, 1765.

which look like quicksilver. In order to see better if various types of silver could be found as the Yutas had told us, we camped on that mountain for two days. We could not learn more because the Yutas explained that what they thought was silver was actually lead....On July 22...Realizing we could not accomplish our objective, we descended the mountain carrying some loose metal ore as we did not have the proper equipment to dig for more other than a chisel for cutting silver.[82]

Disappointed at not finding silver in the mountain, which they ironically called the Sierra de la Plata (Mountain Range of Silver), Rivera left the area. Stories about the Sierra de la Plata and its promise flitted about New Mexico for years. Eleven years later, Domínguez and Escalante corroborated Rivera's story somewhat, probably adding a bit more hopeful information than actually existed. Describing the Sierra de la Plata, Domínguez and Escalante remarked about one of its canyons "in which there are said to be veins and outcropping of metallic ore." In the same entry, Escalante made reference to the Rivera expedition's sojourn through the same country. Hope sprang eternal, as he wrote:

> However, although years ago certain individuals from New Mexico came to inspect them by order of the governor, who at the time was Don Tomás Vélez Cachupín, and carried back metal-bearing rocks, it was not ascertained for sure what kind of metal they consisted of. The opinion which some formed previously, from the accounts of various Indians, and from some citizens of the kingdom, that they were silver ore, furnished the sierra with this name.[83]

---

82 *Ibid.* Entry for July 19-22, 1765.
83 Chávez, trans., and Warner, ed., *The Domínguez and Escalante Journal*, 10.

Although Domínguez and Escalante appeared exuberant in their description, Rivera, on the other hand, never claimed to have found silver. Returning to the Dolores River, Rivera and his men were disappointed not to find the silver deposit they sought.[84] Having learned of a large river further on, probably the Río del Tizón, the explorers returned to New Mexico with the idea that they would undertake another expedition.

Back in Santa Fe, Rivera reported to Governor Vélez Cachupin regarding the many tribes they had met and his encounter with Cuero de Lobo, whom he had found living among the Payuchis. He reported about the many ruins of ancient pueblos he had seen and the many fantastic stories Chief Chino had recounted. Rivera told him about the mountain of lead. Undeterred, Governor Vélez Cachupín, became all the more interested in approving a second expedition in the fall of 1765, as recommended by Chief Chino.

---

84 Cutter, "Prelude," *WHQ*, 8:9.

Chapter III
Rivera's Second Expedition to the Yutas, October 1765

> We asked them if there was water ahead. They said
> there was not much more than a small spring which
> was around the hill from where they stood. From
> there, it would take one day to reach the Tabeguachi
> nation.
>
> — Juan María Antonio Rivera, 1765

Just as Chief Chino had suggested, in autumn 1765 Governor Tomas
Vélez Cachupín approved Rivera's second expedition to the Yuta country.
This time, Rivera was to determine the location of the large river they
had heard about. The governor still hoped to discover whether silver
could be found within its environs. With new instructions in hand,
Rivera hoped to find the Payuchis, who had offered to lead them to the
Río del Tizón and enable them to learn about its land and people. To
that end, Vélez Cachupín instructed Rivera to "ingratiate themselves
immediately with the Payuchi settlement that had offered to show
them the way to the Río del Tizón, winning them over by smoking
tobacco with them."[85] In particular, Vélez Cachupín wanted to know

---

85 Ynstrucción que deverán observar, Juan María Rivera, Antonio Martín, y Gregorio

if there were large towns in the area, what other nations lived along its banks, or about the twice-told tale that flitted throughout Abiquiú that white, bearded men "dressed in a European manner" lived along the river. The expedition's members carried trade goods with them in case they met up with other European traders in the area, they would claim to be trading rather than exploring. Should Rivera deem it safe for his men to cross the river and trade, he was instructed to do so, provided they were accompanied by the Payuchi.

Regarding the Río del Tizón, Rivera was instructed to see if it "originates from the Gran Laguna Copala which the Pueblo Indians call Teguayo that they say is where they come from."[86] The one question that would not go away concerned the Sierra de la Plata. The governor's instructions included one special order: that on his return from the Río del Tizón, Rivera should re-survey the Sierra de la Plata or La Grulla to see whether rich metal could be found there as he had seen what appeared to be virgin silver."[87] Rivera and his men departed Abiquiú in early October 1765, just as the leaves had started to turn. Leaving Abiquiú behind them, the expedition headed northerly with the general idea of finding the Río del Tizón, which meandered westward before turning south to the Sea of Cortez.

With new members added to his second expedition, Rivera felt more confident of his ability to accomplish the goals set by his governor. These other men, who had actively traded illegally with the Utes, were very familiar with the terrain; a few of them spoke Indian languages. Among them were Gregorio Sandoval, Antonio Martín, and the interpreter Joaquín, *indio genízaro*, from Abiquiú. Three names not mentioned in Rivera's diary but who apparently participated in the expedition were

---

Sandoval, con el Ynterprete Joachín, indio genízaro de el Pueblo de Abiquiú con la comisión que por su práctica se les carga in Diarios de reconocimientos de una parte de la América septentrional española, 1766, ASHM. Translation by Joseph P. Sánchez.
86 *Ibid.*
87 *Ibid.*

Andrés Muñiz, his brother Antonio Lucrecio Muñiz, and Pedro Mora, all served as a guides in the Domínguez-Escalante expedition ten years later. Some of the men would later serve as soldiers, guides, and translators for Governor Juan Bautista de Anza in his 1779 campaign against the Comanche.

On a cool October day, deep in the mountains far from Abiquiú, the last Spanish outpost in the region, Rivera again entered the Payuchi settlement along the Río Nuestra Señora de Dolores and met with their leaders and other Payuchi and Mauchi warriors. "We met two captains of the adjoining settlements," he wrote, "...Asigare, who guided us on our first expedition, and the other named Cabezón of the Mauchi nation. We gave them gifts in the best possible way so as to make it possible to converse with them about our desire for them to show us as friends to the other people and nations ahead so that we could trade with them without revealing our real purpose."[88] Their "real purpose," aside from exploring for silver, was to learn as much about the land as possible for future exploration. Suspicious, the Yutas, concerned about possible Spanish intrigue, refused to take them anywhere. Chief Cabezón told them that "The Mauchi decided not to let us pass saying that we were going to reconnoiter their lands and could ruin their trade."[89] The Yutas spoke among themselves about whether or not to trust the Spaniards.

Unexpectedly, Chief Asigare interrupted the meeting and, unbeknownst to Chief Cabezón, had already arranged for a certain Payuchi warrior to guide the Spaniards. With much commotion, the Payuchi warrior appeared among the Mauchi warriors, offering himself as a guide and saying he had no fear of the Spaniards. A scuffle broke out when a Mauchi warrior leaped from the group and struck the Payuchi. Upon seeing the attack on one of his warriors, Chief Asigare announced that he would provide guides to the Spaniards and "that although he was too ill to go, he did not support the immediate disturbance."[90] The next

---

88 ASHM. October 5, 1765, Rivera.
89 *Ibid.*
90 *Ibid.*

day, Asigare sent Rivera the grandson of Chief Chino to serve as a guide. The Spaniards paid him, probably by giving him a horse, and shortly departed, descending the Río Nuestra Señora de los Dolores.

Escorted by Chief Chino's grandson, Rivera and his men left the Payuchi *ranchería* bound for Chief Chino's Payuchi settlement. Meandering northwest, they veered toward the northeast for twelve leagues as they wended their way beyond the Río Dolores. When they reached Chief Chino's settlement, they noted only five campsites. Saying that most of the warriors were out hunting deer, Chief Chino met them and accepted their gifts. He said that his grandson would take them any place they wanted to go within his territory. He advised them that as they were not far from the boundary of his land, they should find a guide from another tribe to take them beyond. After that, Chief Chino departed.

Given the gray gloomy sky, Rivera and his men named the settlement La Soledad.[91] Rivera wrote that the terrain beyond there provided good pasturage for his animals and good shelter for his men. From La Soledad, they traveled over the ridge of a mountain and descended into a canyon.

A day later, after crossing a series of beautiful valleys, with many basins and ridges that were easily traveled with no delays, they reached five Payuchi settlements along a small stream filled with gravel.[92] As the Spaniards approached the settlements, the natives, sounding alarms, fled into the forest. Gregorio Sandoval and the Payuchi guide went out to convince them to return. They "attempted to talk to their guards and calm them by explaining that we were Spaniards of Peace who came to trade with them."[93] After assuring them that they came in peace, they met and arranged for another guide to take them where they wanted to go. Before letting their former guide depart, the Spaniards gave him a horse, and "we bade him take care of it like no other."[94]

---

91 ASHM. October 6, Segundo Diario de Rivera.
92 *Ibid.*
93 ASHM. October 7, Segundo Diario de Rivera.
94 *Ibid.*

Moving eastward their new guide led them for about two leagues before winding around a very steep ridge and turning northward for three more leagues. Veering northwest about a league and a half they reached a stream. Just beyond there, they stopped to rest on the ridge of a mountain they called San Cristóbal. From there, as far as the eye could see, they took in a panoramic view of the country with all its valleys and four branching streams. The next day they went northwest following a wide path to a canyon until they reached three Mauchi settlements. Meeting them, Rivera wrote,

> We asked them if there was water ahead. They said there was not much more than a small spring which was around the hill from where they stood. From there, it would take one day to reach the Tabeguachi nation. On the way, there is a very full river in which one cannot stand, for its canyon-like banks are too steep and narrow. There is no meadow there for one to walk on or to make camp unless one ascends the ridge. Thanking them, we decided to stay there and camp rather than suffer ahead.[95]

Departing the Mauchi settlement the next day, October 10, they went through a very narrow trail. The terrain was rough and difficult. Harassing winds attacked them as temperatures dropped. With much difficulty they finally exited the canyon. Rivera described their ordeal:

> We went west about three leagues through level terrain with little rock. It had some small oak along the route to a short canyon which was very rocky. Getting on the trail which was so narrow that a horse barely fit on it, as from its trail head to the end was three musket shots long. It cost us much work to get through it, having to lift much of our cargo which was made more difficult by the

---

95 ASHM. October 9, Segundo Diario de Rivera.

cold and furious winds from the north that blew through there. It was so strong that the horses and mules balked at it; we had to turn their heads away from the wind. The wind blew for more than a half hour. Had it been longer, we might have frozen to death. Descending a ridge, we looked for a place to get out through another canyon which was between two mountains, but it turned out impossible, for the only way out was the canyon through which ran the river. This was so difficult that the only way out was to stay in the river which reached the chests of the horses. It was that way until we ascended the next ridge of the mountain on the other side which was also steep and narrow like the previous one. In one, we had to remove the cargo from the animals to get through; in the other, we had to wend our way by pulling the animals through (some by the ears), and in another by their tails. Having ascended the ridge, we could see a very pleasant valley as far as the eye could see.[96]

They called the place the Sierra de los Tabeguachis [present Uncompahgre Plateau], a landmark later reached by the Domínguez and Escalante expedition of 1776.

At the Sierra de los Tabeguachis, they met a Tabeguachi warrior who sat and talked with them. He said his people were nearby and warned them of possible Comanche warriors in the area. He said that a few days before, the Tabeguachi had fought a battle with the Comanche and had taken horses from them. After going six to seven leagues through a canyon, the Spaniards reached a Tabeguachi settlement called Passochi, named after three boys of their tribe who had burned to death there. The Spaniards were greeted by Chief Tonampechi and a number of Tabeguachi warriors, who took them to a good camping spot near their settlement. The Tabeguachi shared some of their deer

---

96 ASHM. October 10 in Segundo Diario de Rivera.

meat with them, and the Spaniards responded in kind, giving them some of their provisions. Although the Tabeguachi had planned to celebrate their victory over the Comanche, Chief Tonampechi told his people to cancel their dances that night so that they could gather and talk with the Spaniards.

After sunset, the Tabeguachi sat in a circle with their guests. As a sign of peace, they smoked tobacco and shared their food. In his diary, Rivera wrote that "They told us that Spaniards had never passed through the country where we were going, and the people would be agitated. They asked us not to cross where we planned, for the people on the other side would cause us harm. The chief told us to beware of those who called themselves friends. They already knew that we were going to the big river to see where there might be other Spaniards."[97]

The Tabeguachi told them that, because it was too far north from where they were located, they did not know the way to where the Spaniards wanted to go. They warned that the risk was too great, as they had been at war with the Comanche. It would be better, they said, for them not to go there. Defiantly but politely, Rivera responded that the words of the Tabeguachi were "nothing more than pretenses not to let us go there."[98] He said that they would still go even though they might be killed. Rivera wrote in his diary that, "we still wanted to go forward." He insisted that the Tabeguachi who "knew the land and the way should tell us."[99] Finally, the Tabeguachi , saying that they were indeed friends of the Spaniards, relented. They would be happy, if they were properly paid, to guide them "to the Río Grande del Tizón by way of the north end where many go to trade with the people on the other side."[100]

Rivera and his men remained with the Tabeguachi for three days. During that time, they celebrated and traded. Even though he thought

---

97 *Ibid.*
98 *Ibid.*
99 *Ibid.*
100 *Ibid.*

it a good idea to stay and reinforce his friendship with the Tabeguachi, he complained that

> We did not wish to make them unhappy, but to the point, we did not like wasting two days in the same place participating in their style of trade, which we thought badly done, for our maintenance of food and tobacco was not useful. On the third day, they gave us a celebration with a dance which began at sunrise, wasting in it much food. Nevertheless, we reciprocated with a good meal which left them very amenable."[101] Although the Tabeguachi were somewhat loath to guide the Spaniards saying no one knew the way, "That night they drew us a plan of the Río Tizón showing us the many watering places everywhere on the west side.[102]

A few days later, Rivera and his men, led by their Tabeguachi guide, left the Tabeguachi settlement, moving in a northwest direction.

After two leagues of march, their guide led them off the path, saying that there was little water along it and too much rock which would fatigue their horses and mules. He said it would be better that they cross a smaller mountain that had little rock and much water along the way. The Tabeguachi guide told them that the Tabaguachi often went that way to the big river. Having no contrary argument, and deciding to trust him, Rivera and his men shrugged their shoulders and acquiesced. "We followed his judgment," wrote Rivera, "and we traveled over the mountain about fourteen leagues making certain of what he told us. We continued going to the said watering place which is in the most conspicuous place, but it had such little water that it lasted for only half of our herd; it also had little pasturage, poor shelter, but much firewood. That night occurred such a furious storm of wind and rain that given what had

---

101 *Ibid.*
102 *Ibid.*

gone on before we named this place Purgatory."[103] The impressive place name, "*Purgatorio*," revealed where the Rivera expedition had reached to that point. It would not, however, be the only place with the sobriquet "Purgatory" in Colorado's history.

A day later, they traveled five leagues to the north through an area filled with small cactus plants. Suddenly, Rivera and his men grew animated when their guide told them that they were near the Río del Tizón. Crossing through rough terrain toward the river, Rivera reported that it, "...stretched for three leagues with such great abundance [of cacti] that the horses and mules could not go through it except over a trail until we descended to a very mountainous valley with no pasturage, and no shelter....I agreed with the guide...to go to the watering place that was in a canyon which had a stream...we traveled...a little more than ten leagues. After the horses and mules had been watered, our guide told us that we would climb to the top of a hill which was on the other side of the stream and we would see the Río Grande del Tizón which we sought."[104]

On October 16, the expedition reached the large river called the Río del Tizón. The Tabeguachi guide summoned some of the boys who had come with him. He told them to bid the people on the other side of the river to come and trade with the Spaniards. Seizing the moment, Gregorio Sandoval and Rivera went with them to scout along the river. "We crossed the only ford it has," wrote Rivera, "the high water reached the saddles of our horses....The width of the ford is 60 to 70 *varas*,[105] the rest of the river is boxed with steep banks. It is very enclosed at its deepest part which is three *estados*. Three streams flow into it up river to the east. When it floods, it fills the entire meadow which is more than a league. It reaches the bottom of a hill where it leaves debris."[106]

Doubting that it was the river he sought, Rivera expressed his disappointment that the river did not meet his expectations and

103 ASHM. Entry for October 14 in Segundo Diario de Rivera.
104 ASHM. Entry for October 15 of Segundo Diario de Rivera.
105 A standard vara is approximately 32.5 inches long.
106 ASHM. Entry for October 16 of Segundo Diario de Rivera.

questioned whether it was the Río del Tizón. He told his guide that he felt something was amiss. Rivera could not believe the large river he saw was the river he sought. Finally after meeting other Yutas who seemed to confirm to him that it was the large river he sought, he changed his mind and felt confident that he had reached the Río del Tizón. Still, his doubt persisted. A doubting Rivera wrote:

> Once again, we communicated with our guide telling him that this was not the Río del Tizón which we sought and that he had failed us. To that he responded sadly that there was no other major river in the area than that one. He would never have brought us here had he not heard the people down at the ranchería say that the high river was not passable for it was now reaching the meadow. At the confluence of all the large rivers we had crossed, we met some people and asked them, and we now felt certain about the river: here was the crossing to go to the Spaniards on the other side who were five or six jornadas [days] march. It could be done at great risk owing to hostile tribes in the area.[107]

Concerned, the Tabeguachi guide and other Yutas warned Rivera not to cross the Río del Tizón. Knowing what they knew of the hostile tribes on the other side, Rivera would do so at his own risk. Hoping to scare off Rivera, they said that about a day's march, not far after crossing the river, he would meet a tribe that ate their children because the hunting in their area was so poor.

Beyond them, about a days' ride, the Spaniards would encounter other people, very white with hair the color of straw. They were the most war-like of all the tribes in the area. Their territory was so large it would take two days to cross it. The danger there would be so great that they recommended that the Spaniards cross it only at night. Beyond their land, Rivera and his men would reach the foot of a small mountain with

---

107 *Ibid.*

66

a bountiful lake. In that land lived a people who were like rocks.[108] After crossing their land, they would head toward the skirt of a mountain in which direction they would encounter the Spaniards they sought. "They live on the banks of a small stream with plenty of water," wrote Rivera, "These are the first people one reaches who have houses. They are Spaniards, we are told, because they speak just like us, they are very fair, with heavy beards, and they dress in buckskin, for they do not have clothes like us in our land."[109] Thus, the stories about the "bearded Indians" who lived near the Río del Tizon received a renewed interest.

Momentarily unimpressed and undaunted, Rivera told his guide that if he led them there he would pay him more. He demurred. Consulting with another man who claimed to be his father, the Tabaguache said that the expedition was too small in number to go any further. He told Rivera that, "Upon reaching a ruddy-colored people, they would take each of us by the hand in peace, and we would never again return to our land or ever be seen again. They would kill our guides for having taken us there. As captain, I should go back and bring more people, only that way would it be possible to enter that land."[110] No, he would not lead Rivera there.

The following day, October 17, Rivera unexpectedly found himself communicating with five "Seguaguana" [Sabuagana] messengers. They came to persuade him not to go any farther and informed him that there were no people in the area because they were scattered throughout the mountains hunting. Rivera, still in doubt, asked them about whether this was the large river he sought. Their response seemed to convince him that it was. He wrote, "We asked them about what had occurred with our guide in relation to the river....They confirmed the same, and we were then persuaded that it was the river we sought, although we did not

---

108 Oddly, an old Ute word "Timpanogos" appears to mean "the stone person" in reference to the imaginary figure of a reclining human being formed by the ridges of the presant-day mountain Timpanogos. See Chávez, trans., and Warner, ed., *The Domínguez-Escalante Journal*, 27, fn. 133. Could Rivera have taken literally what the Tabeguachis had told him?

109 ASHM. Entry for October 16 of Segundo Diario de Rivera.

110 *Ibid.*

feel we were at the right part of it."[111] Regarding the Bearded Spaniards he sought, they told him that their leader was Chief Cuchara, who knew about them because he had been in a battle with them. They told him that they had stayed away from him because they thought he was angry at them as they too had killed Spaniards. They said all the Spaniards had been killed in battle. "With that", wrote Rivera, "the talking stopped."[112]

Rivera stayed one more day, long enough to trade with the Sabuagana, who had invited the Spaniards to trade with another chieftain not far from where they were. They stayed at that settlement for two days because their horses were jaded and their hooves needed to be shod. As soon as he could, Rivera called his men together to decide whether they should go on. Evaluating their condition and that of their animals as well as their provisions, they doubted the wisdom of going any further.

On October 20, guided by Sabuaganas, Rivera turned the expedition around, heading eastward away from the river. Traveling through large valleys that had numerous cactus plants for long distances, they reached a large spring and camped for the night. That day, they recounted, that they had traveled twelve leagues, nearly 32 miles, The next day, traveling in the same direction they reached another Sabuagana settlement. Their chief, too ill to accompany them, told them that as soon as he recovered, he would take them to where there was silver, which they called "cuchillo." The Comanche threat was prevalent among the Utes. The chief told Rivera that it was too risky to go as the Comanches in the area had recently attacked them. Although Rivera still wanted to go to the part of the Río del Tizón where the Bearded Spaniards lived, he cautiously decided to stay and trade with the Sabuaganas. Insisting on going beyond the river, Rivera returned to the Río del Tizón. Assessing his options and his odds of survival, he finally gave up his quest and decided to return to New Mexico. In the last entry of his second diary, he wrote: "In the meadow of the Great Río Tizón, on a tree with white bark, I carved a

---

111 ASHM. Entry for October 17 of Segundo Diario de Rivera.
112 *Ibid.*

large cross with the words ˋLong Live Jesus' at the top and my name. At the foot of the tree, I carved the year so that it could be verified at a future time that we had gotten that far."[113]

Back in Santa Fe. Rivera made his last entry in his diary, dated November 20, 1765. He ended it by writing "The return trip took fourteen and a half days by the most direct route with regular marches. It is estimated that the distance from the Villa de Santa Fe to the Río del Tizón is one hundred fifty leagues. I judge that the referenced river empties into the Gulf of California."[114] His conclusion was probably based on knowledge gained about the Colorado River by New Mexican frontiersmen who had figured that the river ran from high in the Colorado mountains through the Grand Canyon and down along the edge of the Mojave Desert. Even so, Rivera confirmed and added new knowledge about what lay in western Colorado and eastern Utah. In his diary, he identified Yuta groups not previously known to the Spaniards. By the same token, he contributed to the mythology of the area, for the stories he heard from the Tabeguachis seemed to conjure up legends of mythical civilizations that had similarly puzzled Spanish explorers since the sixteenth century.

Doubtless the Tabeguachi's stories, piqued Rivera's curiosity, for he believed that some elements of what the Tabeguachi had said were plausible, even though there was plenty of room for skepticism. The persistence of such stories about cannibalistic native groups in North America, and other curiosities upon which European lore fed, surfaced again in the 1770s. In 1775-76, the Franciscan explorer, Fray Francisco Hermenegildo Garcés, while blazing a trail from Mission San Gabriel in the Los Angeles area eastward toward the Mojave Desert and the Colorado River, dispelled the rumor of the possible practice of cannibalism in that area. Garcés wrote: "[Regarding] the Chidumas, who I persuade myself are the Yumas, up to the present time have I not heard that they eat

---

113 ASHM. Entry for October 21 of Segundo Diario de Rivera.
114 ASHM. Last entry in Segundo Diario de Rivera.

human flesh."[115] It seems that Spanish colonials always kept one ear cocked in expectation that they would hear about cannibalism among the tribes of North America. The stories told to Rivera seemed to confirm that possibility.

In 1765, Rivera's exploration of the San Miguel, Uncompahgre, Gunnison and Colorado rivers opened new vistas. They were the first Europeans to describe the Uncompahgre Plateau along with its surrounding mountains, ridges, valleys and rivers. One of the rivers, that the New Mexicans called Río de San Francisco, was called *Ancapagri*,[116] by the Yutas, a word that gives rise to the present-day word "Uncompahgre." New Mexicans, who went there in the middle 1700s and again between 1776 and 1797 wrote it as they phonetically heard from the Yutas with different variations: *Ancapagri, Hancapagari* and *Aricapuaguro*. To the Utes, it meant "Red Lake" so called for" a spring of red-colored water, hot and ill-tasting."[117] Today, the place name "Uncompahgre Plateau" designates a large geographic area that encompassess five counties: Delta, Mesa, Montrose, Ouray and San Miguel. Within the Uncompahgre Plateau are large canyons that bear the names of Escalante, the Big Dominguez, and Tabeguache. Through the canyons, which are separated by ridges and mesas, run the Dolores, Gunnison, San Miguel Uncompahgre and Colorado rivers. The Uncompahgre has an average elevation of 9,500 feet above sea level. Rivera's men seemed to know the area. Indeed, a decade later, while illegally trading in the area in

---

115 Elliott Coues, translator and editor, *On the Trail of a Spanish Pioneer: The Diary and Itinerary of Francisco Garcés (Missionary Priest) in His Travels through Sonora, Arizona, and California, 1775-1776* (New York: Francis P. Harper, 1900, 2 Vols.), 1:474. Coues comments about Garcés's apt remark that the Chidumas were a Yuman tribe "variously called *Alchedomas, Halchedomas, Jalchedomas, Jalchedums,* etc." 1:474, note 23.

116 Ted J. Warner, ed., Fray Angelico Chávez, trans. *The Domínguez-Escalante Journal: Their Expedition through Colorado, Utah, Arizona, and New Mexico in 1776.* Salt Lake City: University of Utah Press, 1995, p. 29.

117 Warner and Chávez, *The Domínguez-Escalante Journal,* p. 29. Also see Proceedings against Cristóbal Lovato, et al, Río Arriba, 2 August to 2 September 1797, SANM, II, Microfilm Roll 14, frame 112.

1775, three of Rivera's guides, Andrés Muñiz, Pedro Mora and Gregorio Sandoval retraced their steps to the Colorado River and crossed it.

In 1776, the Domínguez-Escalante Expedition passed through the same area as it meandered through western Colorado. They confirmed what Rivera had seen. Reflecting on the Rivera Expedition of 1765, Escalante, while camped on the east bank of the Uncompahgre River on August 28, 1776, wrote:

> Farther down, and about four leagues to the north of this Vega de San Agustín, this river joins another, larger one, named San Xavier [today's Gunnison River] by our own, and river of the Tomichi by the Yutas. To these two rivers, already joined together, there came Don Juan María de Ribera in the year of '65, crossing the same Sierra de los Tabehuachis, on the top of which is the site he named El Purgatorio, according to the indications he gives in his itinerary.

> The meadow where he halted in order to ford the river — and where they say he carved on a poplar sapling a cross, the letters spelling his name and the expedition's year — is situated almost near the same juncture on the southern side, as we were assured by our interpreter, Andrés Muñiz, who came with the said Don Juan María in the year mentioned as far as La Sierra de los Tabehuachis. He said that although he had stayed three days' marches behind on this side of the river at that time when he came along its edge this past year of '75 with Pedro Mora and Gregorio Sandoval — who had accompanied Don Juan María throughout the entire expedition mentioned — they said that they had reached it then and from it had started their return, they alone having crossed it when they were sent by the said Don Juan María to look for Yutas on the side opposite the meadow where they stopped and from where they came back — and so, that this was the

one which they then judged to be the great Río del Tizón [Colorado River].[118]

Domínguez and Escalante confirmed that Rivera's men had gone upstream and eastward of the Colorado, hoping to find information regarding silver deposits, which had eluded them. In the end, Rivera and his men had explored over 150 leagues (approximately 380 miles) from Santa Fe, further than any expedition previously recorded, at least officially, of the Yuta country. It was clear even to Rivera and his men, that other traders from New Mexico had seen much of that country before them, and they were not the first Hispanics into that little known wilderness. Equally so, Rivera's guides, Andrés Muñiz, Pedro Mora and Gregorio Sandoval, had gone a little further by crossing the Colorado River in 1775. But, their venture was illegal and not recorded. Still, Rivera left important documentation about southwestern Colorado and western Utah, for he followed on his outward bound trip a route "suggestively identical to the Old Spanish Trail."[119]

Although Rivera's search for silver proved fruitless, his expedition was successful in many other ways. First he had taken the first official step toward finding mythical Teguayo. Second, one of the legacies of his expedition is the place name of the La Plata Mountains which originated from the time of his expedition. From an historical view, however, he accomplished the objectives given to him in the instructions presented by Governor Vélez Cachupín. Indeed, his efforts resulted in a documented description of a land and a route that would become one of the variations of the Old Spanish Trail. Above all, Rivera's expedition served as the impetus for the next major official expedition to the Yuta country, that led by the friars Domínguez and Escalante.

In the intervening eleven years between the expeditions of 1765 and 1776, California had been opened to settlement in 1769. With the rediscovery of Monterey Bay and the fresh discovery of San Francisco

---

118 *Ibid.* 26.
119 Cutter, "Prelude," *WHQ*, 8:14.

Bay, California's importance grew in the minds of Spanish officials. By 1775, the interest created by the Rivera Expedition in a possible westward route resulted in a plan to establish a trade artery between Santa Fe, New Mexico and Monterey, California. Significantly, Rivera's expedition established a line of march to be followed by Domínguez and Escalante in their quest to reach California. Domínguez and Escalante would later provide a clearer explanation of where Rivera and his men had been, for they would not only use some of Rivera's guides, but also better describe the route to the Uncompahgre Plateau and the Colorado River.

Chapter IV
Domínguez, Escalante and Armijo: Western Colorado, Southern Utah and the Road to California, 1776-1830

> ...all the sierras we managed to see in all directions were covered with snow, the weather very unsettled... the passes would be closed to us....the provisions we had were very low by now, and so we could expose ourselves to perishing from hunger if not from the cold.
>
> — Escalante, 1776

Making the sign of the cross, the scruffy looking frontiersmen received the Holy Eucharist from Fray Atanasio Domínguez and Fray Francisco Silvestre Vélez de Escalante, who had celebrated Mass in Santa Fe's church. The congregation prayed for the men of the Domínguez-Escalante Expedition, wishing them safe travel into the heart of Yuta country. It was July 29, 1776. After the Mass, the men walked over to the Plaza de Santa Fe to make one last check of their animals and cargo they carried for trade before departing. The expedition bound for Monterey, California, was led by Fray Atanasio Domínguez and Fray Silvestre Vélez de Escalante, who were accompanied by Juan Pedro Cisneros, chief magistrate from the Pueblo of Zuñí; Bernardo Miera y Pacheco, originally from Burgos, Spain, a cartogapher and retired frontier captain of the militia living in Santa Fe; Lorenzo Olivares from the Villa de El Paso; Andrés Muñiz from Bernalillo; Antonio Lucrecio Muñiz, brother of Andrés from Embudo south of Taos Pueblo; Juan de Aguilar from Santa Clara Pueblo; Joaquín Laín, a blacksmith from Santa Fe; and Simon Lucero, probably from Zuñí, who had served as Cisneros' servant. Andrés Muñiz, who had accompanied Juan María Antonio Rivera to the Gunnison River in 1765, spoke certain dialects of the Ute language. His brother, Lucrecio, had also been with the Rivera expedition and likely spoke, or at least understood, the language of the Yutas.[120]

What experience did Domínguez and Escalante have to lead this expedition? Standing in the Plaza de Santa Fe on that warm summer day, Friar Silvestre Vélez de Escalante must have thought back to the day he first envisioned the possibility of such an venture. Over a year had passed since he had returned from a reconnaissance to the Hopi to test the possibility of a route from Santa Fe through present-day northeastern Arizona south of the Grand Canyon and beyond the western bank of the Colorado River, which he would cross on his way to California. In a letter to Fray Fernando Antonio Gómez dated October 28, 1775, Escalante recounted the purpose of his expedition to the Hopi pueblos. He knew that Governor Mendinueta had expressed interest in learning about the lands beyond the "Province of Moqui" (as noted in Spanish maps) and the tribes that bordered it.[121] His first visit to the "Province of Moqui" in summer of 1775 resulted

---

120 For a complete listing of all participants in the expedition, some of whom joined Domínguez and Escalante while the exploration of the Yuta country was in progress, see pages vii-viii in Ted J. Warner, ed., and Fray Angelico Chávez, trans., with a Foreword by Robert Himmerich y Valencia, *The Domínguez-Escalante Journal: Their Expedition through Colorado, Utah, Arizona, and New Mexico in 1776* (Salt Lake City: University of Utah Press, Reprinted 1995).

121 Herbert S. Auerbach, "Escalante's Letters to Fray Fernando Antonio Gómez, Custodian of the College of Querétaro, and to the Governor of the Province," *Utah Historical Quarterly* (Hereinafter cited as *UHQ*, January, April, July, October 1943, Volume 2, Nos. 1,2,3,4, p. 15.

in meeting a Cosnina Indian who, through an interpreter, had drawn directions in the dirt leading from Oraibe to his land.[122] The Cosnina had given Escalante invaluable information about the land beyond the "Province of Moqui" which would serve him later.

Escalante's expedition to Hopi had, indeed, given him some insights in proposing a plan for a future expedition to Monterrey. In June 1775, Escalante arrived in Hopi with the intention of reaching the Río Grande de los Cosninas, the Colorado River. Finding the Cosninas unfriendly and fearing harm, Escalante did not accomplish his goal, although he spent eight days there. He noted their location, defenses, herds, waters and subsistence of the tribe as well as their population.[123] Given the hostility shown him, Escalante began to think that it would not be a good idea to pass through the land of the Cosininas. He proposed to reach California via the Yuta country.

Francisco Silvestre Vélez Escalante, who rarely used his first name, was born in 1749 in Treceño, Santander, Spain.[124] His parents were Clemente Nicolas Vélez Escalante and María Josefa Fernandez de los Ríos. Little is known about his early life, but by age seventeen, he had taken the Franciscan habit at the Convento Grande in Mexico City. He was sent to New Mexico in the early 1770s,[125] eventually earning recognition among New Mexican officials as an explorer, in addition to his growing reputation as a missionary. In 1780, four years after the expedition, he died in Parral, Chihuahua, Mexico.

Fray Francisco Atanasio Domínguez, actual leader of the expedition, bore the burden of responsibility in planning, making critical decisions on the trail, disciplining members of the party, assuring the safety of

---

122 "Brief of a letter from Fray Silvestre Velez de Escalante, written at the Mission of Nuestra Señora de Guadalupe de Zuni on April 30, 1776, addressed to Fray Isidro Murillo, Provincial Minister," in Auerbach, "Escalante's First Visit to the Moquis," *UHQ*, 2:12.

123 Auerbach, "Escalante's Letters," *UHQ*, 2:15-16.

124 Libro de Bautizados, Parroquia Santa María de Treceño, Año 1736 al 1781, Archivo Diocesano, Santander, Spain.

125 Adams and Chávez, *The Missions of New Mexico, 1776*, xiv.

the men, and the final authority upon whom fell the judgment of his superiors whether the expedition was a success or failure.[126] In this regard, Escalante, as the subordinate to Domínguez, served as the scribe of the expedition.[127] Actually, both men collaborated in the writing of the diary.[128]

Born in Mexico City around 1740, Friar Domínguez had, by age 17, joined the Franciscan Order in the Convento Grande located in the Mexican capital. He served at the Convent of Veracruz in 1772 as commissary of the Third Order. In 1775, he began his assignment to New Mexico as the *visitador* or inspector of the Custody of the Conversion of St. Paul, as New Mexico was known to missionaries. The office of canonical visitor was given only to the most qualified clergyman, a reputation well-earned by the esteemed Father Domínguez.[129]

Having said their prayers and bid goodbye to their friends and families, the Domínguez-Escalante expedition set out from the Villa de Santa Fe. Meandering along the Camino de Taos, they stopped for the night at Santa Clara Pueblo, after an uneventful day. By 30-31 July, they had reached Santa Rosa de Abiquiú. Traveling northwest for the next few days and suffering through heavy rainfall, the expedition passed over rugged terrain in the direction of Arroyo del Canjilón, Río de la Cebolla, and Río de las Nutrias, they reached a small pine forest and descended to the Río Chama.[130] From there, they wended their way over small pine-forested mesas, short valleys and open grassy meadows, they continued northwesterly from sunrise to sunset.

---

126 Chávez, trans., and Warner, ed., *The Domínguez-Escalante Journal*, xv.

127 Eleanor B. Adams, "Fray Francisco Atanasio Domínguez and Fray Silvestre Vélez de Escalante," *UHQ* (Winter 1976), Vol. 44:53.

128 Chávez, trans., and Warner, ed., *The Domínguez-Escalante Journal*, xv.

129 Adams and Chávez, *The Missions of New Mexico, 1776*, xiv-xv.

130 Chávez, trans., and Warner, ed., *The Domínguez-Escalante Journal*, 4-6. For a synthesis of certain place names associated with the Domínguez-Escalante expedition, see Joseph J. Hill, "Spanish and Mexican Exploration and Trade Northwest from New Mexico into the Great Basin," *UHQ* (January 1930), 3:3-26.

To that point, the expedition, following the route traveled by Rivera, had passed and clarified many of the place names passed in 1765. By August 4, they came within sight of Piedra Parada, today's Chimney Rock. Escalante wrote in his entry for that day "a sight known to our people who have traveled through here."[131] That night they camped in a canyon named Cañon del Engaño on Amargo Creek. The next day they left the canyon traveling toward the southwest to the Río de Navajó which flows from the Sierra de las Grullas, a part of the southern Rocky Mountains. The Río de Navajó, today's Navajo River, runs from the northeast to the southwest to a point near Cañon del Engaño where it turns north until it joins the Río San Juan. Crossing the Río Navajó, they continued southwesterly through canyons, over inclines, and over heavy brush country where they lost their trail. Not even their guides could determine where they were. Domínguez and Escalante held a council and decided that without a trail their best guess was to turn northwest. The next afternoon somewhere near present-day Carracas, Colorado, in the vicinity of Pagosa Springs, they stopped and took a reading of the sun's meridian. They reckoned that the place they named Nuestra Señora de las Nieves was at 37^0 51' latitude.[132] Fray Silvestre scouted ahead to the confluence of the San Juan and the Navajo which he said was three leagues in a straight line almost due east

---

131 *Ibid.* 8.

132 Bolton, *Pageant in the Wilderness*, following p. 128, lists all of the astronomical observations made by the expedition as follows:

August 5 Nuestra Señora de las Nieves 37^0 51' August 13 Dolores 38^0 13 1/2' August 19 Cajón del Yeso 39^0 6' August 28 Santa Monica 39^0 13' 22" September 5 San Rafael 41^0 4' September 6 Roan Creek 41^0 6' 53" September 14 La Vega de Santa Cruz 41^0 19' September 14 La Vega de Santa Cruz 41^0 59' 24" September 14 La Vega de Santa Cruz 41^0 19' September 29 Santa Ysabel 39^0 4' October 2 Llano Salado 39^0 34' 35" October 8 Santa Brígida 38^0 3' 30" October 11 Valle de Señor San José 37^0 33' October 15 San Dónulo 36^0 52' 30 October 20 Santa Gertrudis 36^0 30' November 7 La Purísima Concepción 35^0 55'

Note should be taken that the bearings taken by the expedition are not accurate. For correct bearings as calculated by Fray Angelico Chávez and Ted Warner see the footnotes in their translation of *The Domínguez-Escalante Journal.*

of Las Nieves.[133] The two rivers formed a drainage previously unknown to the Spaniards who called it the Río Grande de Navajó. Across it began the Province of the Yuta nation.[134] They described both banks of the river as "leafy and extremely dense thickets of white poplar, scrub oak, chokecherry, manzanita, lemita, there is also some sarsparilla and a tree that looks to us like the walnut."[135]

Traveling westward toward along the river's edge for the next few days, they stopped now and then to allow Bernardo Miera y Pacheco to rest and care for "the stomach trouble" he had been experiencing. Passing near present Ignacio, Colorado, and the flat land along the Pine River south of there, they turned west-northwest and arrived at the Río Florido (the Flowery River) which they crossed.[136] Continuing down a rocky incline they arrived at the Río de las Animas where they camped on its west side not too far south of Durango, Colorado.[137] By August 9, they had reached present La Plata River and took note that the Rivera Expedition had been there before them. They wrote:

> The Río de la Plata] rises at the same western point of La Sierra de La Plata and descends through the same canyon in which there are said to be veins and outcroppings of metallic ore. However, although years ago certain individuals from New Mexico came to inspect them by order of the governor, who at the time was Don Tomás Vélez Cachupín, and carried back metal-bearing rocks, it was not ascertained for sure what kind of metal they consisted of. The opinion which some formed previously, from the accounts of various Indians and from some citizens

133 Chávez, trans., and Warner, ed., *The Domínguez-Escalante Journal*, 9.
134 *Ibid.*, 10.
135 *Ibid.*
136 *Ibid.*
137 *Ibid.*, 11. Also, see footnote 53 in which Chávez speculates that the expedition was "probably somewhat south of Colorado State Highway 172 toward Farmington Hill, which they descended to the Animas River and crossed it."

of the kingdom, that they were silver ore furnished
the sierra with this name.[138]

Suffering through "excessively" cold nights during the months of
July and August, members of the expedition suffered headaches, colds,
fevers, and exhaustion. The heavy downpour of August 10 increased
their maladies and forced them to camp a couple of days at the East
Mancos River near its confluence with the main Mancos River.[139] While
there, Andrés Muñiz, who had been on the Rivera Expedition told them
that the Sierra de la Plata's metallic rocks were a short distance from their
camp. Still, they were too fatigued to go verify his claim.

Once rested, they went west by west-northwest, then changing
course they went north and crossed El Río de Nuestra Señora de los
Dolores (present-day Dolores River) where they took another compass
"bearing on the polar elevation of this site and meadow of El Río de los
Dolores....The bearing was taken by the sun, and we saw that we were
at 38⁰ 13 1/2' latitude." There, they noted an ancient ruin on the river's
south side, writing "there was in ancient times a small settlement of the
same type as those of the Indians of New Mexico, as the ruins which
we purposely inspected show."[140] No description of the ruin is made,
although they did note that water, pasturage, and wooded areas were
characteristically abundant in the area and recommended it suitable for
settlement.

Crossing and re-crossing the Dolores River, they had by mid-
August, realized their need for water which they could not find away
from the river. Somewhere in that wilderness, they were overtaken by
a mestizo named Felipe and an Indian of mixed Plains parentage from
Abiquiú called Juan Domingo. Domínguez and Escalante were not
pleased by their appearance because they had left New Mexico without

---

138 *Ibid.*, 12.
139 *Ibid.*, 13.
140 *Ibid.*, 14. In footnote 69, Chávez comments that their calculations were too high
correcting them to 37⁰. In footnote 70, Chávez notes that the Anasazi site known as
"The Escalante Ruin" may or may not be the one mentioned in the journal.

permission and feared if they sent them back they might run afoul of wandering Ute bands and be killed or captured. Thus, they felt obligated to keep Felipe and Juan Domingo with the expedition.

Meandering along the Dolores River, they entered a canyon they named El Laberinto de Miera "because of the varied and pleasing scenery of rock cliffs it has on either side...and because Don Bernardo Miera was the first one to go through it."[141] That day, August 17, they camped on the Dolores River in Summit Canyon near Disappointment Valley. Near there they found human tracks and followed them hoping they might be those of Tabeguachi Yutas who could guide them, but they failed to make contact with them. In that sortie, they reached present-day Disappointment Creek.

In late August, they continued exploring western Colorado reaching the point the Rivera Expedition called La Sierra de los Tabehuachis, present Uncompahgre Plateau. To get there they had followed the Dolores River past Steamboat Hill to the Little Gypsum Valley at the south end of Andy's Mesa, where they noted they were at 39° 6' latitude.[142] Somewhere southeast of Spectacle Reservoir they entered the west fork of Dry Creek Canyon and camped at a place they named San Bernabé. By the third week in August they had moved northwest of present Naturita, Colorado, as they crossed and followed the San Miguel River which they called Río San Pedro in a northeasterly direction. Having left the San Miguel, they recognized the Sierra de la Sal or present Sal Mountains, known for the salt beds near them. Stopping in a narrow valley they described its pasturage potential, for they had seen little of it since leaving the river. They also described an ancient ruin they saw on one of its ridges. Of it they wrote: "On top of this are ruins of a small and ancient pueblo, the houses of which seem to have been made of the stone with which the Tabehuachi

---

141 *Ibid.,* p. 16.
142 *Ibid.,* 18-19. See footnote 93 in which Chávez notes that they were perhaps closer to 37° 30'.

Yutas have fashioned a weak and crude rampart."[143] Near them, they found pasturage for their mounts. Although the land appeared dry, intermediate rains pelted them along the route. Somewhere along this line of march, they met with a Tabehuachi Ute who exchanged information with them for some food. He agreed to guide them to the Sabuagana tribe Rivera had mentioned. As agreed, the Tabehuachi left them and returned two days later with his family who desired to trade with the Spaniards. After paying their guide with two large knives and sixteen strings of white glass beads, his family members returned to their camps and the Tabeguachi turned to guide the expedition to the land of the Sabuagana.

Crossing present Red Canyon on August 24, they camped near Horsefly Creek which runs through the canyon.[144] From there, they meandered south, southeast, then northeast, they proceeded to a point near Johnson Spring after which they reached the Uncompahgre River, noted on Miera y Pacheco's map as El Río de San Francisco, but which the Utes called the Ancapagari, meaning red lake "because they say," wrote the diarist, "that near its source there is a spring of red-colored water, hot and ill-tasting."[145] Three days later, the expedition was back on course, moving northwest downstream on the Uncompahgre River. Along their march, they met a Ute called the Left-handed with his family from whom they learned nothing of the land in front of them.

As the hot August sun beat down on the expedition, they moved northwestward toward the Gunnison River shown on Miera y Pacheco's map as Río San Xavier; the Utes called it the Tomichi.[146] Near there, Andrés Muñíz told them that Rivera in 1765 had carved a cross, his name, and the year 1765 on a poplar sapling. Muñíz reiterated that he had been there with the Rivera Expedition and had returned there in 1775 with Pedro Mora and Gregorio Sandoval. They had also been there

143 *Ibid.*, 21.
144 *Ibid.*, 23, fn. 116.
145 *Ibid.*, 24.
146 *Ibid.*, 26, fn. 127.

with Rivera and had crossed the Uncompahgre having reached the Río del Tizón, present day Colorado River.[147]

By the end of August, they had contacted the Sabuaganas, who had been exchanging goods with Laguna traders, whom Spaniards knew as the Timpanogotziz from Timpanogos or present day Utah Lake, near Provo, and the Great Salt Lake. Actually, the Timpanogotzis were the present Uintah Utes. Referring to the figure of a reclining human being formed by the ridges of the present day mountain Timpanogos, the old Ute word, Timpanogos, appears to mean "the stone person".[148] At that point, the Spaniards took another reading of the sun's meridian at "39⁰ 13' 29".[149] Near there, they met a group of Utes who attempted to discourage them from proceeding any further west. The Utes said that the Yamparica Comanches would kill them, if they found them. The next day, Spanish scouts brought the Sabuaganas they sought and one Laguna Ute to the expeditionary camp. They, too, told the Spaniards to turn back, for the Comanche would kill them, and besides, none of them knew the way to Timpanogos. Finally, the Spaniards offered the Laguna a woolen blanket, a large knife and white glass beads to lead them to Timpanogos. He readily agreed. Seeing this, the Sabuaganas acknowledged that they too knew the way. Suddenly, all the difficulties with the Comanche disappeared. The next day, they set out for the Sabuagana encampment two days' hence from their camp at a little river they called Santa Rosa, today known as the Leroux Creek.[150] Traveling northeast, then north, they reached a water source they named San Ramón Nonato where they stopped north of the confluence of present Willow Creek and Hubbard Creek in Hubbard Canyon.[151]

In the waning days of August and early September, the weather began to cool noticeably. Somewhere in the Colorado wilderness near

---

147 *Ibid.*, 26.
148 *Ibid.*, 27, fn. 133.
149 *Ibid.*, 27, fn. 135, Chávez notes that it was closer to 38⁰ 45'.
150 *Ibid.*, fn. 138.
151 *Ibid.*, fn. 141.

present Electronic Mountain Hunting Lodge on Grand Mesa, they encountered eighty mounted Yuta warriors "on good horses" from the encampment

> to which we were going. They told us that they were going out to hunt, but we figured that they came together like this, either to show off their strength in numbers or to find out if any other Spanish people were coming behind us or if we came alone; for, since they knew from the night before that we were going to their encampment, it was unnatural for almost all of its men to come out at the very time that they knew we were to arrive, unless motivated by what we have just said.[152]

At the encampment, the Spaniards set about trading for fresh mounts, while the Padres, using Andrés as their interpreter, began to proselytize the natives. Meanwhile, the Utes set up a separate camp for them.

Astute frontiersmen, Domínguez and Escalante perceived that they were being subjected to a ruse played out between the Utes and some of their own men who wanted to turn back. One evening, as the Sabuagana chieftains sat with the Spaniards, they again attempted to convince them to turn around. They said they were certain the Comanches would not let them pass westward. The friars suspected that Andrés, the lead interpreter, and his brother, Lucrecio, had ulterior motives for secretly prompting the Sabuaganas to oppose the plan to proceed westward. Escalante noted:

> Ever since La Villa de Santa Fe, we had reminded all of the companions that those who wished to be part of this expedition were not to take along any goods for trading and that those who did not agree to this condition were to stay behind. All agreed not to bring a thing, nor any purpose other than the one we had, which was God's glory and

---

152 *Ibid.*, 29. Also see note 141 for the location of the confluence of Willow Creek and Hubbard Creek.

the good of souls. For this reason, everything that they requested for their equipment and to leave to their families was rationed out to them. But some of them failed in their promise by secretly carrying some goods we did not see until we were near to the Sabuaganas. And here we charged and begged them all not to engage in commerce, so that the infidels might understand that another motive higher than this one brought us through these parts.[153]

The upsetting issue with the friars is that they felt betrayed by Andrés and Lucrecio because they contradicted the message that the Christian God would grant them safe passage through the lands of the Comanche. By trading for weapons from the Utes as insurance, they showed their lack of faith in divine intervention in the event of an attack. The two men had presumably weakened the friars' message about their Christian God. Escalante felt only sorrow for Andrés and his brother and judged their lack of faith, as he believed their actions proved them "unfit for ventures of this kind."[154] The friars' trust in divine intervention was proven a day later, when the Ute chieftains agreed with the friars and granted them passage through their land exhorting their tribesmen to stop presenting barriers to the Spaniards' desire to travel west.

On September 2, the expedition, led by two Lagunas named Silvestre and Joaquín, continued up Cow Creek crossed over to Dyke Creek westward to Chimney Rock and reached Mule Park on the upper West Muddy Creek.[155] They spent the first week of September wending westward through present Buzzard Park passing along the south face of Bronco Knob and down Plateau Creek to the Meadows in a north-northwest direction until they reached Campbell Mountain, known to the Utes as Nabuncari.[156] Continuing northwesterly, and experiencing

---

153 *Ibid.,* 32-33.
154 *Ibid.,* 33
155 *Ibid.,* 34, fn. 154.
156 *Ibid.,* 35, footnotes 157 and 159.

cold temperatures at night, the expedition passed present Jerry Gulch, reaching the Colorado River by way of Battlement Mesa, east of Castle Peak, then down Alkali Creek to the south bank of the Colorado River. They turned northward seeking a ford near present Una bridge.[157] On September 7, 1776, the expedition approached the confluence of Brush Creek and Roan Creek.

During this part of the expedition, Escalante was disappointed about the continuing intrigue that was going on within the party. He could not help but think that certain members of the expedition still hoped to turn back to Santa Fe, rather than proceed westward. His fears were confirmed when he was confronted by a new threat which he and Father Domínguez had to decide whether their dilemma was real or imagined.

The expedition's interpreters were very concerned that they were being led into a trap set up by the Sabuaganas. They attempted to convince the padres that their Laguna guide, whom they called Silvestre, was leading them into a Sabuagana ambush. They told the priests that they had heard many of the Sabuagana tell Silvestre to walk the expedition in a roundabout way for eight or ten days to make them turn back. Domínguez and Escalante realized that the northerly route they had embarked upon since leaving the Sabuaganas meant a greater detour, but they pondered the contradiction presented to them by their own men. If what they said was true, why did they not say it before?

Apprehensive about the situation, the priests decided to trust their Laguna guide. Not long after their decision, they encountered a lone Sabuagana Ute "of the most northerly ones," and they asked him about the route. He recommended they bear west to get to the great lake because the trail they presently followed went further north. Later, they encountered three camps of Sabuaganas who had been stealing horses from the Comanches. They informed the Spaniards that the Comanches had gone eastward toward the Río de Napeste, present

---

157 *Ibid.*, 37, footnotes 164-165.

Arkansas River. With that report the dissenting voices in the Spanish camp about encountering Comanche warriors subsided.[158]

Near the confluence of Brush Creek and Roan Creek, they climbed to the top of Brush Mountain, thence went to the junction of East Douglas and Cathedral creeks. By September 9, they were in Douglas Canyon south of Rangely, Colorado, where they saw a lofty rock cliff with crudely painted shields, a spear head, and two men depicted in combat. From there they went through the canyon where they saw some iron pyrite, or fool's gold. Traveling north-northwest, they arrived at the White River which they named the Río San Clemente where they camped at the confluence of Douglas Creek and the White River at Rangely, Colorado.[159] The expedition pushed forward, marching west-northwest, passing over arroyos and embankments. Tracking a buffalo on September 12, they crossed into present Utah east of Snake John Reef and K-Ranch, after which they followed Cliff Creek westward to the Green River Valley.[160]

They came to a long river the natives called Seeds-Kee-Dee. The Spaniards called it the San Buenaventura, today's Green River. Near present Jensen, Utah, the Spaniards camped on the east side of the Green River.[161] Up to there, the water sources were scant. The expedition collected water two days after leaving the painted canyon at Fuentes de Santa Clara, about ten miles east of the Green River.[162] Escalante knew a little about the Río San Buenaventura, for he had studied many of the previous Spanish reports of the area. He recounted how Fray Alonso de Posada, the Custos of the Province of New Mexico in the previous century, had written about the river in 1686. Posada had said that the river was the boundary between the Comanche and the Utes. Escalante speculated that the San Buenaventura flowed into the Colorado River.

---

158 *Ibid.*, 38-39.
159 *Ibid.* 40-41.
160 *Ibid.* 42, fn. 187.
161 *Ibid.* 43, fn. 190.
162 *Ibid.* 43.

The expedition spent the middle of September exploring the region around the Río San Buenaventura. Somewhere along the river, Joaquín Laín took an adze and carved on a cottonwood tree the letters and numbers "Year of 1776." After crossing the river, they headed in a south-southwesterly direction. Near present Asphalt Ridge, the Spaniards found horse and human tracks. After studying the indications, they concluded that whoever had been there, had been lying in wait, probably to ambush them and take their horse herd at that place. The priests suspected that it could have been some Sabuaganas who thought to attribute the deed to Comanches, since they were apparently in Comanche territory. Their suspicion again turned on their Laguna guide, Silvestre. They had learned that Silvestre had, the night before, gone off to sleep alone some distance from the camp. They also noticed that throughout the march, he had never once wrapped himself with a blanket. Now they observed that he wore a blanket, even in the daytime. They suspected that if he had negotiated with the Sabuaganas, he wore the blanket so as to be recognized during an attack on the Spaniards. Nevertheless, Silvestre was not confronted with the circumstantial evidence the priests had quietly gathered. Soon, the priests decided that their fears were unfounded and that time had proven Silvestre's innocence.[163]

Apparently, from illegal New Mexican traders, the San Buenaventura had been known for at least 80 years—since Father Posada had written about it in his Report of 1686. To a certain extent, the San Buenaventura River represented all that Spanish officials and explorers knew about that part of the Yuta country. Since 1686 when Father Posada had written about it, albeit vicariously through the eyes of colonial informants, until 1776 when the men of the Domínguez-Escalante expedition saw it and described it, knowledge about the river was hearsay. New Mexican frontiersmen from Santa Fe who had been there before kept what they knew about the area to themselves, for they

---

163 *Ibid.* 46.

had been there without license. Their illegal entry into the area would not have been without penalty, so they kept what they knew about the river and their illegal trading ventures among the Utes and Comanche to themselves. But now, the Domínguez-Escalante expedition, deep in the Yuta country, stood on the threshold of a new land. Beyond the Río San Buenaventura lay Teguayo and Timpanogos, places that only a few New Mexican frontiersmen had seen.

Upon entering present Utah Valley at Provo, Utah, they described the area and named it "El Valle de Nuestra Señora de la Merced de los Timpanogos." They associated Timpanogos and its salt lake with Teguayo. Of Timpanogos, Escalante wrote,

> It is nothing but the land by which the Tihuas, Tehuas and other Indians transmigrated to this kingdom; which is clearly shown by the ruins of the pueblos which I have seen in it, whose form was the same that they afterwards gave to theirs in New Mexico; and the fragments of clay and pottery which I also saw in the said country are much like that which the said Tehuas make today. To which is added the prevailing tradition with them, which proves the same.[164]

Escalante had at last unraveled the mystery of mythical Teguayo. For the small Spanish expedition, myth and reality met on the edge of a place the Yutas called Timpanogos.

Escalante's described the Valley and Lake of Timpanogos (present Utah Lake), and the people, who lived along it. They noted that one of the lakes was quite large (obviously present Great Salt Lake). The Timpanois considered it harmful because of its extremely saturated salt content. Escalante noted that "the Timpanois assured us that anyone who wet some part of the body with them immediately felt a

---

164 Letter of Fray Silvestre Vélez de Escalante in S. Lyman Tyler, "The Myth of the Lake of Copala," Utah State Historical Society, October 1952, Vol. XX, No. 4, pp. 329. Original letter in AGN, Historia, T. 4.

lot of itching in the part moistened."[165]

The Timpanogotzis, according to Escalante, feared the Comanche who attacked them infrequently from the north by northwest through the gap of La Sierra Blanca. Generally the Lagunas (Lake Dwellers), whom Escalante sometimes called the Timpanogotzis, lived in peace with their neighbors. The Spaniards even took note of their language with its variations in pronunciation and vocabulary.[166] Emphazing the differences in inflection, Escalante wrote that the Indians called themselves and the place, Timpanogotzis or Timpanocuitzis. His was the first reliable eye witness account of them. He said that the people there ate much fish. Their neighbors the Sabuagana Utes, were called Fish-Eaters (Come Pescado).[167] Although no figures were given, Escalante noted that the population in the valley was quite large. The sojourn of the Domínguez-Escalante expedition in the vicinity of the Great Salt Lake documented its "official" discovery of the Great Salt Lake, particularly Lake Utah and the Timpanagotzis.

Two days after leaving the southern end of the valley, they turned southwest and came upon "a very old Indian of venerable countenance. He was alone in a tiny hut, and he had a beard so full and long that he looked like one of the ancient hermits of Europe."[168] Influenced by the generalization that Indians lacked facial and body hair and seeing the bearded Indian astonished the explorers. The bearded man told them

---

165 *Ibid.*, 61.

166 *Ibid.*, 60.

167 Fray Angelico Chávez, translator, and Ted J. Warner, editor, *The Domínguez-Escalante Journal: Their Expedition through Colorado, Utah, Arizona, and New Mexico in 1776* (Provo: Brigham Young University Press, 1977), p. 60. Escalante wrote "The Timpanogotzis are so named after the lake where they reside, which they call Timpanogo, and this name is the proper one for this lake since the name or word by which they designate any lake is pagariri," *Ibid.*, 61. This version of the journal is reprinted in Ted J. Warner, ed., and Fray Angelico Chávez, trans., with a Foreword by Robert Himmerich y Valencia, *The Domínguez-Escalante Journal: Their Expedition through Colorado, Utah, Arizona, and New Mexico in 1776* (Salt Lake City: University of Utah Press, 1995).

168 *Ibid.*, 63.

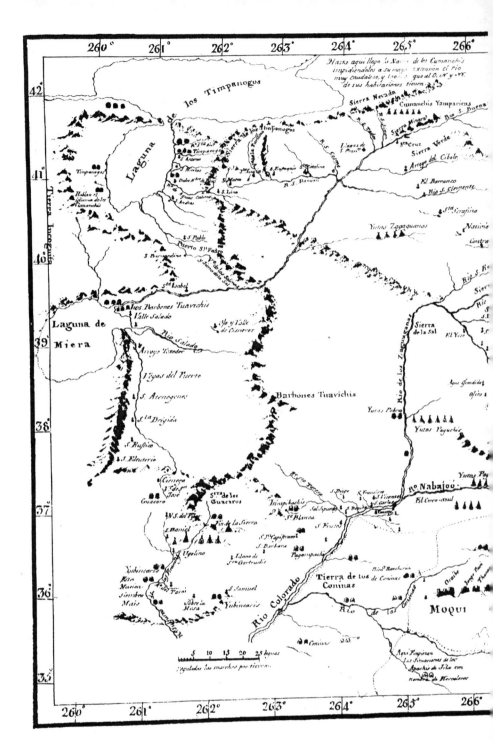

Facsimile of Map of New Mexico drawn by Bernardo Miera y Pacheco 1778.

92

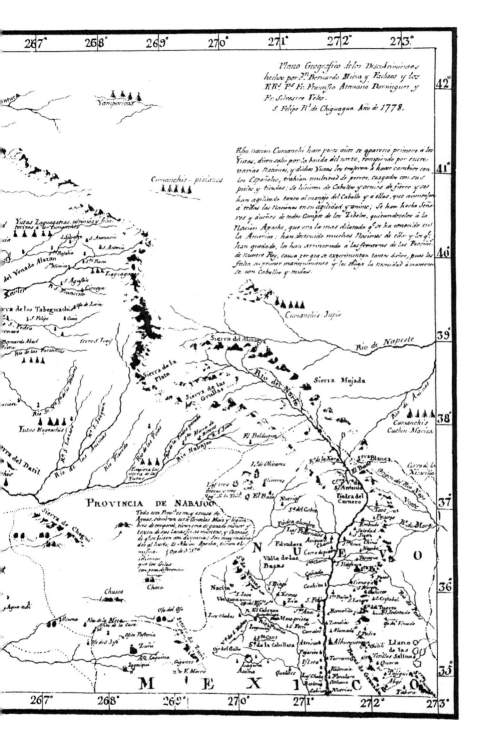

Plano Geografico de los Descubrimientos hecho por D. Bernardo Miera y Pacheco y los RR. PP. Fr. Francisco Atanasio Dominguez y Fr. Silvestre Velez.

S. Felipe Il de Chiguagua. Año de 1778.

that in the direction they traveled, they would come to another river. Upon reaching the river, which they did not see until they were at its very edge owing to the flatness of the land and the undergrowth, they named it the Río Isabel, present Sevier River. There, they met other "bearded Indians." Escalante observed that "In their features they more resemble the Spaniards than they do all the other Indians known in America up to now, from whom they differ in what has been said. They employ the same language as the Timpanogotzis [the Lagunas]. From the river and site of Santa Isabel onward begin these full-bearded Indians, who perhaps gave rise to the report about the Spaniards who were said to exist on the other side of El Río del Tizón."[169]

For a long time, a story, indigenous in origin, about bearded men living somewhere in the Yuta country north of the Colorado River were Spaniards who had been shipwrecked, persisted in the eighteenth century lore of New Mexico. Since the Rivera Expedition to western Colorado in the mid-1760s, the story had been told and retold. New Mexicans believed that they existed south of the the salt lakes. Miera y Pacheco now sketched the "Bearded Indians" with their fur robes on his 1778 map of the expedition, which was the first Spanish colonial cartographical projection to show western Colorado and Utah to the Great Salt Lakes.

The cold October nights, the dwindling supplies, and the scarcity of potable water for long stretches at a time, began to concern the expeditionary leaders. On October 1, searching for water, Escalante wrote, "We thought we saw a marshland or lake water nearby, hurried our pace, and discovered that what we had judged to be water was salt in some places, saltpeter in others, and in others dried alkaline sediment."[170] That day they traveled fourteen leagues (36 miles) without finding water or pasturage for their horses. They stopped at a site they called Llano Salado, Salt Plain, just northwest of Pahvant Butte, Utah, because their horses "could go no farther."[171]

---

169 *Ibid.*, 64.
170 *Ibid.*, 65.
171 *Ibid.*, 65.

From that campsite, the Spaniards decided to continue seeking water as soon as the moon rose offering some night light. The decision almost ended in disaster, for during the night, those who had taken the herd fell asleep in their mission, and the herd got away from them. The next morning, at six o'clock, one of the herdsmen came in to report what had happened. One of the men was still missing. As soon as he reported the bad news, Juan Pedro Cisneros rode off bareback to find herd, which he found half way to the rear toward the Sevier River. No sign of the missing man was found.

Meanwhile, at their camp on the salt plain, they were visited by more "bearded Indians" with pierced-noses. They called themselves Tirangpui. Still in amazement about their beards, Escalante noted that "the five of them who came first with their chief were so fully bearded that they looked like Capuchin padres or Bethlehemites."[172] Upon hearing about the missing Spaniard, the chief ordered four warriors, each one taking a different direction, to go look for him. Just as the warriors were about to set out, the missing man showed up. Still, the chief's gesture to help the expedition was overwhelming. At the camp, the friars spoke about the Holy Gospel to the chief who appeared interested in what was said. Escalante said that the chief and his men wanted them to return with more padres.

Breaking camp, the expedition pursued a south-southeast course to avoid marshes and lakes impeding their path. A few days later, they reached a place they called San Atenógenes, north of present Red Rock Knoll, Utah. San Atenógenes seemed to have enough water and pasturage. The cold increased as winds blew in snow clouds. On the morning of October 6, 1776, the snow fell so unceasingly the entire day and continued into the night.[173] Digging out from the snow compounded by extreme cold and falling temperatures, they were forced to spend another night at San Antenógenes. The next day, 8 October, they broke camp, making slow

---

172 *Ibid.*, 66. Could this tribe have been the Pierced Ears tribe Rivera heard about?
173 *Ibid.*, 70.

progress as a north wind blew cold air beating down onl them all day. Suffering greatly, they stopped at a place they called Santa Brigida, eleven miles north of modern Milford, Utah, where, they concluded that they still had many leagues to travel toward the west. Escalante was afraid of being stranded for months in the bitter cold and wrote of their plans to proceed to California:

> ...all the sierras we managed to see in all directions were covered with snow, the weather very unsettled...the passes would be closed to us.... the provisions we had were very low by now, and so we could expose ourselves to perishing from hunger if not from the cold. We also figured that, even granting that we arrive in Monterey this winter, we could not be in La Villa de Santa Fe until the month of June the following year.[174]

The exhausted explorers began to discuss another plan.

The expedition admitted that by following the well-known route from Santa Fe to Abiquiú toward the mountains and ridges of western Colorado, thence to the Río San Buenaventura (Green River), and by blazing a new pathway from the River to the Laguna de los Timpanogos near present Provo, that they had taken a very long and arduous route. The long distance to Monterey and the cold weather along with their diminishing supplies would cause much suffering along an unknown route through mountainous country where they could perish. Admitting their failing chances to get to Monterey, they decided that their new plan would be to discover a shorter and better route along a lower latitude that would take them back to Santa Fe. Besides, wrote Escalante, there might be other tribes living on the Colorado River that could help them.[175] By backtracking from Santa Brigida to Santa Fe, they would be able to describe an easier route to the Salt Lakes, should anyone ever want to go there, or to the western extreme of the Colorado River.

---

174 *Ibid.*, 70-71.
175 *Ibid.*, 71.

Breaking camp at a place they called Santa Brigida on October 9, 1776, they headed southward. Along their way, their abandonment of their objective to reach Monterrey came up again. Members of the expedition opposed the decision and argued with the priests the entire day. Finally, to put the matter to rest, the priests decided to gamble. By agreement, the members of the expedition would draw lots with two names on them: one the route to Monterey; the other the route to the Cosninas followed by Father Garcés to Oraibe in summer 1776. Also, as part of the agreement, if Monterey were chosen, Bernardo Miera y Pacheco would be the new leader, for it was he who believed that they were closer to California, and "everything started from his ideas."[176] After praying on the matter and offering their fate to God, the casting of lots began. In his entry for 11 October 1776, Escalante wrote "...we cast lots, and the one of Cosnina came out. This we all heartily accepted now, thanks be to God, mollified and pleased."[177] The expedition now planned their "new itinerary."

For the next five days, they moved southward, skirting the vicinity of present Cedar City and, stopping at Indian settlements near there to gather information about what lay ahead. Following present Ash Creek, they crossed El Río Sulfero, present Virgin River. On October 15, they camped at a place they named San Dónulo or Arroyo del Taray near Hurricane Wash, in Utah,[178] close to the Arizona border.

Moving southward, the expedition encountered some Indians who told them that in two days they would reach a very large river, obviously the Colorado. The Indians described the river running through a deep canyon with high rocky walls. They warned the Spaniards that the river could not be crossed at that point. Wondering if these Indians were trying to lead them astray, the Spaniards decided they had no choice but to continue southward to the river.

The nearly exhausted expedition, lacking water, pushed southward

---

176 *Ibid.*, 74.
177 *Ibid.*, 74.
178 *Ibid.*, 79-80.

in search of the Colorado River. Meanwhile, their Indian guides led them to water, which, in that area, was scarce. Their dwindling food supply could not sustain them. With few alternatives, the padres decided to slaughter one of their mounts for food. Meanwhile, their guides who had gone out to find sustenance returned with other Indians with food. Among them a Mescalero Apache, who brought them some wild sheep meat, dried prickly pear cactus, and seeds from wild plants.

Taking an astronomical bearing, on October 20, at a place they called Santa Gertrudis on modern Bull Rush Wash. They noted that they were at 36⁰ 30' north latitude.[179] Crossing the long Arroyo de Santa Gertrudis several times and meandering over hills, the exhausted explorers finally came to a beaten path which, their guides told them, led directly to the big river.

But the path proved unreliable and time-consuming. Relying on their true and tested methods of using ravines and other topographical markers to find their location, the padres and their men left the path. Struggling with exhaustion, they came upon an Indian campsite where they spent the night. Despite the padres' attempt to calm them, the Indians mistrusted them at first. As soon as the friars brought out ribbons and other trade items, the Indians warmed up to them. After four hard days' march, they were finally near the Colorado River. Two days later on October 26, just beyond Coyote Wash (Soap Creek Canyon), not far from present Marble Canyon Trading Post, they reached the big river, which they called *El Río Grande de los Cosninas*, present Colorado River.[180]

Between 1765 and 1776, official Spanish explorations from New Mexico through western Colorado and Utah, including the Grand Canyon, presented an historical panoramic vision of geography and the people who lived there. The early literary tradition of the Yuta country begun in part with the Rivera Expedition of 1765 culminated with the journal of Domínguez and Escalante. Through their written descriptions,

179 *Ibid.*, 88, fn. 342 places the calculation more at 36⁰ 59'.
180 *Ibid.*, 93.

together with the countless unknown Indian Peoples who hunted, lived and died in the Yuta wilderness,and who guided Spaniards across their lands, the histories of these early expeditions are a part of the national story of the United States. Even though the Rivera and Domínguez-Escalante expeditions took much credit for their new "discoveries, they could not have succeeded as they did without the geographical and linguistic knowledge gained by illegal New Mexican traders who had preceded them into that "unknown" wilderness.

The panoramic view provided by Escalante's writings and Miera y Pacheco's maps demonstrated the northern extent of what was known about the Yuta country through southern Colorado and eastern Utah. Its southern extremity, bordered by the Grand Canyon of Arizona, as well as the westernmost extent, lined by the mountains and ridges of the Great Basin, were now better known to Spanish officials. In many ways the Domínguez-Escalante expedition had placed a definitive character on the knowledge about the Yuta country, for Miera y Pacheco had depicted it graphically, thus influencing colonial cartographers of the period.

Knowledge depicted in the maps produced by Bernardo Miera y Pacheco and the written descriptions of the southwestern and western Colorado resulted in the significant contributions of the expedition. They were earned as the expedition meandering its way through the mountains, ridges, and forests of the land beyond present New Mexico-Colorado state line. A few days after crossing the Río San Juan in New Mexico, the Domínguez-Escalante Expedition entered present Colorado, and recorded that on August 8, 1776, they had camped in a valley near present Durango, 1776. Having passed a number of rivers and valleys and circumvented mountains, they reached the Ucompahgre Plateau and wended their way through it past present Montrose and beyond Delta. Having crossed present-day Gunnison River, they continued exploring past Grand Junction, finally exiting Colorado near Jenson, Utah near where they camped on September 16. Furthering the knowledge gained by the Rivera Expeditions of 1765, Father Escalante's description of the terrain of the region brought more of the known geography of western Colorado into focus. Summarizing their meanderings and whereabouts, Escalante wrote:

> DESCRIPTION OF THE SIERRAS SEEN THUS FAR: The one of La Grulla and of the La Plata begins near the site called El Cobre and adjacent to the now abandoned settlement. It runs almost northwest from the place where it starts and, about the seventy leagues there must be from Santa Fe, it comes to a point looking west-south-west and is the one they call Sierra de la Plata. From here it runs north-northeast, turning northward just before La Sierra de los Tabehuachis up to the other small one called Venado Alazán, which is where it ends on the northern side. Along the east side, according to reports, it joins that of El Almagre and La Sierra Blanca. To the west-southwest by west from the original point of La Plata, about thirty leagues, another small sierra called El Dátil can be seen. This sierra sheds westward all the rivers we have crossed up until now, and the ones ahead up to the ones of San Rafael inclusive.
>
> La Sierra de los Tabehuachis, which we have finished crossing, runs toward the north; it must be about thirty leagues in length, and where we crossed over it eight or ten in width. It abounds with good pasturages and is very moist and has good lands for farming without irrigation. It abundantly produces piñon, the ponderosa pine, spruce, scrub oak, various kinds of wild fruit, and flax in some places. On it deer and rose and other animals breed, and certain chicken fowl the size and shape of the common domestic ones, from which they differ in not having combs. Their flesh is very tasty. About twenty leagues to the west of this sierra is the one of La Sal, which likewise appears small. To the west-

southwest, a matter of four leagues or so, another one can be seen, which they call La Sierra de Abajo.

The said Río de San Francisco is medium sized and a bit larger than the Dolores. It is composed of several rivulets which come down from the western flank of the Sierra de la Grullas and run northwest according to what we saw. Here it has a meadow of good land for farming with the help of irrigation. It must be three leagues in size. There is all the rest needed for establishing a good settlement on it. Northeast of this meadow there is a chain of small mounts and hills of a leaden color crowned with yellow ochre earth.

Given the description of the terrain around the Sierra de los Tabehuachis, undoubtedly the Uncompahgre Plateau, the expedition had gone beyond the Gunnison River and had begun to veer northwest beyond present Delta Colorado. Of interest are Escalante's notes on the fertility of the land and his recommendation that it would be an excellent area for settlement and farming.

While the Domínguez-Escalante expedition had contributed much knowledge about the people and geography of the Yuta country, it had failed in its goals of reaching Monterrey and establishing a route to California. The epilogue of the story dealing with the route to California came about decades later — not during the Spanish Colonial period but during the Mexican Territorial period.

After Mexican independence from Spain in 1821, official interest in establishing a route to California was renewed. New discussions had taken place about initiating trade with California. Apparently, with little fanfare, New Mexico Governor José Antonio Chávez had taken the matter into his own hands and communicated the results to Ministro de Asuntos Exteriores in Mexico City. In his letter of May 14, 1830 to the Minister, Governor Chávez reported that a licensed expedition to California had taken place. Of the event, he wrote:

On the eighth of November of last year, a company of about sixty men left this territory for California with the purpose of trading for mules with the products of this country. They have been traveling through unknown deserts until now, and have succeeded in discovering a new way of communication which passes numerous savage tribes, who, from all appearances, fled in terror. The Indians proved no obstacle and this contributed not a little to the success of the expedition.

From the itinerary which I am sending Your Excellency it can be assumed that the distance which separates California from this territory is not great. It should be taken into account that the discoverers often had to retrace their steps and make detours. In short, they had neither map nor compass, and no other guides than the enterprising natives of this country.

I believe that it would be greatly to the advantage of both territories for the Supreme Government to promote the commerce of this region, for which I entreat Your Excellency.[181]

Governor Chávez' letter spelled out the significance of the accomplishment that had eluded New Mexicans for decades.

Finally, a direct trail from New Mexico to California had been blazed in 1829, not by way of Timpanogos, but one farther to the south. Sanctioned by Governor Chávez, the official journey led by Antonio Armijo made in the fall of 1829 from Abiquiú to San Gabriel Mission near Los Angeles took eighty-six days. Carrying blankets and other trade goods, Armijo hoped to barter for mules in California.

Armijo's route quickly became the favored route to California

---

181 Eleanor Lawrence, "Mexican Trade Between Santa Fe and Los Angeles, 1830-1848," *California Historical Society Quarterly* (1931), X:27.

from New Mexico for the next twenty years. New Mexicans used it as a trade and immigration trail to the west coast. Indeed, New Mexicans established the towns of Bakersfield and Riverside as a defensive barrier against Ute raids on the southern California settlements, Other variations developed over time, but Armijo's route served as the basic line of march westward.

Significantly, much of the route was already known, as some of Armijo's men seemed familiar with the country and had been to that portion of the Colorado River, the legendary Río del Tizón, as it makes its bend southward to the Gulf of California. Specifically, in 1828, Rafael Rivera, a member of the Armijo Expedition of 1829, had been to the Colorado River as far as present Hoover Dam near Las Vegas Wash.[182] Doubtless, like many other New Mexican traders, some of the sixty men with Armijo probably had been over the region previously and their collective memory permitted them to "retrace their steps and make detours" as Governor Chávez had reported.

The significant discovery of a practical route from New Mexico to California by Armijo was a culmination of decades of travel to the Yuta country by New Mexican traders and slavers. They had learned about the people and the geography of the Yuta country and had passed it on among each other. Some had learned the language of the Utes and used it for trade. Their cumulative knowledge undoubtly served the Armijo expedition well.

But Armijo's route was more than a trade route. After 1829, New Mexicans began to use the trail as a means to migrate to California. Slowly and quietly, almost without notice among Mexican officials, Armijo's route led to an out-migrations of New Mexicans to California. Some returned, others stayed.

In the interim, between the Domínguez-Escalante expedition and Mexico's independence from Spain, Spanish official interest in

---

182 Hafen, "Armijo's Journal," 99. Armijo noted in his diary that "[Rivera] recognized the ford where he had crossed the Río Grande [Colorado] the previous year in going to Sonora."

the Yuta country was briefly interrupted by the need to consolidate New Mexico's defenses against raiding enemy tribes that threatened to destroy New Mexico as a province. Tribes from the eastern plains of New Mexico continued raiding scattered Spanish villages between the Pecos and Río Grande. Particularly from their *rancherias* along the western confines of New Mexico, Navajo and Apache raiders ravaged New Mexican villages and homesteads almost at will. From the north, New Mexicans were beset by hostile Comanche and Yuta tribes that continually attacked every Spanish village, ranch, farm and place. New Mexico throughout the latter part of the eighteenth century faced possible destruction. During that space of time, Spain sought a military solution to the increased Ute and Comanche raids in New Mexico. In 1778, Juan Bautista de Anza was appointed governor of New Mexico, with instructions from the commandant general of the Provincias Internas to resolve the dilemma caused by incessant Indian raids throughout the province. Anza turned his attention to the north, toward southern Colorado. In so doing, he pointed to the eventual Spanish occupation of southern and western Colorado.

Chapter V
Juan Bautista de Anza's 1779 Campaign Against Cuerno Verde

> There, without other recourse they sprang to the ground and entrenched behind their [fallen] horses made in this manner a defense as brave as it was glorious.
>
> — Juan Bautista de Anza, 1779

Turning his gaze toward La Provincia de Nuevo México in 1779, Teodoro de Croix, Commandant-General of the Provincias Internas, a militarized region of the northern frontier of New Spain, reviewed reports of increased raids by Comanche bands and other tribes against New Mexican settlements. In his assessment, he concluded that the Spanish militia there could not stop the raiders. In 1778, Juan Bautista de Anza was appointed governor of New Mexico. Raised in the perilous Sonoran frontier, he was an experienced military leader. Still, as a Sonoran, he had hoped to establish communications between New Mexico, Sonora and California. Earlier, in 1776, he had led an expedition to settle San Francisco, and had explored possibilities of maintaining a land route from Sonora to California. Anza now saw an opportunity to establish a route from California to New Mexico. In order to achieve the New Mexico end of his plan, he hoped to pacify the Hopis of present northern Arizona, then a part of New Mexico, as they had been a barrier to Spanish passage through their lands. Anza's destiny, however, lay along a different course. Having received instructions from Croix, Anza's purpose in New Mexico, soon took on a completely different direction as increased Comanche raids became evermore violent against Hispanic villages and Indian pueblos.

Anza's appointment to the governorship of New Mexico proved an excellent choice from point of view of Spanish military plans for the area. Anza's military experience in Sonora proved him to be one of the ablest and most experienced frontier administrators of his time. Of Basque origin, Anza was born in 1736 in Fronteras, Sonora. Raised on a war-torn frontier, he was not quite four years old when his father was killed in an Apache ambush. As a teenager, he joined the garrison at Fronteras under the command of Gabriel Antonio de Vildósola, who later became his brother-in-law. By age nineteen, Anza was commissioned lieutenant,[183] and by 1759, four years later, he was promoted to captain of the presidio at Fronteras.[184] Charismatic and inspiring, like his father, he soon became a legendary figure in Sonora because of his military prowess, especially against Apache warriors with whom he had engaged in hand-to-hand combat. Having led numerous campaigns especially the Sonora Campaign (1767-1771), and a settlement expedition to California in 1776, he attracted the attention of Spanish officials. Soldier, explorer and administrator, Anza, who had added new experiences as captain of the presidios at Tubac, Fronteras, Terrenate, and Horcasitas, was destined for greater services to the crown. His appointment to the governorship in New Mexico was no accident, for he was deemed the best person to fulfill the needs of that embattled frontier.

Connecting California and New Mexico continued to stir considerable interest among Spanish officials who hoped to consolidate

---

183 Anza, Hoja de Servicios, 1767, Sección Provincias Internas, tomo 47, f. 263, Archivo General de la Nación (Hereinafter AGN), Mexico City.
184 *Ibid.* 47, f. 263.

the frontier. The dream inspired by Fray Francisco Hermenegildo Garcés in 1774, when he explored a route from the Mojave, via present Needles, to Hopi, was to run a trail to California from New Mexico. That changed when, instead, the Franciscans Domínguez and Escalante proposed expanding the New Mexico mission field to the Ute country.

Not surprisingly, Governor Mendinueta was taken aback when Captain Bernardo Miera y Pacheco rode south to Chihuahua to propose that three new settlements and three new presidios be established to consolidate Spanish control of the area between New Mexico, California, Nueva Vizcaya, and Sonora. Miera even proposed that a presidio and settlement be established at the Great Salt Lake of the Utes, and another on the San Juan River near present Four Corners.[185] Miera's proposal, however, came to naught.

Conversely, the development of a segment of a route from California to New Mexico received inspiration from the efforts of the indefatigable Franciscan missionary, Garcés (1738-1781). Between 1774 and 1776, Garcés, a contemporary of Anza, explored from southern Arizona to Mission San Gabriel, California, near Los Angeles and beyond through the Mojave Desert crossing the Colorado River south of the Grand Canyon and moving eastward to the Hopi villages of northeastern Arizona.[186] As Hopi was within the jurisdiction of the Franciscans in New Mexico, Garcés did not proceed to Santa Fe without Church authoritization, but instead headed back to Sonora. Still, his explorations demonstrated that a direct route from California via present Needles to Hopi could form part of a completed trail from Santa Fe to the Hopi Villages. Some Spanish officials argued that the route was too dangerous as Navajo, Apache, and other hostile tribes stood in the way. Thus, they chose a more northerly route through Ute country. Cognizant of Garcés' explorations, Anza,

---

185 "Miera Report to the King of Spain, October 26, 1777," in Bolton, *Pageant in the Wilderness*, 343-346.
186 Elliott Coues, translator and editor, *On the Trail of a Spanish Pioneer: The Diary and Itinerary of Francisco Garcés Missionary Priest)* in *His Travels through Sonora, Arizona, and California, 1775-1776* (New York Francis P. Harper, 1900, 2 Vols.)

newly appointed governor of New Mexico, considered traveling there by following a route northward along the Colorado River from Tubac, in present Arizona, and following Garcés' route to the Hopi Villages and on to Santa Fe.

Meanwhile, Father Juan Morfi, secretary to Commandant Teodoro de Croix, thinking along the same lines, advised his superior that Anza should, on his way to New Mexico, march from Sonora along the north bank of the Colorado and rendezvous with Fray Escalante at a point in the Sabuaguana Utes territory. Thus, Anza would move toward New Mexico from the west, and Escalante would journey northwest of Santa Fe toward today's Four Corners and, at a certain point, turn eastward until they met. The plan fitted with Anza's earlier hope of running a trail from California to New Mexico. Upon meeting up with Escalante, the two would proceed to Santa Fe via the Hopi Villages thence through Navajo lands all the while making careful observations about the terrain and people for future plans to pacify and occupy the area.

Morfi recommended that a line of presidios be established along the Colorado to protect the route from Santa Fe to Monterey.[187] The plan had a major drawback: the Ute, Apache, Navajo, Comanche and other tribes stood along the path of their projected route. In order to achieve their goals, Morfi hoped Anza would establish peace with the Comanche, Ute and Apache tribes.

Anza's travel plan to New Mexico, however, lay along a different route than envisioned. Departing Sonora for New Mexico, Anza and his men instead marched northeastward to El Paso where he reviewed the militia. He reorganized the El Paso militia by equipping them and creating two new units to guard the area against Apache raids. Marching along the *Camino Real de Tierra Adentro* past Socorro, Belen, Tomé, and the Albuquerque area, Anza could see the devastation caused by Navajo,

---

187 Juan Morfi, Memorial (undated, probably written in 1777) quoted in Charles Edward Chapman, *Founding of Spanish California: The Northwestward Expansion of New Spain* (New York: Macmillan, 1916), 398-402.

Apache and Comanche raiders. At Tomé, for example, 21 settlers had been killed in summer 1777. He noted another 30 dead at the hands of enemy warriors in summer 1778. Upon reaching Albuquerque, Anza, dismayed at the scattered pattern of farms and ranches on land grants that were very isolated from each other, noted that they could not mobilize a quick defense against Apache, Comanche, or Navajo raiders.[188] New Mexico's weakly organized defenses, like those he saw on the Río Abajo (the Lower Río Grande from Socorro to Cochiti Pueblo), shared common problems.

Every where he looked, Anza could not escape the fact that New Mexico continued to be beset by Plains raiders. Apaches on the lower Río Grande continued raiding farms and villages, such as Socorro, from their strongholds in the Magdalena Mountains. Other Apaches still menaced travelers on the Camino Real between El Paso del Norte and the Villa de Alburquerque. The same pattern was common throughout the settlements of the Río Arriba (Upper Río Grande between Cochiti and Taos pueblos. Aside from lack of funding, the settlement patterns were dispersed, and within certain valleys, most homesteads were too far apart to be quickly organized when attacked. Thus the entire province was easy prey to raiding tribes. In northern New Mexico, the Comanches, raiding from southeastern Colorado, dominated the area from the Arkansas River to mountain villages from Taos to Mora, Las Trampas, Pecos, San Miguel, and Villanueva. Comanche warriors raided at will, took captives, and killed whoever stood in their way.

Inspecting the affected areas, Governor Anza implemented his instructions from Croix. Visiting one settlement after another, he convinced frontiersmen who lived in scattered and isolated places to move to towns with defensive walls and watch towers for their safety and protection. At surrounding settlements near the Villa de Albuquerque, Anza virtually forced isolated frontiersmen into the

---

188 Adams and Chávez, trans. and eds. *The Missions of New Mexico, 1776*, 154.

defensive plaza for their own good.[189] Acknowledging that New Mexicans had, for two centuries, effectively defended themselves against Apache, Navajo, Ute, and Comanche raiders, his goal was to make their defenses more efficient. To Anza, the improved defenses in New Mexico were only a part of the solution against raiders. He soon realized that the best plan would require a combination of improved defenses, better equipped militia units, and well-timed punitive expeditions into *comanchería* with Ute and Apache allies, traditional enemies of the Comanche.

Having spoken with many New Mexican frontiersmen, Anza learned that the root of New Mexico's dilemma with the Comanches lay far to the north, in present southern Colorado known to New Mexicans as Comanchería. He quickly realized that he needed to make a decisive strike against the Comanche in their own territory if the New Mexican defenses were to work. Anza met with New Mexican frontiersmen, including Hispanic New Mexican scouts and guides who had been with the José María Antonio Rivera Expeditions of 1765 and 1766 as well as on the Domínguez and Escalante Expedition of 1776, and Indian allies, such as the Utes, who were at war with the Comanche, and the Pueblos, who, themselves, were targets of Comanche raiders. From them, Anza,

---

189 Morfi, Geographical Description of New Mexico...1782, in Alfred Barnaby Thomas, *Forgotten Frontiers: A Study of Spanish Indian Policy of Don Juan Bautista de Anza, Governor of New Mexico, 1777-1787* (Norman: University of Oklahoma Press, 1932), 101. Of Albuquerque, Morfi wrote: "The Villa of Albuquerque was founded in 1706 is distant twenty leagues from the Villa of Santa Fe in a large plain which will be a league from south to north and two and a half from east to west on the banks of the Río Grande. It possesses seven and one half leagues of land for crops and pastures which they irrigate with the waters of the river diverted by means of ditches. The climate is fair with respect to its elevation and very healthy because of the purity of its atmosphere. The land is fertile although it does not produce what it could because of insufficient cultivation for lack of oxen and leisure, the [threat of] enemies not permitting them to absent themselves from the villages for various tasks. Thus the land lies fallow. Scarcity of fuel obliges the settlers to utilize the manure of the horses. The settlement is scattered throughout the entire breadth of the valley. In 1779 the governor, Don Juan Bautista de Anza, reduced it to the regular form. At that time three hundred and eighty-one Spanish settlers lived there."

110

gathered as much intelligence as possible and began to form a plan to counterattack the Comanche in southern Colorado.

Although Anza does not identify the New Mexicans who had been trading with the Utes for at least a generation and who had been with Rivera or Domínguez and Escalante, their names from those expeditions are known. Escalante identified them as Lorenzo Olivares from the Villa de El Paso; Andrés Múñiz from Bernalillo; Antonio Lucrecio Múñiz, brother of Andrés from Embudo south of Taos; Juan de Aguilar from Santa Clara Pueblo,; Joaquín Laín, a blacksmith from Santa Fe; and Cisneros' servant, Simon Lucero, probably from Zuñí. Both Andrés Múñiz and his brother, Lucrecio had been with Juan María Rivera in 1765, and spoke different Ute dialects.[190] For years, Múñiz had, without license, gone with others as far as the Colorado River and the headwaters of the Río Grande to trade.

At least three, if not most, of these men accompanied Anza on his campaign against the Comanche. Anza made good use of them as translators and guides, for they had expert knowledge of the land and people in the area. They guided Anza and identified places in rough terrain reached by the expedition. When they got to the northern portion of the Río Grande drainage system, for example, they identified it as the Río del Norte, and remarked that they were only 15 miles or so from the headwaters of the river. They counseled Anza on other streams and described the land ahead.

With the support of Hispanic frontiersmen and their Pueblo allies, Anza organized an army of one hundred veteran soldiers of the Santa Fe garrison, 203 militiamen and 259 Indian auxiliaries. Among them were the Hispanic scouts who had been on the Rivera and the Domínguez-

---

190 For a complete listing of all participants in the expedition, some of whom joined Domínguez and Escalante while the exploration of the Yuta country was in progress, see pages vii-viii in Ted J. Warner, ed., and Fray Angelico Chávez, trans., with a Foreword by Robert Himmerich y Valencia, *The Domínguez-Escalante Journal: Their Expedition through Colorado, Utah, Arizona, and New Mexico in 1776* (Salt Lake City: University of Utah Press, Reprinted 1995).

Escalante expeditions. The small army was divided into three divisions of approximately 200 men each. Even though the New Mexican militiamen were poorly armed and ill-prepared for forty days of campaigning, Anza decided that the expedition must proceed. By mid-August the punitive expedition against the Comanche was as ready as it ever would be.

On August 15, 1779, about 3 o'clock on a warm Sunday afternoon, Anza and his troops commenced their march against the Comanche.[191] Moving north from Santa Fe, they reached Pojoaque Pueblo, where they halted for the night. At daybreak the next day, Anza and his men continued northward, reaching San Juan de los Caballeros where they camped.

On August 16, at San Juan de los Caballeros, Anza mustered his Sonoran and New Mexican troops. In his review, Anza resolved an issue that had been nagging at him: although these New Mexican frontiersmen were experienced at frontier warfare, they were poorly equipped for the forty-day campaign. Not only were their arms in poor repair, they were inadequately provisioned. The forty-day campaign required that each soldier have three horses, arms, munitions and food to last them for the duration of the expedition. Anza realized that if the campaign had any chance of success, he must share horses and weapons from among his Sonoran troops with the New Mexicans.

Afterwards, Anza regrouped his three divisions. Commanding the first division Anza assigned the second division to serve as the rear-guard. One of Anza's lieutenants commanded the third division.[192] That done, Anza sent out twelve scouts to reconnoiter the land before them and to find out what they could about the Comanche. Anza instructed his scouts not to return for four days, unless they learned something about any movements made by the Comanche.

---

191 Diario de la expedición que sale a practicar contra la nación cumancha el infraescripto teniente coronel, don Juan Bautista de Anza, governador y comandante de la provincia de Nuevo Mexico con la tropa, milicianos e indios in Thomas, *Forgotten Frontiers*, 123.
192 Thomas, *Forgotten Frontiers*, 123.

With his scouts moving ahead of his command, Anza ordered the main troop northward and somewhere along their line of march, they crossed the Río Grande bearing northwest. At the nearly deserted pueblo of Ojo Caliente, they camped for the night.[193] There, Anza noted that nearly thirty families lived scattered in a line nearly ten miles in length. Living in constant fear of attack by Comanche and Ute, almost all of their homes were fortified.[194] Departing Ojo Caliente the next day, Anza moved his troops to the Río de las Nutrias where they camped for the night.

Four days after leaving Ojo Caliente, the three divisions moved over the rough terrain. They marched northward passing the Río de San Antonio, the Río de los Conejos, Río de las Jaras, Río de San Francisco, Río de las Timbres, and Río de San Lorenzo until they again rejoined the Río Grande at a ford they named El Paso de San Barolomé. On Friday, August 20, they reached the Río de los Conejos, where they rendezvoused with their scouts. The scouts reported that up to there, they had not seen any sign of Comanches.

To Anza's surprise, while at his camp on the Conejos, nearly two hundred Ute and Apache warriors came to parlay with him. They wished to make war on the Comanche, their enemy.[195] They talked. Anza, wise in the ways of frontier warfare, understood the complexity of frontier alliances and reasons for them. Firmly, he clarified that should the Comanche be defeated, he would decide how to divide the spoils, meaning that everything would be divided equally between all members of the force under his command. To that, they all agreed. After gaining their trust and assurance, Anza allowed them to join his army as allies against the Comanches.

The next day, Anza's army rose early and broke camp by dawn, marching north-northeast through a series of ravines and crossing the

---

193 *Ibid.*, 124.
194 *Ibid.*, 124.
195 *Ibid.*, 125.

Río del Pino, after which they reached Las Jaras.[196] Quickly, his scouts, finding signs of the enemy, reported that his army was getting closer to the Comanche. To avoid detection, Anza marched only at night. In his account of the campaign, Anza explained that, "It was necessary to make the next march at night so that the enemy might not descry the dust of our troop and horse herd from the sierra, not very distant, which we are keeping on our right. For that reason the march of this day was reserved for the night."[197]

Holding up for the day, Anza and his army waited until sunset before moving forward. As twilight gave way to darkness, Anza and his allied forces moved northward crossing the Río de los Timbres. They marched all that night. By two in the morning, they reached the Río San Lorenzo where they camped for the day. They resumed their march the next night, continuing in northward direction, and then turned northwest until they reached the Río del Norte, the northern end of the Río Grande, at a ford they named San Bartolomé. Anza figured that he was not far, a few leagues[198] south from its source.

Gathering more information about what to expect ahead, his Ute guides and three Hispanic New Mexicans, who had been on the Rivera Expedition ordered in 1765 by Vélez Cachupín, told him that the river "proceeds from a great swamp, this having been formed, in addition to its springs, by the continuous melting of snow from some volcanos which are very close."[199] They also told him that beyond the sierra, one could see seven rivers, which united formed the Río Colorado. Anza deduced that the Colorado was the same one which was fed, further south, by the Río Gila before draining into the Gulf of California. Of the information provided by the New Mexican guides in his force, Anza wrote:

> The same settlers mentioned, who explored the seven rivers referred to, by order of Governor Don

---

196 *Ibid.*, 125.
197 *Ibid.*, 125.
198 A league is approximately 2.6 miles.
199 Thomas, *Forgotten Frontiers*, p. 126.

Tomás Vélez, affirm that on all of them, which are very fertile, they observed that in ancient times they were well populated with Indians, this being demonstrated by the large size of the formal pueblos of three stories and other remains. Among these was [evidence] that the settlers themselves had practiced the art of taking out silver, as their ore dumps and other remains of their use were found. They assured me moreover they delivered these fragments to the aforesaid governor, who, according to other reports, sent them to the city of Mexico."[200]

Who were the New Mexicans? Anza does not say.

Still marching by night, the expedition continued its relentless march toward the Comanche rancherias. That year, fall arrived early. Suffering the bitter cold in the wilderness during the nighttime, the expedition did without warm burning fires so that the Comanche would not detect their presence in the area. The next few nights were spent crossing arroyos they named Santa Xines and El Aguage de los Yutas, a swamp that ran northwestwardly in the San Luis Valley of the Río del Norte that narrowed between two mountains that formed it.

During the night of August 28, snow fell. Yet, they travelled to the Río San Agustín beyond which they crossed the Río de Napestle, present Arkansas River. Near there, they stopped briefly to rest their horses. By the dawn of August 29, a fog formed bogging down their march. Still, they continued their march past daybreak until eight o'clock in the morning when they reached a place they called Las Perdidas because of trouble they had from the weather that dogged them the entire time. Near there, the Anza's men and their allies killed fifty head of buffalo "in less than ten minutes" they said, from the great number they had seen.[201] There, Anza replaced the twelve scouts that

---

200 *Ibid.*, 127.
201 *Ibid.*, 128.

had been out on the trail since August 26 with thirty others who were to report back on August 31.

That day, two scouts returned saying that they had found signs of the Comanche. They reported that a considerable number of the enemy had raised a cloud of dust not far from their scouting encampment that was located near a place the New Mexicans called Río del Sacramento. Hoping to catch the Comanches, Anza quickly moved his men to that place. Anza's army was on high alert and prepared for a fight. When they got there, they discovered that the Comanche had discovered the scouts' camp and fled. Anza realized that he might not have another chance and moved his army forward as quickly as possible to attack the Comanche in the area. The advancing allied force formed a long skirmish line in a semi-circle, which Anza hoped to use as a dragnet entrapping Comanches as they advanced in the woods.

Caught by surprise, the Comanche had never seen this kind of formation before. One chieftain understood it and retreated with his warriors. Others, failing to adapt to the coming attack, most being mounted including women and children, chose to run. Anza's scouts reported that there were probably 120 wooden frames of tents in the area, indicating that the Comanche had left precipitously, if not nearly panic stricken. Within three leagues, the fast moving army caught up with them. In the running battle, eighteen warriors were killed and many others wounded. Over thirty women and children were taken captive. All goods and baggage carried by the Comanche were lost in the flight. Near there, Anza's men rounded up five hundred Comanche horses. Returning to the Comanche camp site, Anza proclaimed a victory and divided the spoils as agreed upon.[202]

Upon questioning his informants, Anza learned that the Comanche he had attacked were going to rendezvous with the chief or captain-general of the Comanches named Cuerno Verde. They told him that Cuerno Verde had returned from a sixteen day raid in New

---

202 *Ibid.*, 130-131, 135, 141, 142.

Mexico and had invited all Comanche bands in the area to join him in a celebration. With that information, Anza decided to pursue Cuerno Verde "to see if fortune would grant me an encounter with him."[203] The following day, Wednesday, September 1, with the aid of scouts and informants, Anza picked up Cuerno Verde's trail. They followed the trail all day from mid-morning until sunset.

Finally, at sunset on September 2, Anza caught up with the Comanche and decided to attack despite twilight was quickly setting in. Attacking in a column, Anza punished his enemy, but night fell, and the Comanche, scattering in all directions fled into the darkness. Anza's army set up camp on the Arkansas River and waited for daylight.

At seven o'clock that morning, Anza broke camp in search of Cuerno Verde. Anza's plan was to feign pursuit of the Comanche to fatigue them and their horses. Then, Anza, with the main body of his troops, turned around as if in retreat. He knew the Comanche were watching and studying his every move. By faking retreat, Anza hoped that Cuerno Verde would stop his flight and make a stand. As his Ute allies pursued the scattered Comanche bands, Anza turned his attention on Cuerno Verde and the main body of Comanche warriors.

In the woods nearby, a group of Comanche warriors fired muskets at the Spaniards, who were out of range. The smoke from their guns dissipated in the air in front of them. Anza's confidence grew when his men identified the insignia and devices used by Cuerno Verde. In the swirl of the battle, they saw Cuerno Verde, mounted on a spirited horse, animating his men forward while defiantly challenging Anza's men to advance.[204] Biding their time, Anza's men attacked and fired. The pungent smell of the black powder from their guns soon filled the air as the battle line filled with smoke from their weapons.

The Comanche settlement lay along Fountain Creek near where it flows into the Arkansas River and meets another drainage that Anza

---

203 *Ibid.*, 132.
204 *Ibid.*, 134.

called Río de los Dolores.[205] There in a gully, realizing he was trapped, Cuerno Verde made a last stand. Anza described what happened next:

> ...without other recourse they sprang to the ground and entrenched behind their [fallen] horses made in this manner a defense as brave as it was glorious. Notwithstanding the aforesaid Cuerno Verde perished, with this first-born son, the heir to his command, four of his most famous captains, a medicine man who preached that he was immortal, and ten more, who were able to get in the place indicated.

> A larger number might have been killed, but I preferred the death of this chief even to more of those who escaped, because of his being constantly in this region the cruel scourge of this kingdom, and because he had exterminated many pueblos, killing hundreds and making as many prisoners whom he afterwards sacrificed in cold blood. His own nation accuse him, ever since he took command, of forcing them to take up arms and volunteer against the Spaniards, a hatred of whom dominated him because his father who also held the same command and power met death at our hands.[206]

Not far from the gully, the defiant Comanche survivors of the battle looked up as Anza approached to talk with them. Without remorse, they told him that they would lament their lost leader. Cuerno Verde had dared to attack Anza's army, nearly 800 strong, with the fifty warriors

---

205 See Plan de la tierra que se anduvo y descubrió en la campaña que hizo contra los comanches el teniente coronel Don Juan Bautista de Anza, governador y comandante propietario de esta provincia de Nuevo México y la victoria que consiguió de los enemigos. [Hereinafter cited as Anza's Campaign Map,1779] AGI, Mexico 577. Copy in Spanish Colorial Research Center, UNM, SCRC-ITEM 176. NEW MEXICO Upper Río Grande & Southern Colorado,1779.
206 Thomas, *Forgotten Frontiers*, 135-36.

who stood by his side. Throughout the battle, Cuerno Verde had defiantly exposed himself to the lively fire from Anza's men. In the midst of the fight, Cuero Verde had refused to load his own musket, while someone else loaded it for him. Cuerno Verde's behavior in battle demonstrated his disdain for the Spaniards. Before leaving the battle site, Anza named the place "Los Dolores de María Santísima" (The Sorrows of Mary, Most Holy) in the vicinity of present Greenhorn Mountains, ultimately named after Cuerno Verde. As indicated by a note on Anza's campaign map, the Comanche settlement was destroyed.[207] Based on Anza's correspondence to him, Commandant Croix wrote to his superior that:

> Twice they attacked the Comanche; destroyed one hundred and twenty wigwams, killed their great chief called Cuerno Verde, his son, his lieutenant-general, Aguila Bolteada, Pujacante, or priest, and fifty-two other warriors; twenty women and children and thirty-four other individuals were taken prisoner along with five hundred head of stock.[208]

Anza, however, understood that the victory meant nothing if peace could not be achieved.

With a wave of his arm, Anza turned his army around, heading south to the Villa de Santa Fe. Three days had passed since the two-day battle. Anza noted in his report that they departed the battle site right at sunset on Thursday, September 3. Passing by Taos Pueblo a few days later, they picked up the old colonial road and followed it southward past the Río Grande gorge. On September 10, Anza and his dusty and tired army entered the Plaza de Santa Fe.

---

207 Anza's Campaign Map (1779), AGI, Mexico 577.

208 Alfred Barnaby Thomas, *Teodoro de Croix and the Northern Frontier of New Spain, 1776-1783* (Norman: University of Oklahoma Press, 1941), p. 109. Also see Anza to Teodoro de Croix, Santa Fe, 1 de Noviembre de 1779 in Luis Navarro García, *José de Galvez y la Comandancia General de las Provincias Internas*, (Sevilla, Publicaciones de la Escuela de Estudios Hispano-Americanos de Sevilla, 1964), p. 336.

Mapa de Campaña de Juan Bautista de Anza, 1779 en "Plan de la tierra que se anduvo y descubrió en la campaña que hizo contra los comanches el teniente coronel Don Juan Bautista de Anza, gobernador y comandante propietario de esta provincia de Nuevo México y la victoria que consiguió de los enemigos." AGI, Mexico 577.

Anza began to explore ways to bring about peace with the Comanche. Not until July 1785 when four hundred Comanches sought amnesty in Taos, Anza's success against the Comanche had not been fully realized. Anza reminded them that lasting peace could not be had until Comanches could united in peace. That fall, the Comanches held a large powwow at a place called Casa de Palo on the Arkansas to unite those tribes present. In the meeting, they chose, as their chief, Ecueracapa, called Cape of Leather or Coat of Chain Mail[209] by New Mexicans. Anza noted that he was the most notable, the most trusted and universally esteemed chief among other Comanche chieftains.[210] Ecueracapa's presence at the meeting signified a willingness among Comanche leaders to, at least, parley with Anza.

Word of Anza's treaty with the Comanche spread to the Utes, who feared a Spanish-Comanche alliance that would unite against them. They sent two chiefs, Moara and Pinto, to protest the arrangement made by Anza with the Comanche. Righteously, they complained that Anza preferred to make peace with unfaithful tribes than with obedient and loyal friends. For hours, they angrily and defiantly refused to smoke from the peace pipe or accept gifts from Anza. Finally, Anza convinced them to join him in the peace ceremony with the Comanches.

Months later, in February 1786, Anza met with Ute and Comanche leaders at Pecos Pueblo and negotiated a peace between the two tribes. In exchange for their agreement to wage war against the Apache, either as auxiliaries of Spanish forces or as individual tribes, Anza offered them trade privileges and promised them justice against abuses by Spanish and Pueblo traders.[211] Anza dearly meant to keep the peace, even if it meant

---

209 Thomas, *Forgotten Frontiers*, p. 384, fn. 108. and fn. 124. Many who have written of him also conclude that the name Ecueracapa also means *Cota de Malla* (Coat of Chain Mail or Coat of Leather). Thomas also noted that he was also known as "El huerfano, the orphan, and because most notable in war, Contatanacapara, Grulla en Cruz (Crane on the Cross), known in New Mexico and Texas by the name Cota de Malla (Coat of Mail)." Thomas, *Forgotten Frontiers*, p. 325.
210 *Ibid.*, pp. 325-26.
211 Eleanor Richie, "General Mano Mocha of the Utes," *The Colorado Magazine*

punishing New Mexican frontiersmen to do it. As all New Mexico's governors had done since the days of Juan de Oñate, Anza doggedly enforced *bandos* providing that anyone going to north to the land of the Utes or to the Great Plains without license be punished under the law. Such laws had been in place to keep the peace between them and tribes, who could overrun the New Mexico Spanish and Pueblo settlements. Anza knew that their defenses could not be sustained indefinitely.

Historically, Anza's Expedition of 1779 to the San Luis Valley through Poncha Pass to the Arkansas resulted in the eventual settlement of present southern Colorado, then a part of New Mexico. Ironically, one of the first settlements in that area resulted from Spanish efforts to settle the Comanche into towns.

In 1787, Anza visited the Comanches one last time. He wanted to see how the peace between New Mexico and the Comanche was working out. Furthermore, he wanted to assure that Ecueracapa and Tosacondata (*Grulla Blanca* or White Crane)[212] had been installed and accepted as "general and lieutenant general of the Kotsotekas" and witness Paruanarimuca (Bear Harness) appointed as lieutenant general for the Jupes and Yamparikas.[213] That summer, Chief Paruanarimuca visited Santa Fe and proposed that the Spaniards create an *establecimiento fijado*[214] (permanent settlement) for his tribe on the Arkansas. In late summer 1787, Anza sent thirty Hispanics and a master mason from New Mexico to construct a Spanish-style village for the Comanche with adobe houses, corrals for sheep and cattle below the Greenhorn Mountains near

---

(January, 1932), Vol. IX, No. 1, p. 153.

212 Thomas, *Forgotten Frontiers*, p. 326

213 Pekka Hamalainen, *Comanche Empire* (New Haven: Yale University Press, 2008), p. 126

214 Thomas, *Forgotten Frontiers*, p. 386, fn. 133 writes: "That this instruction was not an empty gesture is proved by the fact that Anza used this authority to help the Jupes build a pueblo on the Arkansas River. In this project the Spaniards spent almost seven hundred pesos, which covered the cost of materials and labor transported over the mountains from New Mexico to the Arkansas River. There today the stream called San Carlos, near present Pueblo, doubtless marks the spot of this construction which was called San Carlos de los Jupes."

the mouth of the San Carlos River. Several of the Comanche also worked on the village.[215] The Comanche settlement was called *San Carlos de los Jupes*. The settlement was abandoned when one of Paruanarimuca's wives died there and the Comanches, thinking a deadly desease had infested the place, refused to live where such a death had occurred.[216] Despite Spanish efforts to get them to return, they refused.

Not until the 1830s would Hispanic settlers confidently move into present southern Colorado to establish homesteads and land grants, particularly in the San Luis Valley. The expeditions led by Rivera, Domínguez and Escalante, and Anza opened the door to Hispanic expansion northward from the New Mexico settlements along a line of settlements and land grants from Abiquiú, Tierra Amarilla, and Ojo Caliente to Chama. Other settlement patterns ran due north from Santa Fe to Taos to the San Luis Valley. With Anza's Expedition of 1779, the pacification of southern Colorado had only begun; decades would pass before it was completed. Meanwhile, Hispanic traders would continue to follow known trails and routes into western and southern Colorado to trade with the Utes. As they had since the seventeenth century, they continued to push northwestward beyond the La Sal Mountains to the large salt lakes at Timpanogos and, from there, to the Great Basin and, eventually, California.

---

215 Hamalainen, *Comanche Empire*, p. 126.
216 *Ibid.*, 127. López Tushar, *People of El Valle*, p. 22.

Chapter VI
The Colorado Crucible: New Mexican Traders, Ute Raiders, and Military Expeditions from New Mexico, 1779-1845

> Asked: Whether he knows that the journey to the Yuta country is prohibited. He answered that he knows it, but that his debts made him trespass there.
> — Christobal Lobato, 1797

As they had before and after the expeditions of 1765 by Rivera and of 1776 by Domínguez and Escalante despite the *bandos* prohibiting trade with Utes, Apaches and Comanches, New Mexicans turned their attention toward the Yuta country for trade. In reality, trade was a way for both Utes and Hispanic frontiersmen to make a living at a time when barter was the norm. In their wanderings and rendezvousing with Utes for trade, New Mexicans soon looked to the Great Basin as an outlet for commercial dealings. Before long, those involved with the trade knew all of the rendezvous points and routes to the Yuta country as far as the Great Basin and Timpanogos. At first, traders from Abiquiú, Taos, Picuris, and Chama were especially tied to the Yuta trade. Eventually, as settlements spread northward to such places as Tierra Amarilla and Mora, trade with Utes increased. By the late

1770s, Spanish militarists were determined to stabilize relations with the Utes by sternly prohibiting New Mexicans from going to the Yuta country.

Hopes of establishing a route to California gave way to another plan. Although the Domínguez-Escalante expedition sought to establish a route to California through the Yuta country, its outcome was two-pronged. Soon after returning to New Mexico, Friar Atanasio Domínguez proposed a plan to establish a mission field with military outposts in the Yuta country. Still, Spanish officials hoped to create a greater interest in the possibility for trade in the Great Basin, the farthest point reached by the expedition. That delayed plan still held the promise of finding a route to California.

In the thirty years following the Domínguez-Escalante expedition, numerous unofficial trading parties went northwestward from New Mexico to Utah and the Great Basin for trade with Ute tribes. Still, the danger of making enemies of the Utes, or committing an outrage against them that could result in increased Ute raids, motivated Spanish officials to outlaw any expeditions into the area without license. Every step of the way to the Great Basin and to Timpanogos taken by each trading expedition added knowledge about the various tribes, valleys, rivers, mountains and ridges. Finally, after nearly five decades, interest in a direct route to California through southern Utah was revived.

In 1778, New Mexicans were again threatened with another *bando*, this time from a higher official, Teodoro de Croix, commandant general of the Provincias Internas.[217] Croix recognized that the New Mexican practice of trading with the Yutas was longstanding. Too, he was fully aware of previous *bandos* prohibiting trade with the Yutas. Croix's *bando* sought to enforce the law by reinforcing the penalties against the prohibited trade. Focusing his attention on Spanish officials

---

217 *Bando*, Don Francisco Trebol Nabarro, gobernador ynterino y comandante general de este reyno de Nuevo Mexico por el Señor Comandante General Caballero de Croix, (hereinafter cited as *Bando*) September 13, 1778, Spanish Archives of New Mexico (Hereinafter cited as SANM), II, Microfilm Roll 10, frame 1055.

in New Mexico for winking at the violation of the laws, Croix warned officials such as the *alcaldes mayores* and their *tenientes* that they were "seriously obligated to execute and observe the law and punish the transgressors accordingly under penalty of law."[218]

Croix clearly understood that one of the underlying causes of Yuta raids into New Mexico was retaliation against the settlements, which likely originated in some act by illegal traders in the Yuta country. Simply by going there spelled trouble. Trading with them, New Mexicans invariably could, intentionally or not, commit some form of insult against them creating conditions for revenge. Not mincing words, Croix stated that the "Yutas, resenting some bold act or an evil deed against them, commonly break the peace with little reflection."[219] On the other hand, warring tribes had other reasons for attacking Hispanic and Pueblo Indian settlements. Croix hoped his *bando* would curb, if not stop, New Mexicans from going to the Yuta country. Furthering his argument, Croix accused New Mexicans in the illicit trade of impeding the expansion of "*Nuestra Santa Fee Catholica*"[220] among the Yutas because missionaries were fearful of going to them. Basically, Croix accused New Mexican traders of obstructing the work of missionaries.

Croix's *bando* took on a comprehensive character. He expressly prohibited any Spaniard, genízaro, or Indian from trading with the Yutas. That meant that the Pueblos were restricted from trading with the Utes. Aware that wealthy New Mexicans or Pueblos hired people to go trade with the Utes, Croix's *bando* provided that no one would be permitted to go or send someone in their stead to the Yuta country.

So that no one could plead ignorance, Croix ordered that the *bando* be read aloud by a crier and posted in a public area in various plazas in New Mexico. As instructed by the *bando*, the *alcalde mayor* of Taos Pueblo, Manuel Vigil, did so immediately, as did Antonio Baca, *alcalde*

---

218 *Ibid.*
219 *Ibid.*
220 *Ibid.*

mayor of the Villa de Alburquerque, and Nerio Antonio Montoya at Picuris Pueblo. Accordingly, they submitted a response to Croix that they had done so. The *bando* and others similar to it were in effect in New Mexico throughout the rest of the Spanish colonial period.

Penalties for the illicit trade commonly included (1) incarceration, (2) fines of one hundred pesos, which were considerably stiff in a society that depended on barter for trade, (3) confiscation of all items traded, and (4) servitude or public works in government installations for a period of time. Additionally, if a Spaniard were caught breaking the ban on trade with the Yutas, he would be prohibited from holding any public office; if a *genízaro* or Indian broke the law, he would be subject to a fine of one hundred pesos and suffer one hundred lashes.[221]

Much to Croix's dismay, it did not take long for New Mexicans to violate his *bando*. New Mexicans risked their lives to go to the Yuta country for varied reasons. Some New Mexicans lived under the threat of constant peonage. Given their endless debt to creditors in their own communities, some sought sources of income through bartering with native groups on the Great Plains or in the Yuta country. Through such trade, albeit illegal, they found a means to pay their debts that farming and ranching alone could not provide. They risked being caught in order to trade for what was valuable in the wilderness marketplace in those times. The values of the period in animals, produce and other items dictated what could be exchanged. Mules and horses, for example, were traded for slaves held by stronger tribes; a bushel of corn or wheat flour bought a buckskin shirt; and knives and awls were traded for pelts, blankets and saddle blankets. Sometimes New Mexicans did not go to the Yuta country for trade, they went to recover stolen animals or kidnapped kinsmen. Sometimes, Spanish frontiersmen, themselves, undertook unauthorized punitive expeditions into southern Colorado seeking to recover lost property or captured kin. In many cases, their defensive actions often resulted in open warfare with Utes.

---

221 *Ibid.*

128

Despite Croix's *bando*, illicit trade was in full swing. The *bando* did not address the complexity of the problem, but merely offered short-range, stop-gap series of penalties that did not deter New Mexicans from trading with Utes. Like the traders, New Mexican officials too were often caught in the same economic bind that the illegal trade relieved. Disregarding Croix's admonitions as stated in the *bando*, they, themselves, often sent relatives to the Yuta country to carry trade items for them. When their relatives or close friends were apprehended, they, as officials, tended to diminish their crime or reduce their penalty. Sometimes, whenever trading expeditions were reported before they got started, officials obligingly upheld the law before the eyes of the world.

Some traders ventured past the La Sal Mountains and into Utah's canyonlands near Cedar City. The extent of their trading ventures took them to Timpanogos and to the Great Basin in the west. As regards Colorado, much trade took place near the Sierra de la Plata, the Río San Miguel and the Río de los Pinos. Río de las Animas, the Río Navajo as well as the Uncompahgre, Gunnison, Arkansas, and Colorado rivers. Today, some areas of their rendezvous with Utes are marked on maps by such places as Mesa Verde, Dolores, Durango, Mancos, Cortez, Ignacio, Arboles, Pagosa Springs, Montrose, Cimarron, Del Norte, and others.

Oftentimes, the testimony of apprehended traders revealed about where they had gone for trade. Their jumping off points were places like Abiquiú, Taos and Chama. One case in point resulted from the arrest of Marcelino Mansanares, Vicente García, Miguel Sandoval and Cristóbal Salazar, who were arrested on April 10, 1785 for trading with the Utes.[222] Typically, under interrogation, their memories failed them. When asked what they had taken with them to trade, they feigned absence of memory. Predictably, they had taken the usual items: knives, awls, horses, corn,

---

222 Proceso contra Marcelino Mansanares y demás que expresa por infraciones del comercio en el país de los Yutas, y sentenciados come se refiere, 10 April 1785, SANM, II, Microfilm Roll 11, frame 845.

flour and tobacco. When asked how far and where they had gone, they admitted they had gone as far as the Río San Cristóbal, near present Gunnison. Asked whether they had a license to trade Mansanares said he did, but he could not prove it. Given the contradictions about the license, Governor Anza passed judgment on the matter. The men were sentenced to the usual incarceration, fines, confiscation of trade items, and servitude in the *casas reales* in Santa Fe.[223]

Toward the end of the century, the illicit trade was still undeterred. Hundreds of New Mexicans had gone to the Yuta country for trade, many of which were unrecorded as they were not caught. For others who were caught and arrested, they were tried for their "infraction of the law" as Teodoro de Croix had said in his *bando* of 1778. Between 1780 and 1800, numerous cases revealed the inability of authorities to monitor trade with the Yutas. By the end of the 1790s little had changed to stop New Mexicans from going to the Yuta country to trade without license.

While New Mexican frontiersmen ventured to southern Colorado and Utah to trade with the Yutas, others were motivated by different reasons. Although little missionary activity took place in that direction, for example, Father José Vela Prada, the *custos* (custodian), at Abiquiú, said that he had gone among the Yutas when he heard that they were in the area trading. From them, he learned about a young Navajo woman named María Concepción, who had been taken during a raid by Utes and had been brutally mistreated by her captors. In 1805, Father Vela Prada rescued her for humanitarian reasons and he wrote:

> I, as a religious moved by charity, took her from the tyranny of the Yutas who had captured her in just war...but they gave [her] by their barbarity very bad treatment, she had wounds all over her body from the stabs from their arrows....but had I not taken her from their power, without doubt she would be in eternity, and from that hell, that from that loss,

---

223 *Ibid.*

I desired to separate her, bringing to bear the office of the Church, it cost me 1,001 *pesos fuertes*, as she had been bought for two horses....The only thing I did was to take this very unhappy creature from the heavens to where she was on the verge of going, and the tears that she poured out upon being freed...it broke my heart.[224]

Although the Navajos wanted her back, María Concepción chose to stay in Abiquiú.

In September 1805 Manuel Mestas revealed another reason, other than trade, why one would dare go to the Yuta country. A seventy-year old *genízaro* who spoke the Yuta language, Mestas had spent many years traveling from New Mexico via southern Colorado toward the Great Basin for trade. At one point he claimed to have pacified the Yuta of Timpanogos, saying that he was the one who had "reduced them to peace."[225] Governor Joaquín del Real Alencaster, who governed New Mexico between 1805 and 1807, reported that Mestas and his men had attacked the Yutas because they had stolen a number of his horses. In his first attempt, Mestas recovered only eight horses.

Unhappy with the partial recovery of his horse herd, Mestas returned in July 1805 to the Yuta country for several weeks during which time he attacked at least one Ute band. Not only did he retrieve eleven of the animals he sought, but also captured twenty mules and eight horses stolen from other New Mexicans. Mestas claimed that some of the animals had been stolen by Comanche raiders who had been attacked and beaten by Yuta warriors, who took their herds from them. Mestas said that he had gone as far as the area of Timpanogos (Utah Lake), where he identified the animals and retook them. Hard

---

224 Father José Vela Prada, Custos, to Governor Joaquín del Real Alencaster, Abiquiú, 18 August 1805, SANM, II, Microfilm Roll 15, frame 780. Translated by Joseph P. Sánchez.

225 Alencaster to Commandant-General Salcedo, 1 September 1805, SANM, II, Microfilm Roll 15, frame 810.

luck followed Mestas, who, on the way back, appears to have lost most of the animals in southern Colorado to marauding bands, possibly Kiowas who were at war with the Yutas.[226] Governor Alencaster's report revealed that New Mexicans like Mestas were familiar with the Yuta country and often went there.[227] Either Mestas' story is true, or he made up a viable explanation regarding why he went to the Yuta country unlicensed and came back with livestock. Nonetheless, his story is one of many that add to the annals of southern Colorado and Utah about early Hispanic activities in the region.

There were other stories that came down, either through documentation or through the oral tradition. In his report on New Mexico to the *Cortes de Cadiz* in 1812, Pedro Pino told the story about a New Mexican who went to the Yuta country, not for trade but out of curiosity. José Rafael Sarracino, according to Pino, sought a legendary lost Spanish settlement mentioned by the Domínguez-Escalante expedition of 1776. Of Sarracino's adventure, Pino wrote:

> Last year, 1811, Don José Rafael Sarracino, postmaster of New Mexico, crossed that territory in an effort to locate a Spanish settlement which the Yutas have always asserted lay beyond their territory, supposedly completely surrounded by wild Indians. After having traveled for three months, he was finally stopped by a large river. Among the Indians living there he found many articles manufactured by Spaniards such as knives, razors, and awls; he obtained the same information there, that the manufacturers of those articles lived across the river (somewhere between the north and the west). Since they could not tell him exactly where he could cross the river, he decided to return home; he brought back with him a large shipment of beautiful pelts which he had purchased very cheaply; for example, he traded one awl for a

226 *Ibid.*
227 *Ibid.*

perfectly tanned deer hide. At this price he could have afforded to bring as many pelts as he could load on his entire mule train if it had been possible to export them.[228]

Did Sarracino get as far as the Colorado River before turning around? It is not known if he were licensed, and similar to Mestas, could have come up with a viable explanation for why he went to the Yuta country as he did not appear to have led an "officially sanctioned" expedition. Aside from such curiosities, Pino also pointed out the desire of New Mexicans to reach the Pacific coast. Although he did not specifically suggest a California route, he thought that a port along the Sonoran coast such as Guaymas "would be advantageous to Spanish commerce."[229]

In going to the Yuta country, New Mexicans mostly risked their lives for more realistic reasons that were driven by poverty and debt. Most of the proceedings for traders, who had been arrested and tried, were similar. The August 1797 case against Cristóval Lovato, José Miguel Naranjo, and Juan Domingo Sandoval began in the same way. *Alcalde mayor* Manuel García de la Mora presided over the proceedings at Puesto del Río Arriba. Beginning with the order to arrest Lovato and his cohorts, the proceedings included a series of interrogatories in which all answered the same questions. García de la Mora asked Lovato and his men questions from the same interrogatory list.[230] Standing before García de la Mora, Lovato nervously answered each query.

---

228 H. Carroll and Villasana Haggard, trans., and eds., *Three New Mexico Chronicles*, 134. Also see footnote 353 in which the editors state that "Don José Rafael Sarracino was a member of the first and third territorial assemblies of New Mexico. At the fourth territorial assembly he was chosen as a delegate to the national government in Mexico City. He played a prominent part in New Mexican affairs during the two decades immediately following Mexican independence."

229 Carroll and Villasana Haggard, eds., *Three New Mexican Chronicles*, 134. Pino also suggested San Bernardo, possibly on the Texas coast, as an outlet for New Mexican commerce.

230 Proceedings against Cristóbal Lovato, et al., Río Arriba, 2 August to 2 September 1797, SANM, II, Microfilm Roll 14, frame 112. Translated by Joseph P. Sánchez

Asked: With what license did he leave on the journey to the Yuta country? He answered that without one, that he went of his own accord and obligation.

Asked: Who accompanied him? He answered José Miguel Naranjo

Asked: What trade items did he take, he answered one fanega of flour and four almudes of corn.

Asked: What did he buy with the above said items. He answered three gamuzas, and he could not sell the flour.

Asked: How far did he get in this journey. He answered that he got as far as the Río de los Pinos.[231]

Asked: Whether he knows that the journey to the Yuta country is prohibited. He answered that he knows it, but that his debts made him trespass there.

This he said is all he knows and that nothing else happened to him on this journey and whereas he declares and gives in his statement which was ratified by one, two, and three times and which was read back to him, and he did not sign it because he did not know how, and I signed it with my two assistants to which I give testimony.

Manuel García, Assistant José Antonio Martínez, Assistant José Manuel Sanches[232]

---

231 This was the Río de los Pinos crossed by Rivera in 1765 and by Domínguez and Escalante in 1776.
232 Proceedings against Cristóbal Lovato, et al., Río Arriba, 2 August to 2 September 1797, SANM, II, Microfilm Roll 14, frame 112. Translated by Joseph P. Sánchez.

Although tried and convicted, Lovato was not stopped from returning to the Yuta country. In his testimony he said he was accompanied by only one person, but he did not say there were others.

García de la Mora learned that there were indeed other trading parties in the area. Issuing arrest orders, Manuel García de la Mora apprehended a number of other traders. They included José Martín, Andrés Martín, Juan Ballejos, Juan Domingo Sandoval, Asensio Lucero, Juan Esteban Velasques, Gabriel Vigil, Nerio Gómes, Francisco Salazar, Mateo García, Nicolas Martín, Pedro Sisneros, Ramon Saiz, Antonio Maese, Francisco Archuleta, José Manuel Montoya, Silvestre Lopes, Juan de Dios Trujillo, Antonio Torres, Pedro Aguilar, Antonio José Espinosa and Juan Griego. They too were tried and convicted. Their goods were confiscated as was the case for all culprits who violated the *bandos*.

When García de la Mora asked each one how far into the Yuta country they had gone, he was probably surprised how far north they had gone for trade. They told him that they had reached a place called *Hancapagari* or *Aricapuaguro*, present Uncompahgre Plateau, which the Domínguez-Escalante expedition had called *Ancapagri*.[233] One prisoner, Gabriel Vigil, said that he and his companions Gómes, Salazar, and Martín had gone westward as far as the *Sierra de la Sal* (the La Sal Mountains).

While the men were tried and convicted, the law did not stop them from trading with the Utes. Although all were punished accordingly for violating the *bandos* prohibiting trade with the Yutas, those punished in 1797 eventually returned to the Yuta country, sometimes exploring the land in different directions. In their repeated trips to the Yuta country, they had learned about various tribes and some of the traders had become proficient in speaking the different languages and dialects in the area. Without doubt, they contributed new knowledge about the people, geography and resources of southern Colorado as

---

233 *Ibid.*

they probed each river, valley, and mountain and regions that extended from Abiquiú to the Great Basin. Each step they had taken eventually opened the way toward the settlement of the region.

Still, there were other events that led to the eventual settlement of southern Colorado by New Mexicans, who continued to visit the area for trade or other reasons. Each time they went, they left a documentary trail of their explorations as well as a longer list of place names on the map. One of the last efforts by Spain to protect its land from foreign intruders occurred in 1818. The Louisiana Purchase had sent tremors up and down the Spanish frontiers of New Mexico and Texas. While the eastern boundary of the Louisiana Purchase was known, the western boundary was, at best, ambiguous. Diplomats pondered how far west did the Louisiana Purchase extend? Indeed, Spanish efforts to secure the frontier was handled both diplomatically and militarily. Not knowing the route of the Lewis and Clark Expedition (1804-1806), for example, and knowing that almost all expeditions emanating from the United States were carried out by way of the Great Plains, Spanish governors from Texas and New Mexico hoped to intercept them as they crossed through present Kansas and Nebraska. Needless to say, Lewis and Clark went northwestward toward the Mandan villages before turning due west to the Pacific. Still, for the next decade, at least, it was in that atmosphere of events that Spain guarded its boundaries by sending out patrols to find any intruders within the far reaches of its northern claim to the Americas.

Having heard rumors of possible Anglo-American intrusions into Spanish territory, New Mexico's Governor Facundo Melgares placed his commanders on high alert. Of those rumors, Historian James Hanson wrote that, "There was a last shudder of nerves in New Mexico when news arrived in 1818 of the U.S. Army's 'Yellowstone Expedition.'"[234] Indeed, French traders in New Mexico told Melgares that 300 men had been organized in Louisiana under the command

---

234 James A. Hanson, "Spain on the Plains "*Nebraska History* 74 (1993): 17.

of "Teniente Coronel Falbot Chambers" who was poised to ascend the "Río Misouri to the confluence of the *Roche Jaune* or *Piedra Amarilla*,"[235] the Yellowstone River.

Melgares' concerns were not unfounded. Already, two expeditions in the early 1800s from the United States had taken place. The first expedition from the United States was led by Philip Nolan in 1801 to a point near the Brazos River in Texas. Spanish troops from Nacogdoches arrested Nolan's men after Nolan, refusing to surrender, was killed. The second expedition from the U.S. was commanded by Zebulon Montomary Pike in 1806. After one of Pike's men reached Santa Fe and reported that Pike and his men were in distress near present Colorado Springs, and needed help, Facundo Melgares led his men through the San Luis Valley to apprehend Pike. The Pike party, suffering from all kinds of maladies, were taken by Melgares to Santa Fe, and from there, escorted under guard to Chihuahua where they were interrogated for spying and trespassing. Mexican officials there decided to deport them to the United States via San Antonio, Texas.

The new rumors about U.S. expeditions to the Yellowstone River changed things. Thinking that this was a subterfuge for an invasion, and as he had promised the viceroy that he would send an expedition to the Yellowstone River as soon as the weather had warmed, Governor Melgares ordered an expedition northward to scout an area as far as the Arkansas River for possible intruders. In summer 1818, Second Lieutenant José María de Arce led an expedition north from Taos through the San Luis Valley to the Arkansas River against possible foreign intruders into Spanish territory.[236] Given Spain's diligence in keeping foreigners from trespassing into Spanish territory, Arce's instructions, based on recent

---

235 El Virey de Nueva España Conde del Venadito continua dando cuenta de las novedades ocurridas en las costas y Provincias internas de aquel Reyno, 30 de Noviembre de 1818, AGI, Sección Estado, Legajo 33. Numero 24
236 "Diary which Second Lieutenant don José María Arce made and copy of other documents, 1818." translated by Alfred B. Thomas, "Documents Bearing upon the Northern Frontier of New Mexico 1818-1819" in *New Mexico Historical Review*, 1929, Vol. 4: 157-164.

intelligence from French traders, were to apprehend or drive out any foreign enemies crossing into New Mexico as well as to alert the towns and settlements along the way to set up defenses against them. As his expedition progressed, new orders were sent to him instructing him to find out as much as he could about the disposition of the tribes in the area, particularly the Utes and Comanche. His expedition added to information about the land and the people in southeastern Colorado, particularly to the east of the San Luis Valley as far as present Huerfano and Pueblo.

Having left Santa Fe on the morning of August 31 with a small group of armed men, Arce moving quickly, gathered more men along the way and arrived in Taos by 6:30 that evening. Uniting with more armed settlers at Taos, Arce commanded 120 men which included Taos warriors, many armed with bows and arrows. The motley army — armed with thirty-three guns, thirty-nine lances, and 224 paper cartridges — began their march northward in the late afternoon. Within the next few days, messengers caught up with Arce to tell him that Matias Ortiz, the alcalde from La Cañada, was marching to Taos with more than 300 men to join him. Arce requested that 50 of his well-armed men move up quickly to reinforce his troops. At Taos, Arce spoke with José Manuel Hernandez, who had been held captive by Ute or Comanche warriors and had recently escaped. He told Arce that the Indians wanted peace and that he could meet them at a place called Agua Hirviendo or Agua Hirvidora (Boiling Water). Doubtful about Hernandez's story, Arce sent the information to Melgares for evaluation and a possible change of orders.[237]

Within the next few days, Arce and his men had passed places with names well known to them such as Río del Datil, Río de la Culebra and Vallecito del Puesto de Sangre de Cristo. While camped on the Río de la Culebra, ten armed settlers joined Arce's force. They brought two much-needed boxes of ammunition. Moving beyond the Vallecito del

---

237 *Ibid.*, p. 157.

Puesto de Sangre de Cristo, they reached the Sierra de los Yutas. Near there, they encountered hostile warriors, who had evidently been on a raid against New Mexican settlements. José Antonio Martínez, from Taos, and forty horesemen followed their tracks, along with those of stolen animals, to the Sierra de los Yutas. Martínez and his men did not make contact with them.[238]

Meanwhile, Jośe Alari from Santa Fe arrived in Arce's camp to tell him that Juan de Dios Peña and 460 men had been sent to join him. Melgares sent new orders to Arce to proceed to a place called Agua Hirviendo so that he could rendezvous with the Utes and Comanche to talk peace. By the time that word reached him, Arce had crossed the Sierra de Sangre de Cristo and was camped on the Río Huerfano.[239]

There, on September 5, he waited for Peña to join him. In the meantime, Arce sent Martínez forward to scout for hostile warriors. Martínez was ordered to go as far as the place where the Río Napeste (Arkansas River) flows out of the Sierra de los Yutas. Martínez returned without any new information on the whereabouts of the Utes. Still no news from Peña and his men. Arce, left the Río Huerfano and moved some of his men to the junction of the Río del Almagre (probably Fountain Creek) and the Río Napeste near Agua Hirviendo, to wait for Peña and his men. They were near Mosca Pass. Finally, on September 14, Peña arrived with 338 mounted men and 94 foot soldiers. He brought with him a supply of clothes and a box of cartridges sent by Melgares as well as a number of gifts to be given to Indians who wanted peace.

Failing to meet any Yuta warriors at Agua Hirviendo, Arce and his force proceeded to the Río San Carlos where they camped. At that point, Arce and his men were along the Río San Carlos, which flows into the Arkansas River near Pueblo Colorado. On September 16, they scouted the area around the junction of the Río del Almagre and the Río Napeste. Some backtracked and did not find signs of the Utes. Some men reported

---

238 *Ibid.*, p. 158
239 *Ibid.*, p. 159

that they had found Hernandez's old footprints at Agua Hirviendo that showed him to be alone.[240]

On September 16, Arce sent fifty horsemen to scout the area called La Cañada. Four days later, Arce received word that that had reached as far as the Río Chato (South Platte). They had proceeded slowly because some of their horses were jaded. By now, that was the case with most of the horses used on the expedition. Between September 21 and 30, Arce had marched his force down the Río Napeste as far as the Río de las Animas (Purgatoire River) and camped at a place called Las Nutrias. Their route had been determined on September 23, when Arce held a council with the New Mexican settlers on the expedition who had been in that area to trade with the Utes and Comanches. From them Arce learned that some of the settlers had been there a short time earlier to trade at Las Nutrias and that the Utes had told them that they were going to return to their lands along the Río Napeste. Arce wanted to know if the Indians were still in the area and if there was other information they could find out about them. The New Mexican settlers, led by Francisco Sánchez from La Cañada, said they would scout around for two more days. After waiting for their return, Arce set out for the Río de las Animas, which he reached on September 30. When Sánchez reported to Arce on October 1, he said they had gone as far as the Arroyo Tiquin and had found no trace of them. Arce, himself, attempted to find the Arroyo Tiquin, but was unable to locate it.[241]

On October 2, Arce and his men decided to return to Taos. Four days later, after marching for nearly nine hours a day, the men had reached Taos, where Arce dismissed the settlers from Taos and La Cañada. From Taos, he proceeded to Santa Fe, arriving there via the Sierra de Pojoaque on October 10.[242] Aside from the expedition undertaken to secure the lands northeast of New Mexico, the legacy of the Arce expedition is that it added yet another historic moment and had left a written record that

---

240 *Ibid.*, p. 160
241 *Ibid.*, p. 162
242 *Ibid.*, p. 162

140

added to the Hispanic experience and heritage of southern Colorado. As time ran out for the Spanish Empire, Arce's expedition would be one of the last major expeditions into southern Colorado during New Mexico's Spanish Colonial period.

Soon after, in 1819, Melgares dispatched another expedition under Juan Chalvert to the Yellowstone River northward beyond Taos, past the San Luis Valley and across the Arkansas and Platte rivers through the area of present Colorado Springs and Denver to intercept any intruders. Chalvert was probably accompanied by Juan Lucero, as a Comanche and Kiowa translator, who had not only been beyond the Platte River but onto the Great Plains as well. In 1807, Lucero had been trading with tribes near present Colorado Springs.[243] Chalvert reported that "the [Yellowstone] river was farther away from Santa Fe than was St. Louis."[244] Official Spanish reports echoed the notion that the distance through rough terrain was enough of a barrier to an invasion. They estimated that "the referenced heart of Yellowstone was 300 leagues north of Santa Fe and 240 leagues from the headwaters of the Río del Norte (Río Grande)."[245] Still, Melgares had reason for concern. At that time, the Yellowstone Expedition led by Major Stephen Long had stalled in Nebraska. Trusting his instincts, Melgares ordered that mountain passes leading to Santa Fe be fortified.[246]

---

243 Michael L. Olsen and Harry C. Myers, "The Diary of Pedro Ignacio Gallego wherein 400 Soldiers following the Trail of Comanches met William Becknell on His First Trip to Santa Fe," *Wagon Tracks*, Vol. 7 November 1992, Number 1 fn.58
244 James A. Hanson, "Spain on the Plains," *Nebraska History* 74 (1993): 17. Also see Abraham Nasitir, *Borderland in Retreat from Louisiana to the Far Southwest* (Albuquerque: University of New Mexico Press, 1976), p. 156.
245 El Virey de Nueva España Conde del Venadito continua dando cuenta de las novedades ocurridas en las costas y Provincias internas de aquel Reyno, 30 de Noviembre de 1818, AGI, Sección Estado, Legajo 33. Numero 24. Depending on where one stands, the probable mileage is 715 miles. Spanish estimates would have been over 750 miles between Santa Fe and the Yellowstone River and around 640 miles from the Yellowstone to the Río Grande.
246 Hanson, "Spain on the Plains," *Nebraska History* 74 (1993): 17. Also see Nasitir, *Borderland in Retreat*, p. 156.

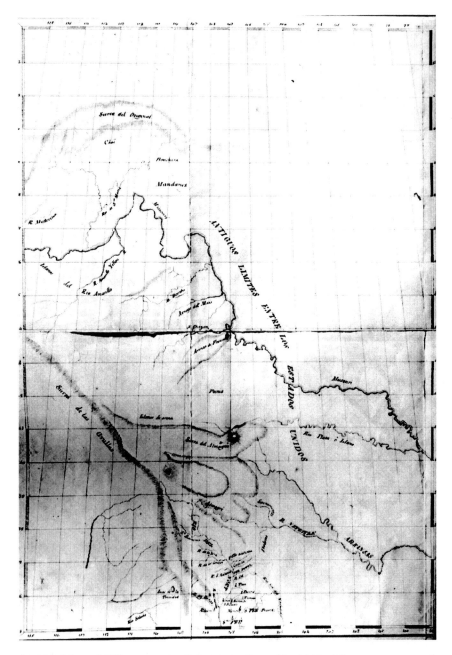

Spanish Map of Yellowstone in Relation to Santa Fe, 1819: *Mapa que comprende el territorio situado entre 35 y 53 grados de Latitud Norte y entre 99 y 115 grados de Longitud Occidental. Se indica el curso de los Ríos Missouri, Colorado.* Según Pedro Torres Lanzas, el plano procede del legajo Estado, 33 [1701] MP-MEXICO, 480

142

Meanwhile, Mexico won its independence from Spain in 1821. A new nation state was born and Mexico took charge, as sovereign over New Spain and its frontier. The problems of frontier defense, however, remained. As predicted by Croix, Ute depredations into New Mexico would continue as long as illegal trading existed to antagonize tribes who felt the need to retaliate when deals went wrong. The pacification of southern Colorado and northern New Mexico continued well into the nineteenth century as Utes, Apaches, Navajos, and Comanches refused to bow to the power of the Mexican nation and, later, to that of the United States.

Throughout the early 1840s, Ute raiders had consistently attacked New Mexican settlements stealing an appreciable number of livestock and captives as well as killing settlers in their paths. In 1841 and 1843, José María Chaves from Abiquiú led two campaigns against the Utes in northern New Mexico and Colorado and the Navajos in northwestern New Mexico.[247] Chaves was no stranger to the Yuta country, for he had traded illegally for slaves taken by Ute warriors from weaker tribes in the area. Like many others, Chaves knew the Yuta country well. His campaign against the Utes, though successful, quieted the frontier for a very short time before the Utes retaliated with a vengeance.

In 1845, Ute raiders again struck New Mexican settlements with increasing violence. This time, Hispanics under Adjutant General Juan Andrés Archuleta organized a large punitive expedition against the raiders. Archuleta commanded over 1000 militia and 100 regulars. That summer, on July 19, 1845, Archuleta's army, with Pueblo allies, mustered at Taos Pueblo and marched into southern Colorado. In a two-pronged attack, Archuleta went directly north from Taos, while the other unit, led by José María Chaves, tracked Utes to the Río Napestle (Arkansas River).

The two armies moved north and northwest. Archuleta marched north from Taos to El Saguache (today's Sawatch Range), a small range

---

247 Rosa Chaves to Governor Prince, Abiquiú, New Mexico, 5 December 1902, Prince Papers: Contemporary New Mexicans, J.M. Chaves #14, New Mexico State Records Center and Archives, Santa Fe, New Mexico.

in the Sangre de Cristos, thence to Poncha Pass,[248] slightly north of Alamosa and the San Luis Valley. Shortly, using experienced traders as his guides, Archuleta found a large Ute encampment and attacked with it such force that the panicked warriors ran as the New Mexicans beset and routed them. Meanwhile, pressing hard against the Utes, Chaves and his militiamen, veering northwest, forced them as far north as the Río Napestle. Once safely across, the Utes were out of reach from Chaves and his New Mexican frontier army. As it turned out, Chaves had realized that the Arkansas River was the boundary between Mexico and the United States for it had been established by the Adams-Onis Treaty of 1819. Immediately Chaves sent a messenger to Santa Fe asking permission to cross the river,[249] but was denied as it would constitute an invasion of U.S. soil. Seeking other Ute encampments, Chaves found them and turned his army loose on remaining Ute settlements. All baggage left behind by fleeing Utes was divided as spoils of war or destroyed as a message to Utes who would, in retaliation, invade New Mexico. For his campaign against the Utes, the Mexican government rewarded Chaves with a handsome sword which he proudly displayed at his home in Abiquiú.[250]

---

248 *Ibid.*

249 *Ibid.*

250 "A Famous Centenarian," Prince Papers, New Mexico State Record Center and Archives, Santa Fe, New Mexico. After the American occupation of New Mexico in 1846 by General Stephen Watts Kearney, New Mexicans became citizens of the United States by dint of the Treaty of Guadalupe Hidalgo. Articles 8 and 9 of the treaty incorporated all Mexican citizens living in the ceded territories as citizens of the United States. Like other Hispanic notables in New Mexico, those under the United States territorial government of New Mexico, served in the territorial military as well as held political offices, inclusive of the Territorial Legislature of New Mexico. Chaves, for example, served as a Brigadier General of Militia. He also served in the New Mexico Territorial Legislature for seven years. In 1851, Governor Jason S. Calhoun appointed him prefect of Río Arriba County, and Governor Merriwether commissioned him Probate Judge of the same county. At the outbreak of the Civil War, José María Chaves, like hundreds of New Mexicans, served on the Union side. The New Mexico Volunteers turned the Union tide against the invading Confederate army and sent them retreating south to El Paso, then west through Texas. Chaves served as a Lieutenant-Colonel of the Volunteer Mounted Regiment. Finally, in 1875, the 74-year old José María Chaves was appointed Río Arriba County School

144

As the Spanish Colonial period came to a close with the Mexican Revolution of 1821 which won its independence from Spain, a new order was at hand. Still, under Mexico, New Mexicans continued to go to the Yuta country for trade. Their interests changed but little as they eked out an existence on that remote frontier area. Knowledge of the land and its people evolved into a familiar pattern. Yet, the warfare continued. As the Mexican nation state developed, New Mexicans became absorbed into a new system of governance. For them, a dramatic change of affairs was in the air.

Commissioner. Given his age, his experiences, his longevity as a settler of Abiquiú and his knowledge of northern New Mexico and southern Colorado, Chaves later served as an expert witness in land grant cases, for his keen memory and his service to the Hispanic community of New Mexico as someone who personally witnessed the establishment of property boundaries.

Chapter VII
Betwixt Governance, Land Grants and Rebellion: A Summary History of the Mexican Period, 1821-1848

> The Territory of Mexico is divided into as many Departments as there were States, with the following modifications: Article 2. That which was the State of Cohuila and Texas is divided into two Departments, each with its own territory. New Mexico shall be a Department.
>
> — Law of December 30th, 1836

New Mexico, as part of Spain's claim to the New World, had been in existence for over 280 years when Spanish power came to an end in 1821. Spain had ruled its frontier provinces in the Americas by establishing the office of the governor, who served as both political boss and military commander. The governors' duties by now were fairly traditional. The Decree of 1843, however, tweaked their responsibilities under Mexican rule. The governor, for example, appointed superior magistrates, judges, and attorneys and employees for positions in government of the Department for review by Congress. He served as ex-officio member of the departmental and territorial assemblies, without voting privileges except on tie votes, and as the chief of the Public

Treasury of departments and territories. In addition, he promoted literacy and other similar duties, as in the past. Governors were limited in legislative powers. They had, on the other hand, eight days to review and comment on decrees passed by the legislative assembly to assure they were in conformity with laws and policies. One new provision called for the reduction of the governor's term from an eight-year term to a five-year term.

Governors still reported directly to the central government and, by law, were "the only and necessary conduct of communication with the Supreme Authorities of the Republic" unless there were accusations of malfeasance against them.[251] They served at the pleasure of the President of the Republic who appointed all the governors in accordance with the law.

During the Mexican Period, 1821-1848, the Department of New Mexico with its capital at Santa Fe was divided into two districts. In turn, the districts were partitioned into jurisdictions called *partidos.* The First District had partido capitals at Taos and San Ildefonso, not the Indian pueblos but Hispanic settlements near them with the same names. New settlements in southern Colorado, particularly the new land grant settlements in the San Luis Valley, would be under the jurisdiction of the Taos partido. In Second District, Albuquerque served as the capital of the first partido. The second partido had its capital at Los Padillas. At the southern end of New Mexico, El Paso served as capital of a partido administered from Ciudad Chihuahua. Las Cruces and surrounding towns in present southern New Mexico were within El Paso's jurisdiction.

During the Spanish Period, all land grants established in New Mexico had elected members to its local council, which made decisions regarding the administration of the partido with the approval of the *ayuntamiento* (town council) and the *alcalde constitucional* (the town mayor). New Mexicans anxiously awaited the administrative changes

---

251 Matthew G. Reynolds, *Spanish and Mexican Land Laws: New Spain and Mexico.* St. Louis, Missouri, Buxton & Skinner Stationery Co., 1895. (Hereinafter cited as SMLL) pp. 246-7.

that emanated from the central government in Mexico City. How New Mexico fit into the larger picture of Mexican rule evolved quickly in a brief, but active, two and a half decades.

Once Juan O'Donojou, the last of the Spanish monarchy's representatives, signed the Treaty of Cordoba on August 24, 1821, Spanish colonial rule in Mexico was forever ended. As Mexican officials took their place at the helm of government, New Mexicans adjusted to participating in a new political system. During the Mexican Territorial Period, definitions related to sovereignty, especially regarding the granting of land, were modified to reflect the budding Mexican nation. The Mexican nation had modeled itself after that of the United States. In fact, the Mexican Constitution of 1824, borrowed much from the U.S. Constitution of 1787, which was framed thirty-seven years earlier.

With an eye toward expanding settlements throughout Mexico, particularly within the region of its far northern frontier, Mexican officials reviewed Spain's policies for colonization and land tenure practices, inclusive of land grants. During the early Mexican Period, legal definitions regarding land tenure under Spain were maintained under the new sovereign that was duly defined by the Mexican Constitution of 1824. Public lands known as *tierras realengas* or *tierras baldias*, for example, theoretically belonged to the monarch. Under Mexico, they belonged to the constitutionally defined sovereign. The king of Spain, as sovereign, granted towns or villages, *tierras concegiles* or *propios*. Public lands were available as common lands provided that, under the *Recopilación de leyes de los reynos de las Indias* (Laws of the Indies), they had water, pasturage for grazing, and wooded areas for use by settlers. Common lands and water rights could not be claimed or alienated by individuals for their own unless they applied for them and were approved. Still, land and water rights were an integral part of land grant concessions.

Grants of land were contracts awarded to individuals, groups of people, or to towns. Land grants were made from public lands claimed by imperial Spain. It should be noted that old Spanish land grants were not affected by the new wave of legislation regarding land tenure under

Mexico. The broad colonization projects of the Mexican Territorial period had little effect on the old Spanish land grants. The usual transactions continued to be worked within members of a given grant. Conveyances, donations, and sales of lands marked the exchange of ownership of such land grants. In general, land grants of the Spanish Colonial period in New Mexico were kept within the ownership of family members, close friends, and extended family relations.

Another category were those lands called *propios*, properties owned by a community or municipalities. *Propios* could be rented out by town councils (*cabildos*) for revenues which were used for public works. The Laws of the Indies regulated the use of *propios*. In the establishment of the Villa de Santa Fe, for example, the instructions of 1609 to Governor Pedro de Peralta similarly provided for the use of *propios*.

In the late eighteenth century, Spanish jurists devised the Plan de Pitic of 1789. The Plan revisited the legal usage of *propios* in the establishment of the town of Pitic (present Hermosillo in Sonora). Later, the Plan de Pitic[252] was applied to the establishment of towns in other areas in New Spain's northern frontier. In effect, the Plan de Pitic was a short, ready-to-use reference of the Laws of the Indies that related to land tenure. The Plan, because it was a restatement of the municipal ordinance contained in the Laws of the Indies, and embodied the regulations used for town founding throughout the frontier provinces of New Spain, is a key document to be studied in understanding Spain's well-established rules for civilian settlement."[253] Under Mexico, the

---

252 For a transcribed copy of the Plan de Pitic, see Joseph P. Sánchez, "El Plan de Pitic de 1789 y las nuevas poblaciones proyectadas en las Provincias Internas de la Nueva España," *Colonial Latin American Historical Review* (Fall 1993), Vol. 2, No. 4. pp. 449-67. As regards the funds raised through rents of *propios*, the document states: "Divididas assi las Suertes de las mas utiles e inmediatas al Pueblo que lo gozen el beneficio del riego se señalaran y amojonaran ocho que quedaren aplicadas para fondo de propios cuyo productos se adminsitraran por el Mayordomo que nombrare el Ayunatmiento con obligación de dar quentas anualmente que se examinaran y aprovaran oyendo previamente sobre ellas al Prcurador, Sindico o Personero del Comun..." p. 460.

253 Iris H.W. Engstrand, "A Note on the Plan of Pitic, *Colonial Latin American*

Plan de Pitic served as a precedent for the establishment of *ejidos*.

Changes were in the wind, as a new political vocabulary blew northward from Mexico City. Colonization policies established under Spain set a precedence and greatly influenced the legalists and officials during the early Mexican period of nation-building. As the transition took place, Mexican officials merged old practices and customs with new policies. Late in the Spanish Colonial period, there occurred a change of mind when Spanish policy allowed Anglo-Americans to enter and settle in Spanish territory. The practice began in Texas, where Spanish officials allowed Anglo-Americans to settle there, provided, of course, that they learn Spanish, convert to Catholicism and settled a prescribed number of families to develop and protect the land. In 1798 Moses Austin had a small land grant in Spanish Louisiana, and in 1821, his son, Spanish-speaking Stephen Austin, became an *empresario* under Mexico in Texas.

Under Spanish law, the new immigrants must also show progress toward cultivating the land. Mexico adopted this policy and allowed Anglo frontiersmen to cross the Sabine River on their way to San Antonio. Mexico desired, as did Spain, to populate the wide open spaces along its northern frontiers of Texas and New Mexico with settlers they hoped would be loyal to Mexico. By awarding land grants to entrepreneurs who promised to colonize its northern frontier under the Colonization Law passed on August 18, 1824[254] [see Appendix A], Mexico aimed to develop

---

Historical Review, (Winter 1994) Vol.3, No.1, 78. For a brief view of the historical precedent of the Plan de Pitic see Jane C. Sánchez, "The Plan of Pitic: Galindo Navarro's Letter to Teodoro de Croix, Comandante General de las Provincias Internas," *Colonial Latin American Historical Review* (Winter 1994) Vol. 3, No. 1, 79-89. Sánchez writes: "The correspondence...discusses the need for formation of the Plan of Pitic for an area in which the laws of the Recomioación de Indias de 1680 could not be applied *in toto*. The correspondence also contains many suggestions about what should be included in the plan, most of which were implemented. Like many legal papers of the period, it draws an accurate picture of the legal values of the colonial culture" p.79.

254 Comp. Laws, Vol., I, page 712, No. 416 in Matthew G. Reynolds, *Spanish and Mexican Land Laws: New Spain and Mexico*. St. Louis, Missouri: Buxton & Skinner Stationery Co., 1895, (herinafter cited as SMLL), pp. 141-142.

and bolster defenses of the area.

The provisions of the Colonization Act of 1824 outlined the procedure to be followed by officials who made the grants within their territories. Although the size of the grant varied among officials who made the grants, the language in the provisions specified the size of the grant. Article 12 stipulated that " It shall not be allowed that more than one square league of one hundred varas of irrigable land, four of temporal land, and six of range land, be united as a property in a single hand." The total number of square leagues per land grant was established as 11 square leagues per person, roughly over 48,800 acres of land.[255] Before long, New Mexico, and later California, began to see land grant activities under the the new Colonization Law of 1824, especially in regard to large grants of land and the settlement patterns in southern Colorado. The provisions stipulated in the Colonization Act of 1824 were reinforced and clarified by the Regulations for Colonization issued in 1828.[256] The Mexican National Congress [See Appendix B], ordered that the provisions of the Act be observed by contractors and settlers of land grants, to wit, articles 10 to 16:

10. No stipulation shall be admitted for a new settlement unless the contractor obligates himself to furnish at least twelve families as settlers.

11. The Political Chief shall set a reasonable time for the settler, within which he must necessarily cultivate or occupy the land in the terms and with the number of families which he has stipulated, in the intelligence that if he does not do so, the grant of the land shall be void, but the Political Chief may, nevertheless, re-evaluate it in proportion to the part in which the party in interest has complied.

---

255 *Treaty of Guadalupe Hidalgo: Findings and Possible Options Regarding Longstanding Community Land Grant Claims in New Mexico. A Report to Congressional Requesters by the United States General Accounting Office* (GAO-04-60), June 2004 p. 71
256 Regulations for the Colonization of the Territories, November 21, 1828 Code of Colonization, Mexico, 1893, p. 237, No. 71 in Reynolds, SMLL, pp. 141-142.

12. Every new settler, after he has cultivated or occupied the land under his stipulation, shall be careful to so show to the municipal authority, in order to consolidate and secure his right to the property to enable him to freely dispose thereof, after the proper record has been made.

13. The aggregation of many families in the settlement, in its formation, internal government and police, shall follow the rules established in existing laws for the other settlement of the Republic, special care being taken in new settlements that they be constructed with the regularity possible.

14. The minimum of irrigable land that may be given for colonization by a single person shall be two hundred varas in a square; the minimum of grazing land shall be one thousand two hundred varas.

15. The land that may be given for a building lot shall be one hundred varas.

16. The vacant tracts that may exist between colonized lands may be distributed between adjoining holders, who have cultivated their own lands with application and have not received the full extent of land the law allows, or the children of said holders who apply for them to consolidate the properties of their families, bearing in mind therefor the the morality and industriousness of the parties in interest.[257]

In 1843, before the end of the Mexican Period, the departments and territories underwent one more revision. The Decree of June 13, 1843 created *asambleas* (legislative assemblies), composed of eleven members with a minimum of seven, in the departments and territories. Eleven alternates were nominated to fill their ranks in case of a sudden vacancy. They could only serve for the remaining time of the vacancy. Members were elected by the outgoing *juntas* so that their terms would be staggered. At first, some of the members

---

257 *Ibid.*, pp. 141-142.

would serve two years while the others served for four. To serve in the *asambleas*, members had to be a full twenty-five years of age.

Concerning land tenure and property rights, the *asambleas* regulated the acquisition, alienation and exchange of property with legislation in accordance with colonization laws. The *asambleas* attended to issues within departments pertaining to infrastructure and issues related to the opening and maintenance of roads. Within the civilian sector, the *asambleas* promoted public instruction, and the establishment of municipal corporations as well as promoted and regulated public health, encouraged agriculture and industry, and established and regulated superior tribunals and inferior courts. The *asambleas* also provided for the recruitment and maintenance of the army, and an urban and rural police force. Each year, the *asambleas* prepared an annual statistical report and an annual estimated budget—both to be presented to the General Congress. In all of it undertakings, the *asambleas* were required to consult the governor on all issues regarding the administration of the Department. The oldest officer of the *asambleas* would also serve as acting governor. The *asambleas* also established taxes with congressional approval, regulated spending, and appointed necessary employees. Over all, Congress retained the right to review and, if need be, annul legislation or actions by the *asambleas*.[258]

In the early days of the new nation, aside from the issues pertaining to governance, much of the reorganization of the office of the government had to to with the administration of lands. Although the governor and the *asambleas* were charged with such administration,

---

258 Decree of June 13, 1843 in Reynolds, *Spanish and Mexican Land Laws*: SMLL), p. 243. It should be noted that soon after the War between the United States and Mexico began in May 1846, officials in Mexico City met and formed the Plan of August 4th, 1846, SMLL, p. 253. In the throes of war and civil war, the central government restored the Constitution of 1824 and suspended the *Asambleas* because they were incompatible with the fundamental codes of that venerable document, Decree of August 22nd, 1846, SMLL, p. 256. In New Mexico, the *Asamblea* remained in force and its members surrendered New Mexico to the Army of the West under General Stephen Watts Kearney.

it was often left to minor officials to do the ground work. It seems that the offices of other minor officials within the Departments appear to have been spared reorganization and revision in 1843. One such minor, but very important, office was that of prefect, the positions held by local officials managing the smallest level of local jurisdictions. The coveted position of the local prefect was jealously guarded. Indeed, local *prefects* could become quite powerful because they affected the lives of those over which they held power.[259] Earlier, the Law of March 20, 1837 empowered *prefects* to "regulate administratively and in conformity with the laws, the distribution of common lands (*tierras comunes*) in the towns of the district, provided there is no litigation pending with regard to them, the right being reserved to the parties in interest to apply to the Governor, who without further appeal, shall decide what is most proper, with the concurrence of the Departmental Council (*Junta*)."[260] Thus, between 1836 and 1843, the office of prefect appears to have been influential regarding land grants throughout the deparments and territories.

While the *prefects* could transfer local lands, sometimes it was done by the *alcalde mayor* of a town or partido and signed off by the governor. Such was the case during the Mexican Territorial period when Martíneztown, a part of present-day Albuquerque, was established. The complexity of land tenure exchanges on a very local level is evident in the following examples. During the late Spanish Colonial period, Hispanic settlers acquired privately owned plots of lands, deeded by the *Alcalde mayor* of Albuquerque, which they lived on and farmed. Sometime in the early 1820s, for example, don Ambrosio Armijo and Antonio Sena acquired land less than a mile east of the Plaza de Alburquerque. In 1823, Juan Antonio Gallegos purchased land near them. In fact, his land bordered theirs. Sometime in the early 1830s, Rafael Martín, another landowner in the area, also acquired land near

---

259 *Ibid*, 215.
260 *Ibid.*, p. 77.

them. He sold his land to his son, Manuel Antonio Martín. Prior to 1835, hard working Simón Perea grazed sheep on the land. In 1835, Perea sold his land to Vicente Otero for 300 sheep. Otero transferred it to Diego García at the end of that year in exchange for 350 sheep. On June 14, 1837, Albuquerque Alcalde Ambrosio Armijo gave Don Mariano Ruiz a deed for a piece of property, whose ownership is corroborated by a note dated June 24th, 1848, by Governor Donaciano Vigil.[261] Other nearby landowners included Don Mariano Armijo, Doña Rosalía Mestas, Antonio Ruiz, and Antonio Santillanes. Such transactions, which demonstrated how land could be acquired, other than through a land grant, similarly occurred throughout Mexico's northern frontier.

The administration of land grants, contracts issued by the central government, continued, as it had been under Spain, accomplished by contracts. Mexico strived to bring laws and practices into better control by issuing legislation to that effect. The Colonization Law of 1823, for example, provided that the central government of Mexico could enter into contracts, land grants, with *empresarios*, a contracted land agent, who would introduce two hundred families into Mexican territories. For his services, the *empresario* would receive three haciendas and two farmfields (*labores*) for every two hundred families he settled. The most an *empresario* could receive was nine haciendas and six labores. Each farmer-settler would receive one *labor*, and each stock raiser would receive at least a *sitio* (six square miles) of land for ranching purposes. The Colonization Law of 1823 authorized the *ayuntamientos* (later called *asambleas*) to grant land within their jurisdiction.[262]

In repealing the Colonization Law of 1823, the Mexican National Congress enacted the Colonization Law of 1824, which provided that

---

261 Joseph P. Sanchez and Larry D. Miller, *Martíneztown 1823-1950: Hispanics, Italians, Jesuits & Land Investors in New Town Albuquerque* (Albuquerque: Río Grande Books, 2009. p. 21.
262 J.J. Bowden, "Private Land Claims in the Southwest," (Masters Thesis, Southern Methodist University: 1969), 71.

the Mexican government would continue to colonize the territories of the Republic. The Colonization Law of 1824 provided for a stronger role by the states in the granting of land. The Colonization Law of 1824 tied into Spanish Colonial practices and a later Mexican policy framed in 1828 [See Appendix B for text] that authorized governors to grant land within their jurisdictions to any Mexican citizen or foreigner who properly requested land for cultivation or settlement.[263] In 1835, the central government attempted to withdraw this authorization from its governors, but found it difficult to do so as it had earlier relinquished this power to the states and territories.[264]

Still, such contradictions in the Mexican land policy seemed to depend on who was in power. The Colonization Law of 1824, for example, applied when Mexico defined itself as a republic. When a dictatorship calling for a centralized system of government was in power, the authority of the states seemed to be curtailed. Under the centralist form, nonetheless, a valid grant could not be made within the provisions of the Colonization Law of 1824 or the regulations of 1828. In an attempt to straighten out the confusion within Mexico, the Mexican government in 1854 declared void all grants made between October 3, 1835 and August 4, 1846 and between March 17, 1853 and July 7, 1854.[265] The second declaration had no authority in lands ceded to the United States between 1848 and 1853, as by that time the Mexican government no longer had jurisdiction over grants made in New Mexico and California during the period 1821-1853, in Texas between 1821 and 1836, and in southern Arizona, which was part of Sonora between 1821-1853 and under Mexican sovereignty. Southern Arizona was annexed to the United States by purchase under the Gadsden Purchase Treaty of 1853.

During the Mexican Period (1821-1848), however, the relationship in New Mexico between the central administration in Santa Fe and the local municipal councils (*ayuntamientos* and later *asambleas*) had

---

263 *Ibid.* 74.
264 *Ibid.* 76.
265 *Ibid.* 82.

similarities to the old Spanish system. During the late Spanish Period, local government was reorganized; and, largely in name, *cabildos* (town councils) were called *ayuntamientos*. In the Mexican Period, the presiding officer of the *ayuntamiento* or *asamblea* was the *alcalde constitucional*, a legally empowered magistrate judge. To most, it seemed, the main difference between the Mexican and Spanish periods was that the title of *alcalde constitucional*, rather than *alcalde mayor*, who was elected and made decisions in consort with the *ayuntamiento* or *asamblea*. Unlike the *alcalde constitucional*, the *alcaldes mayores* were appointed and held judicial, executive, and legislative powers in large districts.[266] *Alcaldes mayores* also exercised military functions as *capitanes de guerra*[267] (war captains). Prior to the establishment of the *ayuntamiento*, the *alcaldes mayores* of the Spanish Period made decisions or recommendations on their own as judicial officers without benefit of a council.

In New Mexico, *alcaldes mayores*, as appointees, were obligated to carry out orders from their governors without question. *Alcaldes mayores* like Francisco Trébol Navarro of Albuquerque, for example, deferred to final decisions made by the governor. More than once, Trébol Navarro was overruled by Governor Pedro Fermín de Mendinueta. Unlike the *alcaldes mayores* of the Spanish period, the *alcaldes constitucionales*, under Mexico, seemed to have developed enough local political strength to overrule their governors. This may have been the result of longevity of tenure held by certain appointed officials, as *alcaldes constitucionales* generally tended to hold office longer than Mexican Period governors. Additionally, the vote of the *ayuntamiento* or *asamblea* usually supported decisions made by the *alcaldes constitucionales*. Given the elective character of government under Mexico, local politics played a greater role in the administration of judicial and economic matters as well as the distribution of land.

At first the linkage between the central Mexican government in

266 Marc Simmons, *Spanish Government in New Mexico* (Albuquerque: University of New Mexico Press, 1968), 219.
267 *Ibid.*, 219.

Mexico City and the other states appeared weak. In 1835, Antonio López de Santa Anna moved to consolidate the country by seizing power and quickly changing the form of government from a federal republic to a dictatorship. Meanwhile, early in 1835, the national congress in Mexico City acquiescsed to his demands by abrogating the self-governing powers of the states. Thereafter, each state or *departmento* was permitted a five-member council which reported directly to the national congress. Territories, such as New Mexico could convene a "provisional" council. In November 1835, a "provisional" Departmental Junta met in New Mexico in conformity with the Mexican directives. Seven months later, the first permanent council for New Mexico was recognized under the Constitution of 1836.

Other changes were meant to bring the entire chain of command into line with the Mexican National Government. The governor, now called a *jefe político*, reported directly to the the national congress. The *jefe político* was the chief political and military figure in his jurisdiction. He appointed the prefects, who reported directly to him. The *jefe político* served as president of the departmental *diputación*, or *asamblea*.[268] Consequently, once the prefect system was established, the chain of governmental command linked local control (*alcalde constitucional*, *ayuntamiento*, *prefectura*, and *diputación* or *Asamblea*) with the central government through the *jefe político*.[269]

When viewed against the relationship between the governor and the *alcaldes mayores* during the Spanish Colonial period, whereby the *alcalde mayor* appealed directly to the governor, the new changes were overwhelming. The administration of justice during the Mexican Period, for example, was further upgraded by the establishment of the *prefecturas*, large districts administered by a prefect with judiciary control. Between

---

268 Daniel Tyler, "New Mexico in the 1820s: The First Administration of Manuel Armijo" (Dissertation, University of New Mexico: 1970), 29.

269 Joseph P. Sánchez, "Año Desgraciado, 1837: The Overthrow of New Mexico's *Jefe político* Albino Pérez," *Atisbos: Journal of Chicano Research* (Stanford University: Summer-Fall, 1978), 183-184.

the office of the *jefe político* who administered the *departmento* and the *ayuntamiento* which oversaw the local affairs of the *municipio*, the *prefectos* with political power over districts called *prefecturias* added another layer of decision making before a given case even reached the governor.

The new bureaucratic administration during the Mexican Period literally changed procedural authority to the granting of land to Mexican citizens. Unlike the Spanish Period when only higher officials like viceroys and governors, as representatives of the king and viceroy, could grant lands to individuals or groups of people, provided they were citizens, Mexican law provided that the governors "are authorized, under the law. . .to grant the public lands of their respective Territories to the contractors, families or private persons, Mexicans or foreigners, who may apply for them, for the purpose of cultivating them or living upon them."[270] The language of the regulations specifically stated that "Every applicant for land, whether contractor, head of family or private person, shall apply to the Political Chief [*Jefe político* or governor] of the respective Territory, with an application which is given his name, country, profession, the number, nature, religion and other circumstances of the families or persons whom he desires to colonize, and shall also mark as distinctly as possible and describe on a map the land he applies for."[271] During the Mexican Period, the procedure changed again, allowing lesser officials to make concessions of land provided they were approved by the governor. Customarily, only the governor of a Department or a higher official in Mexico City could make land grants. Under certain circumstances, however, other government officials could distribute certain lands. As stated earlier, for example, prefects had the power to regulate and distribute common lands within the prefecturia. Interested settlers, however, had to apply to the governor for a grant of land.[272] In any case,

---

270 Regulations for the Colonization of the Territories, November 21st, 1828, in SMLL, p. 141. The purpose of these regulations was to clarify the Decree of August 18th, 1824.

271 *Ibid.*, p. 141.

272 Law of March 20th, 1837, SMLL, p. 221.

the transactions, were subject to the approval of the governor. For each grant, they made a certified copy validating their actions, usually it got the approval of the governor.

Centralization of political power had been the aim of Mexican authorities under Santa Anna. When, in 1822, Santa Anna overthrew Iturbide, the new Congress moved to restructure the governments of the states by abolishing state legislatures and replacing them with departmental councils called *Juntas*. Before dissolving, the legislatures appointed "a Departmental Board" composed of five former legislators. The Departmental Board acted as the council of the governor,[273] who reported directly to Mexico City.

The Departmental structure continued to evolve during the Mexican Territorial period. Under the Decree of December 29, 1836,[274] the Republic was divided into Departments which, in turn, were divided into districts, and those, in turn, were divided into precincts. Even though the Departments nominated three individuals for governor, the selection was made by the General Government. In the case of frontier Departments, such as New Mexico, the General Government was not obligated to consider their nominations and could appoint its own choice without any other consideration.

The powers of the governor were prescribed under the Decree of December 29, 1836.[275] Each Department would be entrusted to a governor who was subordinate to the central or general government in Mexico City. Accordingly, the governors "shall be appointed by the latter [that is, the central government]…and shall hold office eight years and may be re-elected."[276] The duties of the governor were outlined. He would attend to "the preservation of public order," could deploy a military force, comply with all decrees and orders of the general government as well as those by the Departmental Junta, and transmit

---

273 Law of October 3d, 1835 in SMLL, p. 195.
274 Decree of December 29, 1836 in SMLL, pp. 203-204.
275 *Ibid.*, pp. 205-206.
276 *Ibid.*, p. 203.

"all enactments of the departmental Junta to Mexico City." Locally, the governor would appoint *prefects* and approve the appointments of *sub-prefects* of the Department. He would confirm appointments of justices of the peace made by the Departmental Junta. He had the power to remove any official "after first having heard the opinion of the Departmental Junta." With the consent of the Departmental Junta, the governor could suspend common councils in the districts or *prefects* of the Department. In regard to elections of common councils, he served as arbiter in case of a contested election or as the deciding vote in case of a tie in an election. The governor could accept or reject the resignations of members of the common council.[277]

The Departmental *Juntas* chiefly proposed laws related to taxes, public education, industry, commerce, municipal administration. It could propose amendments to the constitution in conformity with constitutional law. Within the Department, the Departmental Junta was charged with establishing schools for primary education in all the towns, providing funding for schools from municipal revenues and levying moderate taxes if no municipal funds were available. Even though the Departmental Junta could provide for "institutions of learning and public charity as well as those dedicated to promoting agriculture, industry, and commerce," approval from the Mexican Congress would be required if "these provisions should in any manner prove burdensome to the towns." The Departmental Junta was also charged with opening and maintaining roads and establishing moderate tolls to cover their cost. All accounts, particularly those dealing with municipal revenues, were to be examined and approved by the Departmental Junta. With the governor, the council was to formulate municipal ordinances of common councils, as well as regulations pertaining to departmental interior police, subject to congressional review. In all, the Departmental *Juntas* were "to promote, through the medium of the Governor everything that may contribute to the

---

277 *Ibid.*, pp. 205-206.

prosperity of the Department in all its branches; and to the well-being of its towns [and]….advise the government on all matters on which it may require it of them."[278]

The central government did warn both the governors and members of the Departmental *Juntas* that they could not levy taxes without congressional approval. The Decree of December 29, 1836 stated that monies could only be used for the purpose for which they were enacted. The governor and the Departmental Junta were prohibited from raising an armed force "except in the case in which they are expressly authorized by the general government." Commitment to the Department was required, members of the Departmental *Juntas* could not resign, except for legal cause, without the approval of the Departmental Junta itself and the governor.[279]

Perhaps the most notable feature of the Departmental *Juntas* under the Law of December 30, 1836, was that they would divide the Department of New Mexico into smaller districts. As in all other departments in Mexico, the districts would be subdivided into precincts or *partidos*. Each district would be governed by a *prefecto* and the *partidos* would have *sub-prefects*. Common councils and justices of the peace in each of them would form the governing authorities. As such, New Mexico was already divided into two districts, one in the Río Arriba north of Cochiti Pueblo, the other in the Río Abajo, south of Cochiti. Each one had been sub-divided into two *partidos*, each one with a capital. Santa Fe would, of course, host the *Departmental Junta*. The partido governments would have their own capitals: San Ildefonso (Hispanic settlement) and Taos (Hispanic settlement) in the north; and, Alburquerque and Los Padillas in the south. They would serve as capitals akin to seats of government with an *ayuntamiento* and an *alcalde constitucional*. That provision was supported by constitutional law.

These changes would have profound meanings to the frontier

---

278 *Ibid.*, pp. 207-207.
279 *Ibid.*, p. 208.

Department of New Mexico. Through the Law of December 30, 1836, New Mexico became a Department—not a state of Mexico.[280] The Department would now be subject to rules governing all Departmental *Juntas*. As a frontier area not accustomed to intense regulation, New Mexico would begin to re-evaluate, as would Sonora and California, the rebellious path taken by Yucatan and Texas. New Mexican watched the changes with interest. They were keenly aware that Texas and Yucatan had rebelled over issues related to their status. Changes were in the wind—and New Mexicans would soon be drawn into the swirl of Mexican politics.

Although Mexican rule, in its quest for a more efficient government, offered much tightened political reorganization to New Mexico, it also proved troublesome. The Law of March 20th, 1837,[281] for example, defined and added tighter management controls for a more efficient governing. Too, it initiated a new national debate in regard to how centralist was the general government becoming. Article 1 spelled out the powers of the departmental governments comprised of governors, *juntas*, *prefects*, *sub-prefects*, common councils, *alcaldes*, and justices of the peace. Governors could now "use the armed force which the law may give to them for that purpose, and in the absence or insufficiency thereof to apply for the force needed to the military

---

280 Law of December 30th, 1836 in SMLL, p. 209. Article 1 of the provision reads: "The Territory of Mexico is divided into as many Departments as there were States, with the following modifications: Article 2. That which was the State of Cohuila dn Texas is divided into two Departments, each with its own territory. New Mexico shall be a Department. Upper and Lower California shall be a Department. Aguas Calientes shall be a Department with the territory it how has. The Territory of Colima is annexed to the Department of Michoacan. The Territory of Tlaxcala is annexed to the Department of Mexico. The capital of the Department of Mexico is the city of that name." Regarding Texas, which had rebelled in early 1836, Article 4 read: When order is re-established in the Department of Texas, the government shall dictate the necessary measures for the organization of its authorities, and shall fix the capital in the place it considers most suitable."
281 Law of March 20th, 1837 in SMLL pp. 211-221.

commandant, who cannot refuse it."[282] The governor could now decide "without appeal" on questions raised in elections. He was now to "take particular care that in all the towns of the Department there shall not be lacking schools for primary instruction, and that the male and female teachers shall be not only of sound morals and good behavior, but also competent." The governor had the right to suspend employees of the department for as long as three months and deprive them of half their salaries. His powers were increased to suspend the common councils with the concurrence of the Departmental Junta; and, he could impose, without appeal, fines reaching $200 for disobedience of laws and sentence offenders to jail or public works. He could also fine members of the Departmental Junta $50, without appeal, for failing to follow the law. And to solve a widespread social problem, the governors of the Departments could send vagrants to workhouses or fields. The Decree of 1836 provided for a host of other detailed powers[283] and also increased the membership of the *juntas* from five to seven members. By the middle 1830, Mexican frontiersmen in the far north, opposed to change, began to question the tightened political changes that to them seemed so radical in comparison to the seemingly laissez faire approach under Spanish colonial rule.

The political atmosphere created by a vigorous Mexican authority in a frontier circumstance proved stressful to New Mexicans. So too in far away Yucatan, which rebelled in 1834, Texas in 1836, Sonora in 1837, and California in 1837. California had rebelled several times before and after 1837. Frustrated and angry about changes which appeared abusive to them, New Mexicans openly rebelled against the Centralist Mexican government in 1837. Appointed to the military-governorship of New Mexico by Antonio López de Santa Anna in 1835, Albino Pérez, a native of Veracruz, was an outsider to Santa Fe's politics. Consequently, New Mexicans opposed him in public. In the

---

282 *Ibid.*, p. 211.
283 *Ibid.*, pp. 213-214.

Rebellion of 1837 that followed, Governor Pérez was killed along with several of his supporters. After his untimely death, archrival Manuel Armijo became governor of the politically fragmented north Mexican department until the American invasion of 1846.

The instability in Mexico during the dictatorship of Santa Anna allowed New Mexico to revert to its customary pattern of isolation. Just prior to the occupation of New Mexico by the United States, a series of events regarding the distribution of land took place. The distribution of land in New Mexico during the Mexican Period took on a history of its own. Authorized by the Colonization Law of 1824, the states and territories were permitted to enact laws providing for the colonization of lands within their respective boundaries as long as they were consistent with national policies. Moreover, Mexican law prohibited the granting of lands within twenty leagues of an international boundary and ten leagues of coastlines without consent of the central government in Mexico City.[284] The law stipulated that individuals could not receive more than eleven square leagues of land.[285]

During the 1840s, New Mexican officials used land grants to influence private enterprises and create defensive barriers against marauding Indians, Texans, and Anglo-American intruders. New Mexicans were encouraged to settle lands in river valleys on the northeastern and eastern peripheries bordering the Republic of Texas.[286] Other New Mexicans looked to lands north of Tierra Amarilla and Taos for settlement.

During the administration of Governor Manuel Armijo, large tracts of land were granted. Between 1837 and 1846, Governor Armijo gave away an estimated 16,500,000 acres of the 31,000,000 acres[287] of land in southern Colorado and northern New Mexico. Among those receiving

---

284 Decree of August 18th, 1824, Article 5, in SMLL, p. 121.

285 Bowden, "Private Land Claims in the Southwest," 73.

286 Twitchell, *The Leading Facts of New Mexican History*, II:196-7. Also, see Alan Ward Minge, "Frontier Problems in New Mexico Preceding the Mexican War, 1840-1846" (Ph.D. diss., University of New Mexico, 1965), 306.

287 Victor Westphall, "Fraud and the Implications of Fraud in the Land Grants of New Mexico," *NMHR*, (July 1974), 49:199-200.

land were Guadalupe Miranda and Charles Beaubien, who requested and received lands from the Armijo in 1841 east of the Sangre de Cristo Mountains along the Cimarron and Canadian rivers. They received the land for ranching purposes as well as farming as they had planned to cultivate cotton and sugar beets, cut timber, and prospect for minerals. That grant later became subject of one of the largest land grant claims when Beaubien's son-in-law, Lucien Maxwell, claimed nearly two million acres in northeastern New Mexico and southeastern Colorado.[288]

Particularly selecting land grant recipients to meet the defensive policies for New Mexico, Armijo generally chose foreigners, that is immigrants from the United States, who had married Mexican women or foreigners who had lived in New Mexico since the 1820s. On the other hand, most foreign grantees had New Mexican partners. During his administration, Armijo authorized grants to New Mexicans and their foreign-born partners in New Mexico. Those receiving grants drew settlers from the Hispanic population of New Mexico as well as Anglo-American immigrants. One such grantee, in 1845, was Gervasio Nolan, a French Canadian, and two New Mexican partners, who received lands on the Canadian River, neighboring the Beaubien-Miranda Grant.[289] Too, Charles Beaubien's thirteen year old son, Narciso and a partner Stephen Louis Lee, a fur trapper from St. Louis, received the Sangre de Cristo Grant in the San Luis Valley straddling present New Mexico and Colorado border.[290] Cerán St. Vrain and Cornelio Vigil received a grant along the Cucharas, Huerfano, and Apishapa rivers in eastern Colorado, known as the Animas Grant; and, John Scholly and his Mexican and

---

288 Lawrence R. Murphy, "The Beaubien and Miranda Land Grant, 1841-1846," *NMHR*, (January 1967), 52:27-46. William A. Keleher, *Maxwell Land Grant: A New Mexico Item* (Santa Fe: 1942). Jim Berry Pearson, *The Maxwell Grant* (Norman: 1961).

289 Morris F. Taylor, "The Two Land Grants of Gervacio Nolan," *NMHR* (April 1972), 47:151-84.

290 Herbert O. Brayer and William Blackmore, *The Spanish-Mexican Land Grants of New Mexico and Colorado, 1863-1878* (Denver, 1949), 59-62.

Anglo-American partners received a grant northwest of Las Vegas.[291]

Armijo's land policies alarmed many New Mexicans because of the large tracts of land granted to foreigners. The famous Father Antonio José Martínez of Taos openly opposed Armijo and questioned his granting of New Mexico's land to foreigners. In February 1844, when an ailing Armijo was replaced briefly by interim governor Mariano Martínez, Father Martínez urged him to annul the Beaubien-Miranda grant. Arguing that a Law of March 11, 1842, permitted foreigners to acquire property anywhere in the Mexican Republic except in departments contiguous with other nations requiring special permission to do so, Father Martínez persuaded the interim governor to oust Beaubien from his land. As it turned out, Beaubien, a naturalized Mexican citizen, had as his partner in the land grant Charles Bent, a foreigner, which under the Law of March 11, 1842 would be illegal. In late spring 1844, Governor Martínez ordered Beaubien to vacate his grant. It seemed the issue was settled. Father Martínez's victory, however, was short-lived, for the next governor, José Chávez, reinstated the rights of Beaubien to settle foreigners on the Beaubien-Miranda Grant. The controversy took on a new twist, when, in 1845, General Francisco García Conde, a representative of the central government inspecting New Mexico, ordered all foreigners in the Cimarron area to leave their lands. Manuel Armijo, once again, assumed the governorship of New Mexico for a second term, and encouraged the foreigners to ignore the order. Motivated by his one-fourth interest in the grant, Governor Armijo supported foreign settlers in their desire to remain on the Beaubien-Miranda land grant.[292]

Supported by Mexican officials who desired opened colonization of the northern frontier by anyone who would swear allegiance to the Mexican government, become a Roman Catholic, learn the Spanish

---

291 Harold H. Dunham, "Cerán St. Vrain," in Leroy Hafen, ed., *The Mountain Men*, V:310-11, and, Twitchell, *The Spanish Archives of New Mexico*, I:276-277.

292 Murphy, "Beaubien and Miranda" 32-33, 35; Twitchell, *Spanish Archives*, I:276-77; J.J. Bowden, "Private Land Claims in the Southwest," 6 vols. (LLM thesis, Southern Methodist University, Dallas, 1969), III:775-76.

language, and promise to bring additional settlers into the area, Armijo's grandiose land grant policies attracted new settlers into New Mexico. Still, the larger number of settlers, to the New Mexico and Colorado grants were drawn from the Hispanic population of New Mexico, many of whose ancestors had been through those lands as traders, explorers, or on military expeditions. As private property owners of their land, they could acquire their land in various ways [See Appendixes A and B]. By 1821, New Mexico's population had virtually reached 65,000 people.

The Mexican Period was truly a period of transition. In the short twenty-seven year period of Mexican rule, New Mexicans participated in the political system thrust upon them by Mexico. Their novitiate in Mexican politics prepared them for the next cycle of change. Between 1846 and 1848, New Mexicans watched the outcome of the war between Mexico and the United States with disquieting interest. As the Army of the West under General Stephen Watts Kearney occupied New Mexico, a new order was at hand. Mexican acting-Governor Juan Bautista Vigil y Alarid's words of acquiesence echoed with *tristés* throughout New Mexico:

> Do not find it strange if there has been no manifestation of joy and enthusiasm in seeing this city occupied by your military forces. To us the power of the Mexican Republic is dead. No matter what her condition, she was our mother. What child will not shed abundant tears at the tomb of his parents?...Today we belong to a great and powerful nation....we know that we belong to the Republic that owes its origin to the immortal Washington, whom all civilized nations admire and respect.[293]

With those words, New Mexico quietly slipped into U.S. hands.

---

293 For full text see William A. Keleher, *Turmoil in New Mexico, 1846-1868* (Santa Fe: Rydel Press, 1952), p. 20

Chapter VIII
History's Hispanic Legacy: The Land Grants of Southern Colorado

> All grants of land made by the Mexican government
> or by the competent authorities, in territories
> previously appertaining to Mexico, and remaining
> for the future within the limits of the United States,
> shall be respected as valid, to the same extent that
> the same grants would be valid, to the said territories
> had remained within the limits of Mexico.
> —Article X of the Treaty of Guadalupe Hidalgo
> deleted by U.S. Congress, 1848

Large land grants issued during the Mexican Territorial Period such as
the Miranda and Beaubien Grant, the Las Animas Grant and the Sangre
de Cristo Land Grant were made to New Mexicans and their partners.
During the Mexican Territorial Period, officials chose to concede land
grants to recipients who would not only develop the land, but who would
accept lands in strategic areas in order meet the defensive needs for New
Mexico. Governor Manuel Armijo generally chose foreigners, that is
immigrants from the United States, who had married Mexican women or
foreigners who had lived in New Mexico since the 1820s. Carlos Beaubien,
a Canadian fur trader, for example, had married María Paula Lobato in
1827 at Taos. Most foreign grantees had New Mexican partners. During

his administration, Armijo authorized grants to New Mexicans and their foreign-born partners in New Mexico. In 1845 one such grantee, for example, was Gervasio Nolan, a French Canadian, who with his two New Mexican partners received lands totaling 275,000 acres neighboring the Beaubien-Miranda Grant on the Canadian River.[294] Nolan's grant was approved by the Surveyor General in 1860.[295] Too, Charles Beaubien's thirteen year old son, Narciso and a partner Stephen Louis Lee, a fur trapper from St. Louis, received the Sangre de Cristo Grant in the San Luis Valley, straddling present New Mexico and Colorado border.[296] Cerán St. Vrain and Cornelio Vigil received a grant, known as the Animas Grant; and, John Scholly and his Mexican and Anglo-American partners received a grant northwest of Las Vegas.[297]

Between 1837 and 1846, Governor Manuel Armijo granted large tracts of land in southern Colorado.[298] Governor Armijo reasoned that only a liberal land grant policy would lure settlers to southern Colorado to defend against raiders and the oncoming immigration from the United States that had resulted in Mexico's loss of Texas. Armijo hoped that settlers would already have established the area and be poised to defend it. New Mexican settlers, hoping for a new life, were willing to take a risk in settling land so remote without the security of military assistance. Perhaps Bent's Fort, established in 1832 on the edge of that isolated and perilous stretch of land, was the only saving grace. Bent's Fort was on the

---

294 Morris F. Taylor, "The Two Land Grants of Gervacio Nolan," *NMHR* (April 1972), 47:151-84.

295 See No. 12, Decision of the Surveyor General in the Case of Gervasio Noland, signed by William Pelham, Surveyor General, Santa Fe, July 10, 1860, United States Congressional Serial Set , Vol 1067, p. 19.

296 Herbert O. Brayer and William Blackmore: *The Spanish-Mexican Land Grants of New Mexico and Colorado, 1863-1878* (Denver, 1949), 59-62.

297 Harold H. Dunham, "Cerán St. Vrain," in Leroy Hafen, ed., *The Mountain Men*, V:310-11, and, Twitchell, *The Spanish Archives of New Mexico*, I:276-277. Also see, Joseph P. Sánchez, Robert L. Spude, and Art Gómez, *New Mexico: A History*, University of Oklahoma Press 350 pp. (2013), p. 97.

298 Victor Westphall, "Fraud and the Implications of Fraud in the Land Grants of New Mexico," *NMHR*, (July 1974), 49:199-200.

last segment of the Santa Fe Trail before entering New Mexico proper.

Bent's Fort was constructed as as trading post by William and Charles Bent and their associate Cerán St. Vrain, who was involved with the fur trade and was owner of the St. Vrain Company. Located near Lamar between La Junta and Las Animas, the fort was the only settlement on the Santa Fe Trail between the Mississippi River and New Mexico. Bent's Fort was a stopping point for travelers as well as a trading post where traders, trappers, travelers, and the Cheyenne and Arapaho tribes came together in peace to trade. The fort was abandoned in 1849 due largely to cholera disease that had spread from Oklahoma among the plains Indians as well as Santa Fe Trail travelers.

In 1960, the United States Congress designated the fort as Bent's Old Fort National Historic Site. When the fort was reconstructed in 1976, its authenticity was based on archaeological reports, excavations, paintings, original sketches, diaries and other historical records from the period. Today, Bent's Old Fort is a reconstructed replica in situ of the original adobe structure. In many ways, today its museum tells a checker boarded story about how it served as a resting place for travelers, and as a jumping off point into New Mexico by Colonel Stephen Watts Kearney and his Army of the West, that occupied Santa Fe during the U.S.-Mexico War of 1846.

Bent's Fort was not the only settlement in the area. New Mexican traders, known as Comancheros, usually went out into the Texas and Oklahoma plains to trade with Comanche, Apache and other tribes. Often, some Comancheros went north from Taos into the San Luis Valley and over to the Arkansas River before moving northeastward to trade with the Cheyenne and other northern plains tribes. Some Comancheros passed by Bent's Fort and stayed on as employees. Others continued north and established small settlements, some of which did not last long due to Indian attacks. One such settlement founded by New Mexicans was a place called El Pueblo, a fortified settlement on the south bank of the Arkansas River about five miles north of Bent's

Fort.[299] Thomas Farnham, a trader, passed by "Fort El Pueblo" sometime in 1839.[300] He said that the settlers lived in one-story adobe structures built around a fortified plaza. Near the Arkansas, they raised grains and vegetables on plots of land irrigated from the river by acequias. Farnham said they had a "few head of livestock." One other traveler, Matt Field, left behind a description of El Pueblo after having stayed there overnight. He wrote that it had about "30 houses of small dimensions, all built compactly together in an oblong square, leaving a large square in the center and the houses themselves forming the walls of the fort. Into which there was but one entrance through a large and very strong gate."[301] Field remarked that the settlers lived by hunting and traded "now and then with friendly Indians." He remarked that the settlers had a number of goats, which they milked, and that the "men were as brave and daring as the Comanches." The settlers of El Pueblo, who called their town "El Pueblo de la Leche," supplied Bent's Fort with milk and vegetables.[302] Some travelers referred to it as "Fort Milk"—to them, a well-known landmark. Field also noted that the men were "as expert with the bow as the Indians."[303] Field observed that they were peaceful and wrote that once or twice a year they traveled to Santa Fe for supplies.

During that period, Comancheros established small settlements along the Arkansas where they lived under constant threat of attack by warring tribes. Life on that perilous frontier was hard and filled with heartbreaks. On Christmas Day, 1854, a large number of Utes and Jicarilla Apaches struck Fort Pueblo, a trading post established in 1842 by Anglo and Hispanic settlers and traders that was located on the Arkansas River near present Pueblo. Under Chief Tierra Blanca, the Utes and Jicarilla

299 Charles L. Kenner, *The Comanchero Frontier: A History of New Mexican-Plains Indian Relations* (Norman: University of Oklahoma Press, 1969) p. 91.
300 *Ibid.*, p. 91.
301 Stephen Garrison Hyslop, *Bound for Santa Fe: The Road to New Mexico and the American Conquest, 1806-1848* (Norman: University of Oklahoma Press, 2002), p. 225.
302 López Tushar, *People of El Valle*, p. 22.
303 Kenner, *The Comanchero Frontier*, pp. 92-3.

Apaches killed seventeen men, captured a woman, who they killed, and her two children, and rustled two hundred head of livestock.[304] The two boys were the only survivors of the seventeen killed, Rafael Chacón, who served on one of the punitive expeditions against the Ute and Apache wrote:

> It is believed that thirteen men were killed outright, that the only woman at the post, a Mrs. Sandoval and her two sons were taken captive, and another man escaped to a nearby ranch but died shortly thereafter, unable to communicate because he had been shot through the jaw and his tongue severed. After a few day's captivity, the woman was killed by the Indians beause they claimed that she grieved excessively and would not be comforted. Within the next day or so it was reported that the Indians killed some other men in the vicinity, stole a number of horses and cattle, and also ambushed and killed nine Cherokee Indian teamsters who had been in the employ of some American traders.[305]

Chacón theorized on two possibilities leading to the attack. One theory was that the trading post was probably attacked because the Utes believed that a smallpox outbreak among their people was caused by the Superintendent of Indian Affairs who had given them blankets, which they thought were infested with the germs. On the other hand, Chacón also considered the possibility that, as the thirteen men were killed outright after they had been celebrating with "spirits" with the Indians, things went wrong and the Indians attacked.[306]

Military expeditions were sent north from Santa Fe to pursue the Apache. In February 1855, Captain Francisco Gonzales and his cousin,

---

304 López Tushar, *People of El Valle*, p. 22. Kenner, *The Comanchero Frontier*, p. 93
305 Jacqueline Dorgan Meketa, ed., *Legacy of Honor: The Life of Rafael Chacón, A Nineteenth-Century New Mexican* (Albuquerque: University of New Mexico Press, 2000), pp. 97.
306 *Ibid.*, p. 97-98.

First Sergeant Rafael Chacón, joined troops under Colonel Thomas T. Fauntleroy to find and attack the Utes and Apaches responsible for the attack on Fort Pueblo and other settlements. Chacón wrote:

> We received our arms at Fort union and immediately started in pursuit of the Apaches who had stolen a herd of mares from Don Juan Vigil of La Cueva in the county of Mora. We followed the trail of the Indians through what is now Wagon Mound; they crossed the Río Colorado at Piedra Lumbre, and entered the Sierra Grande, and recrossed the river at Casa del Aguila in the neighborhood of what is now Otero in Colfax County. We followed them by the same route and caught up with them in what is now Long's Canyon....From here we started and traveled through Taos, Río Colorado, Costilla, Culebra, and to Fort Massachussetts, now Fort Garland, where the campaign was organized. In the first encounter we had with the Apaches in Saguache, March 19, 1855, they were undoubtedly waiting for us to give us battle; they...fought with reckless valor....Finally they were put to flight, and had to abandon the field, leaving several of their dead, who were buried by order of Colonel Fauntleroy...On the 21st we crossed over the Puerta Del Punche [Ponche Pass] and the valley between the Río Almagre [Fountain Creek] and the Napeste [sic] [Arkansas River] we had another encounter with the Ute Indians. They did not make much resistence.[307]

From there, they moved northward from Ponche Pass past the Sierra Mojada (Wet Mountain) to Salida. Following Indian tracks along the Arkansas River, they fought the Utes at Rosita. Moving through the Puerto del Mosco (Mosca, Colorado), they returned to the road to Fort Massachusetts and made their way through El Vallecito and La

---

307 *Ibid.*, pp. 100-103.

Veta to Río del Oso and Trujillo Creek in Animas County. They again fought the Utes. Ranging far and wide, they encountered the Apache at Ponil and chased the Apache into New Mexico as far as the Montoya Grant near Tucumcari. From there they returned to Abiquiu and Taos where the campaign ended.[308]

Undaunted, after generations of trading with tribes in southern Colorado, albeit illegally, New Mexicans had begun to establish settlements in the area. Some, like that settlement near present Pueblo, were short-lived, while others became more sustainable when settlers, under land grant contracts, began to move in in greater numbers, especially into the San Luis Valley.

The area of the grants in southern Colorado stretched from the Arkansas River to the La Plata Mountains, inclusive of the rich San Luis Valley. The names of most of the grants are part of the history, legend and lore of southern Colorado. The grants, under Mexico, as they had under Spain, required that the contracts for lands be given to individuals, groups of people, and under Mexican law, to an *empresario*, that is, an individual who promised to colonize an area in return for a large land grant. The contracts for the land grants also required that sustainable resources such as water, pasturage, and wooded areas be located as a part of the selection of the area to be settled. Too, the settlers had to develop the land for ranching and/or farming within a specified time, usually five to eight years. It should also be noted that the southern portion of Colorado was a part of New Mexico until 1861, when the Territory of Colorado was created with its southern boundary along the 37⁰ north parallel.

By that time, land grants were already spread across the vast expanse of southern Colorado. County by county land grants were listed within the boundaries of each county as it evolved. In the eighteenth century those land grants had become well-known place names. The Maxwell Grant fell within Las Animas County once the county was created. The

---

308 *Ibid.*, pp. 102-103.

Las Animas Grant stretched across four counties: Las Animas, Otero, Pueblo, and Huerfano. The Sangre de Cristo Grant lay within Costilla County, while the Los Conejos Grant was located in Alamosa County. Other portions of the Conejos Grant lay in Río Grande, Mineral, and Conejo counties. The boundaries of the Río Don Carlos Grant were well defined within Pueblo County. Saguache County held Baca Tract No. 4, one of several "Baca Float Grants" that were located in Arizona and New Mexico as well. While the large portion of the Tierra Amarilla Grant was situated in New Mexico's Río Arriba County, a part of it stretched into Archuleta County. Other small grants dotted lands that were overlapped by the larger grants.

During the Mexican Territorial Period, the Las Animas Grant, awarded to Cornelio Vigil and Cerán St. Vrain, both from Taos, encompassed an area along the Cucharas, Huerfano, and Apishapa rivers "to their junction with the Arkansas and Animas rivers" in eastern Colorado. Assuring [Governor Armijo] "that it is public land," both men, furthermore, said that "we have not hesitated to apply to your excellency, praying you to be pleased, by an act of justice to grant to each one of us a tract of land in the above mentioned locality, protesting that in the coming spring we will commence operations, which will be continued until the colony shall be established and settled." In their petition they explained that they would use the land "to encourage the agriculture of the country to such a degree as to establish its flourishing condition...and finding sufficient fertile land for cultivation, and abundance of pasture and water, and all that is required for a flourishing establishment, and for raising cattle and sheep, and being satisfied therewith."[309] Soon after the petition was made and heard by Governor Armijo, he wrote an order in the margin directing Alcalde José Miguel Sánchez of Taos to deliver possession of the land to the petitioners. Armijo noted that

---

309 J.J. Bowden, "Private Land Claims in the Southwest," (Masters Thesis, Southern Methodist University: 1969), Section X, p. 1795.

178

he made the grant as an official of the government in order to foster agriculture and the arts.[310]

On December 25, 1843, Vigil and St. Vrain appeared before Alcalde Sánchez and petitioned that he sign the document giving them possession of the land. The next day, Sánchez posted a public notice to deliver possession of the land to the two men unless anyone protested the proceedings. On January 2, 1844, Sánchez and the two men travelled to the land, marked it off, and placed monuments to establish the boundary. Sánchez' field notes describe the occasion:

> Commencing on the line (north of the land of Beaubien and Miranda) at one league east of the Las Animas River a mound was erected thence following on a direct line to the Arkansas River, one league below the junction of the Las Animas and the Arkansas, the second mound was erected on the banks of said Arkansas River; and following up the Arkansas to one and one-half leagues below the junction of the San Carlos River, a third mound was erected; thence following in a direct line to the south, until it reaches the foot of the first mountain, two leagues west of the Huerfano River, the fourth mound was erected; and continuing on a direct line to the top of the mountain to the source of the aforementioned Huerfano, the fifth mound was erected; and following the summit of said mountain in an easterly direction until it intersects the line of the land of Miranda and Beubien, the sixth mound was erected; from thence following the dividing line of the lands of Miranda and Beaubien in an easterly direction, I came to the first mound which was erected.[311]

In the tradition of the act of possession, Sánchez performed the customary ceremonies necessary to deliver possession of the land.

---

310 *Ibid.*
311 *Ibid.*

Probably reminiscent of the act of possession ceremony performed during the Spanish Colonial period, Sánchez probably did the same.[312]

Promptly, between 1844 and 1847, Vigil and St. Vrain were busy hiring drovers to herd 1,500 head of livestock to the area. Meanwhile, William Bent and a number of employees attempted to farm at Purgatoire on the Las Animas River, but were driven off by raiding tribes before the first harvest. After the 1847 Taos Rebellion when Cornelio Vigil was killed along with Governor Charles Bent, Vigil's heirs joined St. Vrain in attempting a second colony on the Huerfano River in 1852. Not long afterwards, warriors violently struck the area leaving eight settlers dead.[313] Discouraged, they pulled back. Eventually, Bent's Old Fort became a monument to their efforts.

During his lifetime, Cornelio Vigil had played an important role in several grants made in southern Colorado. One of them was a large grant made in 1841 to Carlos Beaubien and Guadalupe Miranda by Governor Manuel Armijo and it had a history of its own. Their grant was later known as the Maxwell Grant. That year, Beaubien and Miranda requested and received lands east of the Sangre de Cristo

---

312 The ceremony is described in Statement signed by Francisco Trébol Navarro, *Alcalde mayor* of Albuquerque, 9 May 1768, Población de San Fernando en el Río Puerco, Record of the Surveyor General 145, #1047. Translation by Joseph P. Sánchez. In 1768, Alcalde Francisco Trébol Navarro took Joseph Hurtado de Mendoza by the hand, "and in the name of the king, our Lord and in the name of the Royal Jurisdiction which I represent by virtue of the commission conferred on me by the Governor of this kingdom, I gave him royal and personal possession of the said site. I took him through the land pulling up weeds, throwing dirt, and making other demonstrations as a sign of true possession, and figuratively on behalf of the other grantees who were present. In loud voices they declared `Long live the King!' `Long live our Lord!' `Viva!' Then they placed themselves under the advocacy of Saint Joseph, their patron, thus ending the proceedings. Together they pledged that no one of them should ever cause injury to any of the settlers of San Fernando. Afterwards Trébol Navarro assigned the lands to the appropriate grantees. See Joseph P. Sánchez, *Between Two Rivers: The Atrisco Land Grant in Albuquerque History, 1692-1968* (Norman: University of Okalahoma Press, 2008.)

313 Bowden, "Private Land Claims in the Southwest," Section X, p. 1797. Also see, H.R. Report No. 457, 35th Congress, 1st Session, 1858, pp. 275-277.

Mountains along the Cimarron and Canadian rivers from Governor Manuel Armijo. They said that the land would be used for ranching purposes as well as farming as they had planned to bring settlers into the grant to cultivate cotton and sugar beets, cut timber and prospect for minerals.[314]

On February 22, 1843, Alcalde Vigil met the grantees and witnesses to survey the boundary and place monument to make them. Vigil's notes described in detail where the monuments were placed.

> Commencing on the east side ot the Colorado River, a monument was erected; from whence, following in a direct line in an easterly direction to the first hills, another mound was erected at the point thereof; and continuing from south to north on a line nearly parallel with the Colorado River, a third mound was erected on the north side of the Chico Rica or Chacuaco Mesa; thence turning towards the west, and following along the side of the said table land of the Chacuaco to the summit of the mountain, where the fourth mound was erected; from thence following south to the Cuesta del Osha, one hundred baras north of the road from Fernandez de Taos to the Laguna Negra, where the fifth mound was erected, from thence turning again to the east towards the Colorado River, and following along the southern side of the table lands of the Rayado and those of the Gonyalitos on the eastern point of which the sixth mound was erected; and from thence following in a northerly direction, I again reaching the river on its western side, where the seventh and last mound was erected opposite the first.[315]

314 Lawrence R. Murphy, "The Beaubien and Miranda Land Grant, 1841-1846," NMHR, (January 1967), 52:27-46. Also see William A. Keleher, Maxwell Land Grant: A New Mexico Item (Santa Fe: 1942), and Jim Berry Pearson, The Maxwell Grant (Norman: 1961).
315 Bowden, "Private Land Claims in the Southwest," Section VI, p. 852.

Completing the survey, Vigil performed the customary ceremony of the *entrega* (delivery) of legal possession of the land to the grantees. To show that they had taken physical possession of the land, Vigil said "I took them by the hand, walked with them, caused them to throw earth, pull up weeds and show other evidences of possession...."

Hoping to colonize the land as soon as possible, there was a change of governors and a challenge to the grant by the people of Taos. The new governor, Mariano Chávez, issued a decree on February 27, 1843, suspending the grant. The chief protest came from Father Antonio José Martínez, who protested the grant because Beaubien was a foreigner and not entitled to hold an interest in the grant. Furthermore, the grant had appropriated pasture and hunting lands belonging to the Pueblo de Taos. Beubien fired back. Addressing the *asamblea* in Santa Fe, he admitted that he was born in Cañada, but he had become a naturalized Mexican citizen who resided in New Mexico. Having checked the southern boundary of the grant, it was found that it did not overlap onto lands occupied by Taos. The grant was reissued in 1844. The boundaries of the grant, as written, read:

> Beginning at a point on the summit of the hill below the junction of the Rayado River with the Colorado River; thence easterly in a direct line to the first hills; thence in a northerly direction and parallel with the Colorado River to a point and continuing in a northerly direction along the same hills to the summit of the table land, thence northwesterly along said summit to the top of the mountain which divides the waters of the rivers; running towards the east from those running to the mountain to the intersection of the first hill south of the Rayado River; thence easterly following the summit of said hill to the place of beginning.[316]

---

316 *Ibid.*, p. 850.

Before long, over 200 acres had been farmed by private land owners whose scattered settlements and towns were a large part of the bucolic scene reported by travelers, as in most other land grants in the area. In 1860, the grant was confirmed by Congress, apparently unbeknownst to congressmen regarding its size, for 1,714,764 acres.

As fate would have it, the grant had one last chapter to include in it short history. When Kearney entered Santa Fe with his Army of the West, Miranda and others chose to serve under Governor Manuel Armijo who had intended to fight for Mexico. Seeing that his ill-prepared army could not stand up to the U.S. troops, Armijo chose to abandon the battlefield. He realized that many of the men he led were related to him in one way or another, and he did not wish them killed or harmed, so he retreated. Armijo and his followers fled south to El Paso del Norte. Miranda took up residency there. Of Armijo's decision not to engage the U.S. Army of the West, Rafael Chacón, recalled that:

> General Armijo and our poor people had no other resources than that of 'going to fight,' being used to the summons for a campaign against...Indians... ready to obey orders. What could Armijo do with the undisciplined army and without leaders to direct the men?...Had he rashly rushed to give battle, it would have been equivalent to offering his troops as victims to the invading army; the result would have been a useless effusion of blood...The guerrillas which Armijo sent out to observe the advance of the enemy brought back information to him of how well provided and equipped they came and of the perfect order they kept in their march, being a well disciplined army. It was then he realized he could not give them battle nor capitulate without effusion of blood, either with the enemy or his own people.[317]

---

317 Meketa, ed., *Legacy of Honor: The Life of Rafael Chacón*, pp. 63-64.

Originally from Albuquerque's Old Town, Armijo returned to live out his years in Lemitar near Socorro. Later, Rafael Chacón wrote his memoirs. Chacón served in campaigns against the Apache and Utes in the San Luis Valley and later served in the Civil War in New Mexico. For five years, during the middle 1850s, he traded with the Arapaho, Comanche, Ute, Cheyenne north of the Río Napeste and along the Río Conejos.[318] He died in his early 90s in Trinidad, Colorado, in 1925.[319]

While Miranda later prospered in El Paso, times for several years were difficult for him. Finally, in 1858, Miranda wrote to Beaubien telling him he needed money to survive and would sell out his part of the grant to him. Beaubien did not take up the offer, but his son-in-law, Lucien Maxwell, did. He purchased Miranda's part for two thousand seven hundred forty-five dollars. When Beaubien died in 1864, Maxwell bought out his heirs. It was said that Maxwell paid less then $53,000 for the entire grant. In 1869, the surveyor general reviewed the grant and found that the grant had greatly exceeded the maximum eleven square leagues per individual grantee allowed under Mexican law.[320] Therefore, it appeared that at some point in time, the grant would be reduced to 11 square leagues per claimant, which amounted to 97,650 acres.[321] How much of this information was shared publicly is not known, nor does it appear that adverse claimants were notified of such proceedings if the justice due would be served. However, the discussions held were not yet part of an adjudication, which would have made the difference in inviting public involvement.[322] In 1870, the grant was confirmed as the Maxwell Land Grant. Anticipating that his large grant would be reduced to 11 square leagues, especially following

---

318 *Ibid.*, pp. 104-106.

319 *Ibid.*, pp. 334-35.

320 Ebright, *Land Grants and Lawsuits*, p. 39.

321 *Ibid.*, p. 41. Also see *Treaty of Guadalupe Hidalgo: A Report to Congressional Requesters by the United States General Accounting Office* (GAO-04-60), June 2004 p. 73

322 *Ibid.*, p. 39.

the Tameling case of 1876, Maxwell sold nearly all of his lands within the grant to the Maxwell Land Grant and Railway Company for over $1,000,000. Although innuendos of fraud and conspiracy[323] attended the dealings with the sale and disposition of the grant, in the end the issues were settled by the proper authorities in both Colorado and New Mexico. Such agitations, along with those that Hispanic settlers protested against behind the scenes dealings, procedures and protocols contributed to the creation of the Court of Private Land Claims, which inherited more problems than could be imagined.[324]

Another important grant in southern Colorado is the Conejos Land Grant. In 1833, José Celedon Valdes and several other individuals petitioned for a grant of land that came to be known as the Los Conejos Grant. Acknowledging that the grant would be for colonization purposes, Governor Francisco Sarracino conceded the grant that would be located along the Conejos River. The grantees were unable to take possession of the grant for nearly nine years. During that time, hostilities with Indian tribes, particularly the Navajo, waged war relentlessly. Finally, in 1841, they were forced to seek peace. The grantees knew that they had lost their rights to the grant for failure to meet its terms. Explaining that the Indian hostilities had prevented them from settling the land, the grantees approached the Prefect of the Northern District of the Department of New Mexico, Andres Archuleta, to reinstate the terms of the grant. Given the situation, Archuleta revalidated the grant and instructed Cornelio Vigil, the Alcalde of the Spanish town of Taos, to place them in legal possession of the grant. On October 12, 1842, Vigil accompanied eighty-three settlers to the grant where

---

323 Bowden, "Private Land Claims in the Southwest," Section VI, p. 862. Bowden's research shows that some charges were made, but that the charges could not be proven. Thus, "As a result of these findings, the court dismissed the government's suit. The government appealed the case to the United States Supreme Court, which completely exonerated the Commissioner of the General Land Office, the Surveyor General and the Deputy Surveyor...by holding there was not the slightest evidence that they had been governed by fraudulent or improper motives..."
324 *Ibid.*, p. 856.

they surveyed the boundaries and the land. The designated boundaries approved by Vigil were "on the north—Garita Hill, on the east, the Río Grande, on the south, the San Antonio Mountains, and on the west, the Sierra Montosa."[325]

Once having established the grant, Vigil instructed the settlers that "the tract shall be cultivated and never abandoned, and he that shall not cultivate his land within twelve years or that shall not reside upon it will forfiet his right...."[326] Vigil further instructed them that they would eventually have to fortify and wall their settlement. Meanwhile, they were to "move upon the said tract and build their shanties...."[327] Upon receiving their promise and agreement to those terms, Vigil performed the traditional ceremonies necessary to place them in legal possession of the grant. Despite their good faith, the Navajo again took to attacking the settlement and forced the settlers to abandon the area. Four years later, in 1846, another attempt was made. Finally, toward the end of 1851 or the beginning of 1852, they returned to permanently settle the Conejos Land Grant.[328]

The subsequent history of the Conejos Grant was one shared with other grants. In 1861, for example, José María Martínez, on behalf of himself and his fellow grantees, petitioned Surveyor General William Pelham for confirmation of their grant. Considering that the grant was located in Colorado, Pelham referred the petition to the surveyor general in Denver. No record of the appeal or response appears to have resulted from that effort. Once the Court of Private Land Claims was established, Cresencio Valdes, an heir to the grant, filed suit as an individual against the U.S. government (Valdez v. United States, No. 109. Court of Private Land Claims) seeking confirmation of the grant, which he claimed amounted to two and a half million acres. By that time, a number of towns had been established within the Conejos Grant, and over 1,000

---

325 *Ibid.*, p. 1814.
326 *Ibid.*, p. 1814
327 *Ibid.*, p. 1815
328 *Ibid.*, p. 1815

claimants had "conflicting claims under the public land laws."[329] Valdez refused to include the other heirs as defendants in his suit. On August 14, 1900, the Court of Private Land Claims dismissed Valdez' petition. Of the dismissial of the case, Bowden, a land grant historian, concluded:

> This claim was one the most important filed for consideration by the Court of Private land Claims, not only on account of the vast size but because of the immense value of the mineral and agricultural lands located within the boundaries of the grant. The rejection of the claim dispelled the apprehensions of the thousands of *bona fide* settlers as to their holdings and removed the cloud which had rested upon their titles to land in one of the most prosperous sections of the Southwest.[330]

The subsequent twentieth century history of the Conejos Land Grant is tied to that of the San Luis Valley. Much had happened to the Conejos Grant and the San Luis Valley beginning in the late nineteenth century. Themes of that history are entangled within that of the Sangre de Cristo Land Grant, the movement of other settlers into the San Luis Valley, inclusive of Mormon settlers, and the carving up of the land grant in which the U.S. Forest Service incorporated many of its lands within the Río Grande National Forest.

Gervasio Nolan, a resident of Taos, claimed to be a naturalized Frenchman, when in 1843 he petitioned Governor Manuel Armijo for a grant of land located in the Valle del Río de Don Carlos. Nolan described the land as fertile where he would establish a farm with cattle and sheep. Nolan said he would colonize the land within the prescribed time. Armijo made the grant, and, after the Prefect Andres Archuleta received the instructions, he ordered Cornelio Vigil, the *alcalde mayor* of Taos, to proceed to the site and deliver the land to Nolan following the customary ceremony of possession. Vigil carried out the ceremony on December 15,

---

329 *Ibid.*, p. 1815.
330 *Ibid.*, p. 1815.

1843.[331] Vigil walked of the boundary of the grant and recorded that it was located within the area. Vigil field notes described the grant as

> Commencing on the south bank of the Arkansas River, a league and a half below the confluence of the Don Carlos River with the former river, where the first landmark was placed, thence following up the same Arkansas River five leagues above the confluence of the Don Carlos River, where the second landmark was placed, thence running half-way up the brow of the mountain, where the third landmark was placed; and thence following from north to south the brow of the mountain to a point opposite the first landmark, where the fourth and last landmark was placed.[332]

Vigil noted that the survey did not show the granted area in conflict with any previous grant. The ceremony completed, grantee Gervasio Nolan was given legal possession of that land.

As it turned out, Nolan never lived on the grant, but his employees built their homes and successfully farmed the land. Travelers through the grant commented on the large crops that grew there. When Brigadier General Kearney began to record the land grants, Gervasio Nolan's Río Don Carlos Grant was one of the first recorded.

After Gervasio Nolan died in 1857, his heirs sought to confirm the grant. Appealing to the Surveyor General, the grant was found to be valid. Like all other large grants, Congress confirmed the grant, but reduced its size to the "eleven square leagues" rule. On march 3, 1875, the grant was confirmed for 48,778.5 acres despite that the original grant contained 595,978 acres.[333]

One of the most fascinating solutions to a land grant problem was resolved in a very creative way. The land in question spanned both the

---

331 *Ibid.*, p. 1806.
332 *Ibid.*, p. 1807.
333 *Ibid.*, p. 1807.

Spanish Colonial and the Mexican Territorial periods. The Las Vegas grant, for example, consisted of 496,446 acres surveyed in 1860[334] in the Gallinas Valley. Although the Las Vegas grant was given in 1835, and not effectively occupied until 1838,[335] the heirs of Luis María Cabeza de Baca claimed that the land had been granted to them in 1820, at the end of the Spanish colonial period. As, later, the Surveyor General had recognized that Cabeza de Baca's heirs were legal claimants, a deal was made in which they would take other lands in lieu of their claim. In 1860, Congress confirmed grants, known as Baca Floats, in other areas including New Mexico, Arizona and Colorado. Thus, Baca Float Number 4 would be in Colorado. Congress confirmed the Baca Floats in 1869 and a Supreme Court decision upheld the patent to the town of Las Vegas in 1893.

Two days after Christmas, 1843, thirteen-year old Narciso Beaubien, son of Charles Beaubien and María Paula Lobato, in partnership with Stephen Luis Lee, a Mexican citizen, petitioned Governor Manuel Armijo for a grant of land for the purpose of settlement, farming, and ranching, Armijo agreed and, on December 30, 1843, referred the petition to Juan Andres Archuleta, the prefect of Río Arriba. Archuleta, in turn, assigned the Alcalde of Taos, José Miguel Sánchez, to survey the area and present the grantees with title to the grant, that is, as long as the grant did not adversely affect the rights of other property owners. Sánchez' survey indicated that the boundaries and monuments were located within the following description of the land:

> Commencing on the east side of the Río Grande, a mound was erected at one league distance from its junction with the Costilla River, thence following

---

334 Malcom Ebright. *Land Grants and Lawsuits in Northern New Mexico.* Albuquerque: University of New Mexico, 1994, p. 204. Also see, *Treaty of Guadalupe Hidalgo: Findings and Possible Options Regarding Longstanding Community Land Grant Claims in New Mexico. A Report to Congressional Requesters by the United States General Accounting Office* (GAO-04-60), June 2004., p. 73,
335 *Ibid.*, p. 182.

up the river, on the same eastern bank to one league above the junction of the Trinchera River, where another mound was erected, and continuing from west to northeast, following up the current of the Trinchera River to the summit of the mountain, where another mound was established, and following the summit of the mountain to the boundary of the lands of Miranda and Beaubien, the fourth mound was established, and continuing on the summit of the Sierra Madre, and following the boundary of the aforementioned lands to opposite the first mound erected, on the Río Grande, where the fifth and last mound was erected, from thence in a direct line to the place of beginning.[336]

Having surveyed and marked the boundary of the grant, Sánchez, pursuant to the customary ceremony, delivered legal possession of the land to the grantees.

The grant sat along a series of plunder trails and was subject to attacks by Ute warriors, who had wreaked havoc on other land grants and settlements in the area. The Utes and Comanches had for decades driven off aspiring settlers. In 1845, the grantees and their settlers were similarly driven off. Fear of attacks by these tribes was enough to discourage settlement of the area, but as intrepid frontiersmen, they persisted in returning to the grant whenever they could to pasture cattle and sheep in the area.

In the meantime, it would not be the Utes or Comanches who would change the ownership of the Sangre de Cristo Grant. As the U.S. Army occupied New Mexico during the U.S.-Mexico War of 1846, a civilian government was established. Unsatisfied with the newly established government, a rebellion erupted in Taos on January 19, 1847. Governor Bent, along with Cornelio Vigil, Narciso Beaubien and Stephen Luis Lee, were among those who happened to be visiting with the governor,

---

336 Bowden, "Private Land Claims in the Southwest," Section VII, p. 886.

190

when a number of attacking Taos Indians and Hispanic New Mexicans killed them.[337]

Charles Beaubien inherited his son's share of the Sangre de Cristo Grant. Lee had been in debt and his "estate" had insufficient monies to pay them off. His friend, Joseph Plaey, who acted as his administrator, agreed to sell Lee's half to Charles Beaubien for $100. As the new owner of the grant, Beaubien moved to settle the area. In 1849,[338] he led Hispanic settlers to establish a settlement on the Costilla River. Again, in 1851, he led settlers to the Culebra River where they successfuly established farms, ranches and towns within the San Luis Valley.

On June 21, 1860, Congress approved Beaubien's Sangre de Cristo Grant. But a dark cloud hovered over it as John G. Tameling forced himself onto the land by attempting to homestead on a 160 acre tract within the grant. He argued that the Mexican Colonization Law of 1824 had limited the amount of land granted to individuals to eleven square leagues and that the Sangre de Cristo Grant should be considered void. Tameling also argued that as Narciso Beaubien and Stephen Lee were deceased, that they could not have owned more than twenty-two square leagues combined. Therefore, Charles Beaubien could only be in possession of twenty-two square leagues and not the amount of land claimed in the Sangre de Cristo Grant, which originally totaled 998,780.46 acres.

Meanwhile, Beaubien had sold a piece of the grant known as the Costilla Estate to the United States Freehold Land and Emigration Company. The owners of the company filed an ejectment suit against Tameling in the District Court of Pueblo County, Colorado. The District Court upheld the plaintiffs and Tameling appealed to the Supreme Court of the Territory of Colorado. Land Grant Historian Bowden summarized the Court's finding by writing that "the [Territorial Supreme] Court concluded that the 1860 confirmation of the grant by

---

337 Sánchez, Spude, Gómez, *New Mexico: A History*, p. 109-111.
338 Bowden, "Private Land Claims in the Southwest," Section VII, p. 888.

Congress "amounted to a grant *de novo* of the whole claim without regard to the question of whether or not the claim was originally valid. This desision subsequently was affirmed by the Supreme Court."[339] Although the size of the grant had been altered, Beaubien was still recognized at the legitimate holder of the Sangre de Cristo Grant.

The Sangre de Cristo Grant would survive a turbulent history of exploitation of the land and water rights of grantees by speculators, squatters, and other politically motivated investors. In the long run, however, the U.S. Supreme Court ruling in Tameling Case[340] would result in reducing the size of the grants to a maximum of eleven square leagues as stipulated in the Mexican law of 1828. Consequently, the U.S. Supreme Court decision was "based on the fact that all land in excess of 11 square leagues belonged to the United States as part of the public domain. In effect, therefore, the Supreme Court confirmed 11 square leagues based on the amount allowed to each grantee under Mexican law and granted an additional 1.6 million acres of the Maxwell Grant to the United States."[341] The Sangre de Cristo grant and others were similarly reduced in size.

As the history of land grants in southern Colorado has demonstrated, land grants of the Mexican Territorial Period, 1821-1846, constitute one of the most difficult land problems in New Mexico. Mexican period land grants, like those of the Spanish Colonial period, may be divided into three groups: community grants, that is, those made to settlements or groups of people, small size grants claimed by individuals and large size grants conceded to individuals and their partners, such as *empresarios*, to encourage settlement, especially for defensive purposes. Under the Treaty of Guadalupe Hidalgo, claimants rights to lands were guaranteed to them as part of the contractual terms made in each land grant.

---

339 *Ibid.*, p. 889. Also see Tameling v. United States Freehold & Emigration Co., 2 Colo. 411 (1874)

340 Tameling v. U.S. Freehold & Emigration Co., 93 U.S. 644 (1876)

341 *Treaty of Guadalupe Hidalgo: Findings and Possible Options Regarding Longstanding Community Land Grant Claims in New Mexico* (GAO-04-60), June 2004, p. 73

Under U.S. sovereignty, claimants had to produce documentation to title of the land they claimed to be theirs. In many cases, proof of ownership was generally lacking in the form of documents that definitely defined the rights of the claimants as well as the boundary markers on the land, and maps indicating the boundaries and configuration of the boundaries. The burden of proof naturally fell on the claimant.

Problems related to documentary proof of ownership of the land emerged during the early days of the U.S. occupation of New Mexico. Under Brigadier General Stephen Watts Kearney, land grant heirs were encouraged to turn in their documents so that they could be registered. Many such documents were lost and their disappearance remained a mystery. In many cases, the register was the only evidence that such a grant had been made, but no details could be gleaned from the register. Many claimants based their arguments on the right of occupancy by dint of the fact that their ancestors had been on the land since time immemorial. The complications were many. To be sure, forgeries, such as that seen in the well-known 1895 Peralta-Reavis suit[342] which claimed 12,467,456 acres, were the exception. James Addison Reavis of Missouri made the claim. He said his name was Peralta-Reavis. He was tried and found guilty of fraud and sentenced to a prison term.

In the first decades following the take over of lands ceded to the United States by Mexico following the U.S.-Mexico War of 1846, the U.S. Congress confirmed, on the recommendation of the Office of the Surveyor General, a number of titles to large grants. Issues revolving around the smaller grants would wait their turn and grantees would take their chances, particularly, after the Court of Private Land Claims was established in 1891. The court provided a new method of deciding whether to approve or reject a grant: adjudication through court proceedings.

Despite the efforts by the United States government to assure fairness and equity in the disposition of land grants, there were other

---

342 Ebright, *Land Grants and Law Suits*, p. 236

factors that stacked the odds against a fair and just conclusion to the processes of approving land grants. In his book *Land Grants and Lawsuits in Northern New Mexico* (1994), Malcom Ebright cites the conduct of Thomas B. Catron and others as being unethical. He concludes, "As more study is done of these and other lawyers' involvement in other land grant partition and quiet title suits, we may learn of other instances of unethical or fraudulent conduct. Enough evidence has been unearthed so far, however, to establish the activities of these lawyers...." Another major cause of Hispanic land loss was unfair adjudication of land grants due in part to the conflict between the Hispanic and Anglo legal systems. Too, as has been argued, that an ethnocentric viewpoint or a biased interpretation of Spanish Colonial and/or Mexican land ordinances of the period in question seemed prevalent. Ebright aptly writes: "This ethnocentric viewpoint was also expressed by Americans toward the entire system of Hispanic Civil Law."[343] Yet, in these considerations, one must also factor in the attitudes of political and bureautcratic authorities in the decision making that went against the rights of claimants by enforcing or enacting measures contrary to guarantees made under the Treaty of Guadalupe Hidalgo.

Indeed, the door was left open when Article 10 of the Treaty of Guadalupe Hidalgo was struck down by the U.S. Congress during ratification of the Treaty. Article 10, as written by Mexican officials, provided that "All grants of land made by the Mexican government or by the competent authorities, in territories previously appertaining to Mexico, and remaining for the future within the limits of the United States, shall be respected as valid, to the same extent that the same grants would be valid, to the said territories had they remained within the limits of Mexico."[344] Without that important wording, the

---

343 *Ibid.*, p. 268

344 ARTICLE X of the original draft of the Treaty of Guadalupe Hidalgo. Cited from Center for Land Grant Studies, Guadalupita, New Mexico, http://www.southwestbooks.org/treaty.htm. The wording is as follows: "All grants of land made by the Mexican government or by the competent authorities, in territories

adjudication of land grants changed and would be governed, as it turned out to be the case, by a seeming trial and error or, at least, an amorphous approach by the U.S. Congress, the Office of the Surveyor General, the Court of Private Land Claims as well as by the capriciousness of those in position to approve or reject land grants. Caused largely by agitation among claimants, who not only desired but needed confirmation of their land tenure rights during the late nineteenth century, Congress created the Court of Private Land Claims for the final settlement of all Spanish and Mexican land claims in New Mexico, Colorado and Arizona[345] on March 3, 1891.

Previously, between 1854 and 1891, the Office of the Surveyor General had investigated land grants and made recommendations to Congress for confirmation or rejection of claims based on sound proof or lack thereof. Congress approved certain land grants without knowing their size, in terms of acreage, or their specific boundaries. The Secretary

---

previously appertaining to Mexico, and remaining for the future within the limits of the United States, shall be respected as valid, to the same extent that the same grants would be valid, to the said territories had remained within the limits of Mexico. But the grantees of lands in Texas, put in possession thereof, who, by reason of the circumstances of the country since the beginning of the troubles between Texas and the Mexican Government, may have been prevented from fulfilling all the conditions of their grants, shall be under the obligation to fulfill the said conditions within the periods limited in the same respectively; such periods to be now counted from the date of the exchange of ratifications of this Treaty: in default of which the said grants shall not be obligatory upon the State of Texas, in virtue of the stipulations contained in this Article.

The foregoing stipulation in regard to grantees of land in Texas, is extended to all grantees of land in the territories aforesaid, elsewhere than in Texas, put in possession under such grants; and, in default of the fulfillment of the conditions of any such grant, within the new period, which, as is above stipulated, begins with the day of the exchange of ratification's of this treaty, the same shall be null and void.

[Seal] Luis de la Rosa"

345 See "Excerpts from the 1854 Act Establishing the Office of the Surveyor General of New Mexico," and "Excerpts from the 1891 Act Establishing the Court of Private Land Claims" in *Treaty of Guadalupe Hidalgo: Findings and Possible Options Regarding Longstanding Community Land Grant Claims in New Mexico* (GAO-04-60), June 2004, pp. 183-188.

of the Interior also had a bearing on some decisions, especially as they regarded common lands which the United States considered belonged to the public domain. When the Court of Private Land Claims stepped in to adjudicate remaining land grants, it was hoped, among claimants, that the agitating features of past decision making regarding land grants would change. The Court of Private Land Claims, for example, required that a survey be made before its approval could be given. Appeals to negative decisions allowed the claimants to plea their case before the United States Supreme Court. In the end, claimants, whose petitions were rejected or whose lands were reduced in size felt that justice was not served in their best interests. The historical perception is that those claims remain unsatisfied today.

The histories of land grants in specific areas of the Greater Southwest are well known. In New Mexico, southern Colorado, California, Arizona and Texas, descendants of early settlers still live in those areas, and their cultural imprint is seen throughout the region. The role of early Hispanic settlers as participants in the historical process of developing the land and establishing a cultural imprint and political institutions in the area is, in part, buried in the history of land grants. In southern Colorado, those land grants, following the historical legal traditions of their predecessor Spanish Colonial land grants, were created during the Mexican Territorial Period of New Mexico, 1821-1846. Their legacy lives on in the cultural landscape and Hispanic people of southern Colorado.

Chapter IX
The Office of the Surveyor General, the Court of Private Land Claims and Colorado's Land Grants: A Synopsis.

> The United States owes a duty to Mexico to confirm to her citizens those valid grants that were saved by the treaty, and the long delay which has attended the discharge of this duty has given just cause of complaint.
>
> The entire community where these large claims exist, and indeed, all of our people, are interested in an early and final settlement of them.
>
> — President Benjamin Harrison, 1889

The Treaty of Guadalupe Hidalgo (1848) had obligated the U.S. Congress to recognize valid land claims. The process to recognize land grant claims had begun as early as 1846, when General Stephen Watts Kearney, commander of the Army of the West, issued the Kearney Code. As New Mexico was under military occupation, such an order obligated New Mexicans to register their land grants with the territorial secretary, Donaciano Vigil. The registration of grants created an abstract of land titles. The treaty, however, required that New Mexicans were required to give up their original documents. Vigil, then, created a list, or register of land grants and their documents. That action, however, worked to the detriment of land grant owners and resulted in the loss of documents for the original titles. Some documents disappeared and all that was left of them was the register. Those that were not "lost" became unavailable and, as a consequence, could not be drawn upon later for title investigations or defense. Of that catastrophic event, Historian Richard Wells Bradfute wrote "Evidence exists that land titles were carted away and new ones created; at any rate, there was no assembling of titles in New Mexico as there was in California."[346] The land registration under the Kearney Code was repudiated by the New Mexico Territorial Legislative Assembly in favor of the act to establish the offices of the Surveyor General of New Mexico, Kansas, and Nebraska, which was passed by Congress on July 22, 1854.[347] Many members of the territorial assembly hoped that the Surveyor General's office, charged with examining land claims and making recommendations to Congress would fulfill the treaty obligations of the United States. That would not, however, be the case.

Despite its efforts in setting up the Office of the Surveyor General to investigate the land grants and, later, in establishing the Court of Private Land Claims, the United States government properly failed to adjudicate titles and ownership of many Spanish and Mexican land grants in the nineteenth century. History has shown that to be one of the most shameful episodes in American history. For Hispanic New Mexicans, the Territorial Period (1850-1912) was one of change and uncertainty. During that time Hispanic New Mexicans would struggle to assert their citizenship and property rights guaranteed under the Constitution and the Treaty of Guadalupe Hidalgo against a system managed by unscrupulous, deceitful and racist, if not, at least,

---

346 Robert Wells Bradfute, *The Court of Private Land Claims: The Adjudication of Spanish and Mexican Land Grant Titles, 1891-1904* (Albuquerque: University of New Mexico Press, 1975), p. 12.
347 J.J. Bowden, "Private Land Claims in the Southwest," Masters Thesis, Southern Methodist University, 1969, 249.

ethnocentric, individuals. New Mexicans had seen their ilk before, but this time, the stakes were high. The players, usually in the form of Anglo-American lawyers and politicians with the deck stacked in their favor, played for keeps. New Mexicans, under Spain and Mexico, had learned to defend their land claims in those courts against all comers. Too, they had learned to guard, jealously, historical documents proving their ownership to their land. This time, however, they must deal with a system that was managed by self-interested individuals who were not dedicated to seeking justice. The failure of the system eventually led to the creation of the Court of Private Land Claims,[348] but not before havoc had been visited upon the civil and property rights of New Mexicans. Even then, the Court of Private Land Claims left much undone.

For four decades, the U.S. Congress luke-warmly acted to recognize legitimate titles to land grants that fell within the provisions of the Treaty of Guadalupe Hidalgo. In California in 1852, Congress created a commission to investigate and settle eligible claims there. The stakes were different there. California's economic importance due to the "Gold Rush" of 1849, and the fact that California had become a state, the commission moved Congress and the California Legislature to confirm 618 of 813 claims. That process took nearly thirty years.[349] As regards New Mexico, southern Colorado, and Arizona, Congress failed to act, in earnest, on grants until 1854, the year that the office of the surveyor general was created.

In the creation of the office of the surveyor general, the legislation provided that land claimants could submit their claims to the surveyor general who would then investigate the claim and make recommendations to Congress. While the surveyor general could investigate a claim, he could not initiate a survey of the boundaries of a grant until or unless Congress approved it. That would later prove

---

348 Bradfute, *The Court of Private Land Claims*, vii.
349 *Ibid.*, 12.

to be a drawback. No time limit was specified for the presentation of a claim. Congress held the power to make the final determination or confirmation of a grant. Meanwhile, the legislation provided that any land grant claim under consideration by Congress would be reserved from the public domain until it was rejected or confirmed. For the next four decades, 1854 to 1891, Congress confirmed grants singly or in groups, preferring to deal with each case individually. Still, no other legislation or provisions was made by Congress to deal with land grants during this period.[350]

Congresses inability to act decisively placed many, if not all, land grants in limbo. Corrupt groups of politicians, referred to as land grant rings such as the Santa Fe Ring, gained as much control of grants as possible. Like the carpetbaggers of Reconstruction South, these groups, largely composed of politicians, lawyers, railroad administrators, and businessmen, gained control of the Territorial government of New Mexico. It has long been speculated that Governor William A. Pile was a member, or, at least, in cahoots with the rings, as were at least three surveyors general and certain Territorial delegates to Congress. So successful were these rings that the lawyers may have received as much as 80 percent of their fees in land grant property.[351] Seeing their land holdings dwindle, New Mexicans asked Congress for relief and reform.

Four years later, it seemed, luck favored their cause. The situation appeared bound for a new beginning, it at least provided room for New Mexicans to develop a strategy. On February 26, 1891, the Territorial Legislative Assembly passed "An Act Relating to Community Land Grants, and for Other Purposes." The law provided for the incorporation of community land grants. Section 38, as amended, provided that "This act shall not operate to divest any private rights or affect any private titles, but shall extend only to land grants made to a pueblo

---

350 *Ibid.*, 12-13.
351 *Ibid.*, 2-3.

or colony or for the public use of a community."[352] The significance of the law is that it broke the legal gridlock in which New Mexican land grant owners and their heirs had been placed. The definitions in Section 2 of the Act provided the needed wording, to wit:

> Sec. 2. Any ten or more of the owners and proprietors of any such land grant or real estate so held in common as a colony community or town grant, as aforesaid, may within five years from and after the passage of this act, and not afterwards, file in the office of the clerk of the district court of the county in which such land grant or real estate (or the greater part thereof, if the same be situate in two or more counties) is situate, a petition setting forth the names and places of residence of all persons claiming or owning any interest in the said land grant or real estate who are known to the petitioners, a description of the said land grant or real estate by metes and bounds according to an actual survey thereof, if the boundaries of such land grant have been definitely fixed by an actual survey, but if no such survey has been made by the proper authority, then such land grant may be described by any other description which will reasonably designate the land grant and the name by which it is commonly known in the vicinity of its location, and the nature and extent of the title under and by virture (sic) of which such land grant or real estate is held and claimed, and praying that the owners and proprietors of such land grant or real estate may be created a body politic and corporate under the provisions of this act.[353]

---

352 An Act to Amend Section 38 of An Act of the 29th Legislative Assembly of the Territory of New Mexico, Entitled "An Act Relating to Community Land Grants, and for Other Purposes." II. B. 200; Approved February 26, 1891. Laws of New Mexico, 1891, Chap. 86, p. 174, University of New Mexico Law School Library, Fiche 55 and 56.
353 Section 2, An Act Relating to Community Land Grants, Laws of New Mexico,

Lacking authorized surveys, New Mexicans saw a ray of hope that their land grants could be recognized. Too, the Act allowed them to incorporate and form a body politic that would give them the power to act in unison and keep some of their lands intact. To that end, some land grants were successfully incorporated as towns or townships.

Less than a week later, on March 3, 1891, the U.S. Congress proposed the creation of the Court of Private Land Claims. The two actions proved significant. For many, they began the juridical process under which New Mexicans would gain permanent possession and official recognition of their ancestral lands owned since the Spanish Colonial and Mexican Territorial periods. Soon, several owners and proprietors of land grants were consulting lawyers and filing petitions with the office of the Clerk of the District Court in the various counties on behalf of claimants of private ownership of lands within their respective land grants. Some of their petitions called for the incorporation of both grants into townships.

The Court of Private Land Claims had a history of its own. Territorial Governor Edmund G. Ross was appalled by the chaotic situation regarding land claims and the increasing demand for a final determination of land grant titles by heirs and other interested persons, including the railroads and other commercial groups. Seeking a solution, he initially suggested the creation of a land commission similar to that of California. By the end of his administration, he advocated that a court of private land claims be established.[354]

Frustrated by the situation, grantees, settlers, and businessmen alike, who needed to have land grant questions resolved, appealed to President Benjamin Harrison to bring about the adjudication of the land grant issue in the ceded territory. Typically, debates spun about the kind of adjudication that would be needed. The questions whirled about whether it should be through a commission or a special

---

1891, Chapter 86, 164.
354 Bradfute, *The Court of Private Land Claims*, 14.

judicial tribunal. In his State of the Union address on December 3, 1889, President Harrison included the proposition, but Congress did not take up the cause. Pressured by the Mexican government, which insisted on the observance of the rights of its former Mexican citizens under the Treaty of Guadalupe Hidalgo, Harrison delivered a special message urging Congress to act on the issue. Addressing Congress, he said:

> The United States owes a duty to Mexico to confirm to her citizens those valid grants that were saved by the treaty, and the long delay which has attended the discharge of this duty has given just cause of complaint.
>
> The entire community where these large claims exist, and indeed, all of our people, are interested in an early and final settlement of them. No greater incubus can rest upon the energies of a people in the development of a new country than that resulting from unsettled land titles.[355]

Harrison urged Congress to introduce the necessary legislation to resolve the issue.

A year passed and still Congress had not acted on Harrison's recommendations. Antonio Joseph, the Territorial delegate from New Mexico, along with several other Senators and Congressmen, presented a compromise bill[356] in early March 1891. The Act of March 3, 1891, created the land grant tribunal known as the Court of Private Land Claims. As Hispanics in New Mexico and southern Colorado had urged, the establishment of the Court of Private Land Claims came about as a result of the need to reform the land claims process which was fraught with corruption on the part of Territorial administrators.

---

355 *Ibid.*, 15.

356 Twitchell, *The Leading Facts of New Mexican History* (Cedar Rapids: The Torch Press, 1912), II:464-65.

The enabling legislation for the Court of Private Land Claims repealed the Act of July 22, 1854, which created the office of the surveyor general. Congress had finally taken a positive step toward resolving the land grant issues of Hispanics in the ceded territory.

The Act of March 3, 1891, which President Harrison immediately signed, provided for a court comprised of five justices — one chief justice and four associate justices — for the purpose of adjusting perfect and inchoate land claims in the ceded territory which had not yet been adjudicated. The court was empowered to "adopt all necessary rules and regulations" for the transaction of its business, and hold sessions within its jurisdiction. With the exception of the first session, which required ninety days notice to the people of the ceded territories, the court was instructed to publish announcements of all its sessions in English and Spanish languages "once a week for two successive weeks" in one newspaper in the capital of the state or territory where it presided.[357]

In the end, the actions of the Court of Private Land Claims was short-lived, lasting thirteen years. During its term, the Court of Private Land Claims was successful in quieting some land titles against the United States, although it lacked the power to completely settle the land grant issues at hand. Even though the term of the Court of Private Land Claims was originally chartered for five years ending on December 31, 1895, it was extended from time to time, ultimately expiring on June 30, 1904. The court originally convened for business in Denver, Colorado on July 1, 1891, but soon relocated to Santa Fe, New Mexico, for lack of a government building to house it in Denver. Nearly a year and a half later, on December 6, 1892, the Court of Private Land Claims began holding special sessions from time to time in Tucson and Phoenix, Arizona. The main business of the court was twofold: the adjudication of the validity of land claims, and the approval of surveys made to confirm said claims.

Despite its provisions, there were loose ends that the authors of the Private Land Claims Act did not address, understand, anticipate, or

---

357 Court of Private Land Claims Act, Chap. 539, 26 Stat., 854 (1891).

resolve. While provisions appeared to cover situations of ownership that could emerge as issues, it failed to understand the intricacies of land grant ownership. For example, the Act held that all claims of inchoate lands, that is, those grants that had not been made perfect under their original charter that derived from Spain or Mexico within the ceded territory not filed by March 3, 1893, were forever barred.[358] The act, moreover, provided that people, likely squatters, who had been in actual and continuous adverse possession of land not exceeding 160 acres for twenty years were to be given patents following a survey of their land ordered by the court.[359] Persons making adverse claims, however, could not apply for lands to "any city lot, town lot, village lot, farm lot, or pasture lot held under a grant from any corporation or town the claim to which

---

358 *Ibid.* Regarding the date of expiration for filing petitions for land claims, Section 12 states: "That all claims mentioned in section six of this act which are by the provisions of this act authorized to be prosecuted shall, at the end of two years from the taking effect of this act, if no petition in respect to the same shall have then been filed as hereinbefore provided be deemed and taken, in all courts and elsewhere, to be abandoned and shall be forever barred: Provided, that in any case where it shall come to the knowledge of the court that minors, married women, or persons *non compos mentis* are interested in any land claim or matter brought before the court it shall be its duty to appoint a guardian *ad litem* for such persons under disability and require a petition to be filed in their behalf, as in other cases, and if necessary to appoint counsel for the protection of their rights."

359 *Ibid.* In that regard, Section 13, Part 16 states: "That in township surveys hereafter to be made in the Territories of New Mexico, Arizona, and Utah, and in the States of Colorado, Nevada, and Wyoming if it shall be made to appear to the satisfaction of the deputy surveyor making such survey that any person has, through himself, his ancestor, grantors, or their lawful successors in title or possession, been in the continuous adverse actual bona fide possession, resident thereon as his home, of any tract of land or in connection therewith of other lands, all together not exceeding one hundred and sixty acres in such township for twenty years next preceding the time of making such survey, the deputy surveyor shall recognize and establish the lines of such possession and make the subdivision of the adjoining lands in accordance therewith. Such possession shall be accurately defined in the field notes of the survey and delineated on the township plat with the boundaries and area of the tract as a separate legal subdivision. The deputy surveyor shall return with his survey the name or names of all persons so found to be in possession, with a proper description of the tract in the possession of each as shown by the survey, and the proofs furnished to him of such possession."

may fall within the provisions of section eleven of this act."[360] Another provision maintained that subsoil rights containing mineral wealth were also exempt, for such rights were vested in the sovereign state.[361] The United States only quitclaimed its interest to surface rights—not subsoil rights.[362] Another drawback was that the court could not confirm inchoate claims exceeding eleven square leagues as specified by the Colonization Act of 1824 by Mexico. Any unresolvable or unfavorable decisions could be appealed directly to the United States Supreme Court.[363] Favorable

---

360 Section 16 of Court of Private Land Claims Act, Chap. 539, 26 Stat., 854 (1891).

361 Court of Private Land Claims Act, Chap. 539, 26 Stat., 854 (1891). Regarding subsoil mineral rights, Section 13, Part 3, states: "Third. No allowance or confirmation of any claim shall confer any right or title to any gold, silver, or quicksilver mines or minerals of the same, unless the grant claimed effected the donation or sale of such mines or minerals to the grantee, or unless such grantee had become otherwise entitled thereto in law or in equity; but all such mines and minerals shall remain the property of the United States, with the right of working the same, which fact shall be stated in all patents issued under this act. But no such mine shall be worked on any property confirmed under this act without the consent of the owner of such property until specially authorized thereto by an act of Congress hereafter passed."

362 Although the history of land grants in Texas differs from what occurred in New Mexico, southern Colorado, and Arizona, the issues in Kerlin v. Sauceda, 263 S.W.3d 920 (Tex. 2008) are representative of the complexity faced by land grant descendants in those states. Texas differed because like California, it was a state and not a territory. Under the concept of states' rights, they were governed by different laws, precedences, and policies. A number of cases involving the Balli family that had in the eighteenth century been granted South Padre Island went unresolved. Top soil and subsoil issues were involved as well as issues that revolved around boundaries and ownership. In Kerlin v. Sauceda, in a case involving subsoil royalty rights received a positive verdict for the Balli family living in Tamualipas, Mexico, but was overturned. The news commentary included such statements to the effect that: Almost 300 descendants of Padre Nicolas Balli hoped to recover oil and gas royalties from a New York attorney who they claim defrauded them for more than 60 years. The decision reversed an earlier decision that the Balli family had won in 2005. Also see State v. Balli Tex.Civ.App. June 23,1943."

363 Ibid. Regarding appeal to the Supreme Court, Section 9 states: "That the party against whom the court shall in any case decide — the United States, in case of the confirmation of a claim in whole or in part, and the claimant, in case of the rejection of a claim, in whole or in part--shall have the right of appeal to the Supreme Court of the United States, such appeal to be taken within six months from the date of

decisions depended on a survey to be made by the Commissioner of the General Land Office, who in turn, would return the survey to the court for final approval.

The problem, in general, was that the Surveyor General could not survey land grants until Congress approved them. Therefore, Congress confirmed grants without knowing their size, for they had not been surveyed. Then, when the Surveyor General surveyed them, he discovered the discrepancies and the conflicts between large grants overlapping small grants. Wherever a large land grant had been confirmed even before a survey had been done, the small grant, which in most cases had not been confirmed, lost out. Thus, as a rule, large land grants that had been confirmed prevailed in boundary disputes with those that had not been confirmed. The Las Vegas Land Grant case supported that premise or so it seemed.

Then there were issues that revolved around whether common lands should be part of the equation of the amount of land within a land grant. That issue, associated with the extent of the Las Vegas Land Grant that overlapped into several grants including the Town of Tecolote Land Grant, the Antonio Ortiz grant and the John Scolly grant in New Mexico raised questions. The issue later included the eastern boundary of the San Miguel del Bado grant that had yet to be surveyed. The problem lay in a tangled mess of surveys and opinions between the Surveyor General Office and the General Land Office. The 1860 survey showed 496,446 acres were in question. This type of situation, where large land grants overlapped with small land grants,

---

such decision, and in all respects to be taken in the same manner and upon the same conditions except in respect of the amount in controversy, as is now provided by law for the taking of appeals from decisions of the circuit courts of the United States. On any such appeal the Supreme Court shall retry the cause, as well the issues of fact as of law, and may cause testimony to be taken in addition to that given in the court below as truth and justice may require; and on such retrial and hearing every question shall be open, and the decision of the Supreme Court thereon shall be final and conclusive. Should no appeal be taken as aforesaid the decree of the court below shall be final and conclusive."

soon manifested itself in southern Colorado where large land grants conflicted with other grants.

Once the controversy between large and small grants erupted, Congress which had confirmed grants on the recommendation of the Surveyor General, stopped doing so. As it turned out, the Supreme Court resolved the issue in its 1876 decision in Tameling v. United States Freehold and Emigration Co., 93 U.S. 644. The Court upheld previous decisions that under Mexican law, Mexican governors could grant a maximum of 11 square leagues (approximately 48,800 acres to an individual).[364]

The issue swirled around the question, how large should a land grant be? In the 1876 Tameling decision, the Supreme Court, furthermore, declared that once Congress had confirmed a grant, the courts could not dispel that confirmation, even if a title had been passed to the grant through an erroneous confirmation.[365]

The Maxwell and Sangre de Cristo grants are examples of the problems created by the Tameling case and its precedents. Although the grants had not been surveyed, Congress confirmed them in 1860 unaware that the Maxwell grant contained 1.7 million acres and the Sangre de Cristo grant consisted of 1 million acres. For nearly ten years (1860-1870), the claimants of each grant petitioned that their grants be surveyed using the descriptions of the Surveyor General's reports, but the U.S. government, namely the Department of the Interior, rejected the requests and ordered that surveys be made for only 97,000 acres

---

364 *Treaty of Guadalupe Hidalgo: Report to Congressional Requesters by the United States General Accounting Office* (GAO-04-60), June 2004 p. 71.

365 Malcom Ebright, *Land Grants & Lawsuits in Northern New Mexico*, (1994, p. 206. See also *Treaty of Guadalupe Hidalgo: Findings and Possible Options Regarding Longstanding Community Land Grant Claims in New Mexico. A Report to Congressional Requesters by the United States General Accounting Office* (GAO-04-60), June 2004, p 70. See also Joseph P. Sánchez, Jerry Gurulé, and Mario Milliones, translators, *El Tratado de Guadalupe Hidalgo: Hallazgos y Opciones Posibles Con Respecto a Los Reclamos de Larga Duración de Mercedes de Tierras Communitarias en Nuevo Mexico*. GAO, June 2004. 250 pages. GAO The Treaty of Guadalupe Hidalgo

as prescribed by the Mexican Law of 1824 that would allow 11 square leagues times two claimants or 22 square leagues, which translated to 48,500 acres per claimant or 97,000 acres in total.

There were other issues: the earlier fights in Las Vegas over common lands as well as water rights issues, for example, spilled into other land grants well into the early 20th century. In the end, the complicity inherent in the adjudication and disposition processes regarding land grants and their common lands in the territorial and, later, state and federal governments and courts contributed to the loss of the common lands of the Las Vegas Grant[366] as well as others in the Greater Southwest.

In the course of thirteen years, the Court of Private Land Claims dealt with 290 claims that had been filed covering an aggregate area of 35,491,019 acres.[367] Two hundred twenty-eight cases were in New Mexico; 17 in Arizona; and 3 in Colorado. Of them, 158 cases were rejected. Only 21 cases were confirmed for the entire land claimed. In other cases, the court recognized titles, in whole or in part, covering a total of 2,051,525 acres of which 116,539 were in New Mexico. A total of 33,439,494 acres of rejected claims reverted to the public domain. Some grants which exceeded the eleven leagues limitation or were smaller than what had been claimed were substantially reduced in size. Seventy-three cases, 58 in New Mexico and 15 in Arizona, were appealed to the United States Supreme Court. Of them only 39 appeals were passed upholding 23 decisions made by the Court of Private Land Claims, reversing five others, and reversing or remanding 11 cases. The U.S. Government had been the appellant in 26 cases. It was able to secure a reversal or a reversal and remand in 10 cases. Only one payment in the amount of $513.63 was made.[368] Thirteen years after its creation, the Court of Private Land Claims had, according to Congress, discharged the obligations of the

---

366 *Ibid.*, pp. 189-193 and 216-217,
367 Bowden, "Private Land Claims in the Southwest," 243. The following statistics are taken from Bowden, pp. 243-248
368 *Ibid.*, 248. Also see Chaves v. United States, No. 57 (Mss., Records of the Ct.Pvt. L. Cl.).

United States under the 1848 Treaty of Guadalupe Hidalgo and the 1853 Gadsden Purchase Treaty. During the thirteen year period of the Court of Private Land Claims, Hispanic land grant heirs had been busy defending its boundaries, just as they had under Spain and Mexico in New Mexico, southern Colorado and Arizona.

Chapter X
A Legacy of Mistrust: The Treaty of Guadalupe Hidalgo and Hispanic Citizenship Rights

> Mexicans now established in territories previously belonging to Mexico, and which remain for the future within the limits of the United States, as defined by the present Treaty, shall be free to continue where they now reside, or to remove at any time to the Mexican Republic retaining the property which they possess in the said territories, or disposing thereof and removing the proceeds wherever they please; without their being subjected, on this account, to any contribution, tax or charge whatever.
>
> — Article VIII,
> Treaty of Guadalupe Hidalgo, 1848

It was now after the peace confirming the conquest and its consequences and engendered among a people foreign in language, laws, customs, and religion, with the pride of kindred and race peculiar to all Spanish races, in the midst of those who had lately,...`risen against the government and the American name and blood in the country,' and when risen, whose steps and deeds were marked with murder, robbery, and

fiendish atrocity in the village of Taos, and who,...
did not cease to conspire.

— Carter v. Territory, 1859 1 NM 317

The land grant issues in New Mexico and Colorado must be seen
against the backdrop of a larger plight faced by Hispanics in the newly
ceded territories inclusive of California, which had been made a state
in 1850 and was no longer subject to Congressional oversight as a
territory. In the first half century following ratification of the Treaty
of Guadalupe Hidalgo, hundreds of state, territorial, and federal legal
entities produced a number of conflicting opinions and decisions
interpreting the treaty's provisions, particularly those dealing with
citizenship rights of Hispanics living in the Mexican Cession.[369] Under
the ostensible protection of the treaty, Hispanics quickly learned within
just one generation to use the court system to challenge perpetrators
who violated their citizenship rights. Their legal status, granted
through their incorporation as citizens of the United States under the
Treaty of Guadalupe Hidalgo, was based on the Constitution of the
United States. In general, they hoped to gain recognition of the Treaty
of Guadalupe Hidalgo in the courts in order to strengthen their pleas.
Indeed, in 1899 one District Court judge in New Mexico remarked
that "reference to the treaty rights of defendants are immaterial."[370]

---

369 The Mexican Cession comprised of lands ceded by Mexico to the United States
under Article 5 of the Treaty of Guadalupe Hidalgo. Generally they encompassed
the present states within the Greater Southwest of the United States among them
New Mexico, southern Colorado, Arizona, and California, Utah, Nevada and a part
of Wyoming. See Alfredo Jiménez Nuñez, *El Gran Norte de Mexico: Una frontera
imperial en la Nueva España* (1540-1820) (Madrid: Editorial Tébar, 2006), p. 138..
After Texas had been annexed and granted statehood by the United States Congress,
Hispanics there suffered similar inequalities in society and before the law.

370 In the District Court of the First Judicial District of the Territory of New
Mexico within and for the County of Santa Fe, the Albuquerque Land & Irrigation
Co., Plaintiff vs. Tomas C. Gutierres, et al., Defendants. And Tomas C. Gutierres,
et al., Cross-complainants, vs. The Albuquerque Land and Irrigation Co., Cross-
defendants, Judgment, October 13, 1899, Part VII, New Mexico State Record
Center and Archive (Hereinafter cited as NMSRC), Case 858, Box 85.

Overall, Hispanics relied on the Treaty of Guadalupe Hidalgo to protect land and water rights they held prior to and in conformity with the U.S. citizenship rights stipulated in articles 8 and 9. For nineteenth century Hispanics, justice was not always served.

Early in the legal history to enforce the Treaty of Guadalupe Hidalgo, Hispanics asserted their rights as citizens of their newly adopted country, the United States of America. In regard to land issues, Hispanics had filed 1,000 claims by 1880, but the federal government had only considered 150 of them.[371] Many cases, however, were not appealed beyond the jurisdictions of the district courts where, it appeared, justice was final.

Distrust of the court system by Hispanics encouraged the belief that the Anglo-American judicial system — administered by Anglo-American politicians, legislators, and judges — often worked against Hispanic interests to protect themselves under the law, particularly in the district courts. Citizenship rights seemingly guaranteed in Articles 8 and 9[372] of the treaty were not all they seemed. Thus, property rights

---

371 Richard Griswold del Castillo, *The Treaty of Guadalupe Hidalgo: A Legacy of Conflict* (Norman: University of Oklahoma Press, 1990), p. 78.

372 Article VIII is as follows: "Mexicans now established in territories previously belonging to Mexico, and which remain for the future within the limits of the United States, as defined by the present Treaty, shall be free to continue where they now reside, or to remove at any time to the Mexican Republic retaining the property which they possess in the said territories, or disposing thereof and removing the proceeds wherever they please; without their being subjected, on this account, to any contribution, tax or charge whatever.

"Those who shall prefer to remain in the said territories, may either retain the title and rights of Mexican citizens, or acquire those of citizens of the United States. But, they shall be under the obligation to make their election within one year from the date of the exchange of ratifications of this treaty; and those who shall remain in the said territories, after the expiration of that year, without having declared their intention to retain the character of Mexicans, shall be considered to have elected to become citizens of the United States.

"In the said territories, property of every kind, now belonging to Mexicans not established there, shall be inviolably respected. The present owners, the heirs of these, and all Mexicans who may hereafter acquire said property by contract, shall enjoy with respect to it, guaranties equally ample as if the same belonged to citizens of the

of former Mexican citizens in California, Arizona, New Mexico, and Texas proved vulnerable to interpretation by district and territorial courts. Despite their misgivings, Hispanics used the court system for redress of grievances. The Hispanic experience in legal matters, nonetheless, had, by then, been honed by their active participation in the legal systems of Spain and Mexico for more than 200 years.

Between 1849 and 1900, the main issues affecting the lives of Hispanics living in the ceded territories, revolved around articles 8 and 9 of the treaty. These articles pertained to approximately 100,000 Mexicans, including a large number of Hispanicized and nomadic Indians living within the area encompassed by present New Mexico, Arizona, and California.[373] Texas, which became a state in 1845, was theoretically exempted from the treaty's provisions.

Under Article 8, the treaty provided that persons living in the newly acquired territories had one year to elect United States citizenship or after one year they would automatically be considered to have decided to remain within the U.S. domain. They would, according to the provision be free to continue their residency within the ceded territory or move at any time to the Mexican Republic. Those who preferred to remain were given two options: to "retain the title and rights of Mexican citizens, or acquire those of citizens of the United States." The provision specified that property, real or personal, belonging to Mexicans not living in the ceded territory would be inviolably respected. The owners and their heirs, and all Mexicans who would

---

United States."

Article IX is as follows: "The Mexicans who, in the territories aforesaid, shall not preserve the character of citizens of the Mexican Republic, conformable with what is stipulated in the preceding article, shall be incorporated into the Union of the United States and be admitted, at the proper time to be judged by the Congress of the United States to the enjoyment of all the rights of citizens of the United States according to the principles of the Constitution; and in the mean time shall be maintained and protected in the free enjoyment of their liberty and property, and secured in the free exercise of their religion without restriction."

373 Griswold del Castillo, *The Treaty of Guadalupe Hidalgo*, p. 62.

thereafter acquire property by contract in the United States, would be guaranteed rights to their property "equally ample as if the same belonged to citizens of the United States."

Article 9 provided for the protection of property rights. Mexicans living in the said territories would "be maintained and protected in the free enjoyment of their liberty and property." Absentee Mexican landowners holding property in the ceded territories would have their property "inviolably respected." Furthermore, this article reiterated that Mexicans who remained in the said territories "shall be incorporated into the Union of the United States…and be admitted, at the proper time to be judged of by the Congress of the United States to the enjoyment of all the rights of citizens of the United States according to the principles of the Constitution; and in the meantime shall be maintained and protected in the free enjoyment of their liberty and property, and secured in the free exercise of their religion without restriction."

At the onset, the provisions of the treaty conferring citizenship rights on Mexicans living in the ceded territories seemed clear. The evolving practice of denying or suppressing these rights would prove otherwise. In the context of nineteenth century United States, where nativism and racism enjoyed a long history vis-a vis white-black relationships, Hispanics would have to fight for their rights. The struggle took on many forms from armed resistance to alienation with Anglo-American society, to direct involvement using the intervention of the court system in the United States.

Citizenship was the main crux of the provisions of the treaty. Everywhere in the ceded territory, Anglo-Americans who hoped to despoil Hispanic successes to advance their own interests, challenged Hispanic citizenship. In 1869, for example, Pedro de la Guerra, a landholder who had been a signer of the California Constitution, ran for district judge. His right to hold office was challenged on grounds that his citizenship had not been perfected, for he had only elected to become a citizen of the United States as provided by the treaty. His opponents argued that Hispanics were not citizens because Congress had not yet formally granted them citizenship.

In *People v. de la Guerra* (1870), the California Supreme Court ruled in de la Guerra's favor by declaring that the admission of California as a state of the United States conferred citizenship on former Mexican citizens who had remained within the territory as provided in the treaty.[374] Inferentially, the status of the treaty had, in effect, been challenged. The principle was that statehood, as an act of Congress, had with one broad sweep conferred on all legal residents full rights as citizens of the United States.[375]

In New Mexico, it was different. Its territorial status running from 1848 to 1912 created a distinct, yet ethnocentric, ambiance. There, the franchise was limited to Anglo-Americans only. Hispanic New Mexicans attempted to broaden political rights by participating, as members, in the convention of 1849 aimed at drawing up an organic act to create the Territory of New Mexico as a step toward statehood. The majority of delegates were from old Hispano families. Regarding the issue of citizenship, they provided that citizenship should be limited to "free white male inhabitants residing within the limits of the United States, but who [had been residents] on the 2nd

---

374 *Ibid.*, p. 69.

375 *People v. de la Guerra* is significant for Hispanics for at least three reasons. First, it demonstrated their ability to influence the judicial system through the use of the Treaty of Guadalupe Hidalgo. The California Supreme Court's decision to recognize de la Guerra's rights to political office as a new U.S. citizen affirmed the importance of the 1848 Treaty as a vehicle for securing Mexican Americans' rights. Second, the case signified the California Supreme Court's willingness to provide new U.S. citizens protection from discriminatory state policies through the use of federal treaty law without waiting for Congress to act first. Third and finally, *People v. de la Guerra* reminds contemporary human rights activists not to neglect the power of the state court system to secure greater protection for individual rights than the federal government is sometimes willing to grant. Also see, Richard Griswold del Castillo, *The Treaty of Guadalupe Hidalgo: A Legacy of Conflict*. Norman: University of Oklahoma Press, 1990. T. Luna, Guadalupe, "Beyond/between Colors: On the Complexities of Race, the Treaty of Guadalupe Hidalgo and Dred Scott v. Sanford." University of Miami Law Review 53 (1999): 691–716.

day of February 1848."[376] As a compromise, they agreed that former Mexican citizens would be required to take a court-approved oath of affirmation, renouncing their allegiance to the Mexican Republic as a condition of citizenship in the Territory of New Mexico. The U.S. congress approved the statement the following year.[377] In theory, the treaty had promised that they would "in the meantime be maintained and protected in the free enjoyment of their liberty and property, and secured in the free exercise of their religion." But the territorial status granted New Mexico relegated New Mexican Hispanics to a second-class citizenship.

As early as 1848, official efforts were made to remind the general public that Hispanic New Mexicans were U.S. citizens. Other efforts required Hispanics to publicly declare their intent to become citizens of the United States or remain citizens of Mexico. For example, Acting Governor John M. Washington issued a controversial proclamation in April 1848[378] requiring Mexican residents to declare publicly their intent to remain Mexican citizens.

> Whereas, I, John M. Washington, governor of the territory of New Mexico, do hereby ordain, that the clerks of the probate courts in the different counties of this territory shall immediately open, at the prefectures, records, which shall be handed as follows: 'We elect to retain the character of Mexican citizens;' in which those of each county who shall so elect may personally record their names, and those who do not appear and sign said declaration, on or before the thirtieth day of May next, will be, in conformity with the treaty, considered citizens of the United States. Within six days after the thirtieth of May, the record shall be sent, with the certificates of

---

376 Robert W. Larson, *New Mexico's Quest for Statehood, 1846-1912* (Albuquerque: University of New Mexico Press, 1968), p. 19.
377 Griswold del Castillo, *The Treaty of Guadalupe Hidalgo*, p. 70.
378 *George Carter v. Territory of New Mexico* (1859), 1 N.M. 317.

the clerks of the prefectures of the several counties, to the secretary of the territory, that they may be published and distributed to the different tribunals of justice in the territory. Given under my hand and seal, at Santa Fe, the twenty-first day of April, 1848. (Signed) J.M. Washington.'[379]

Generally, however, jurists agreed that such a public declaration was not necessary because the Treaty of Guadalupe Hidalgo had prescribed that permanence in the territory would be sufficient. The Territorial Supreme Court declared that Washington's proclamation on the subject was considered unnecessary because a voluntary, formal, but private, declaration before any court would have been enough.[380]

Others, as in *George Carter v. Territory of New Mexico* (1859), felt, on the contrary, that "The filing of a declaration of intention to become a citizen of the United States by a Mexican who resided in this territory at the date of the Treaty of Guadalupe Hidalgo, is not evidence that such Mexican had previously elected to retain his Mexican citizenship under that treaty." Even so, it was argued that the mere signing of such a declaration would be insufficient, especially in cases where the signatures had not been authenticated or certified in the absence of an appointed deputy.[381]

The issue of such declarations was probed in the District Court case against George Carter.[382] In 1858, Carter was indicted for "assault with intent to kill and murder" Juan Duro. Witnesses stated that on December 31, 1857, George Carter "willfully and maliciously" shot Juan Duro, who was apparently unarmed, at close range, with intent to kill him.[383] The facts seemed clear and straightforward. The Santa Fe

---

379 *Ibid.* 321.
380 *Ibid.* 317.
381 *Ibid.* 317.
382 George W. Carter vs. Santa Fe County District Court, March Term 1858, Criminal, NMSRC, Case 25, Exp. 3. See also, *Carter v. Territory* (1859), 1 N.M. 319.
383 Based on testimony by Jesús María Sena y Quintana, Juan Duro, Jesús María

District Court ordered Sheriff Jesús María Sena y Baca to arrest George Carter on March 18, 1858 and charge him with "assault with intent to kill."[384] The investment in time and money in Carter's trial and appeals would prove costly. To begin, the initial cost to arrest Carter, jail him, and present him at court was $300.[385]

The grand jury members were drawn "from a body of the good and lawful men of the district...elected, empannelled [sic], sworn and charged...to inquire in and for the district...upon their oath at present, that George Carter" had committed the crime.[386] The members of the grand jury were Anastasio Sandoval, Santiago Armijo, Agustín Durán, Juan Felipe Ramírez, Nepomuceno Apodaca, Anisetto Abeyta, Fernando Delgado, Visente García, José Salasar, Ignacio Quesada, Antonio Tafoya, Luis Alarid, Lorenzo Tafoya, Juan Antonio Rodrigues, Marcos Quintana and Francisco Sena.[387]

Presiding Judge Kirby Benedict stated that he had them swear that they

> had resided in the United States since the seventh[388] of February A.D. 1848 and that it is their *bona fide* intentions to become citizens of the United States and to renounce forever all allegiance and fidility [sic] to any foreign Prince Potentate or sovereignty whatsoever and particularly to the Republic of Mexico of which they are subjects, whereupon it is ordered by the court that certificates of their

---

Baca y salazar, and Luciano Ortega Territory vs. Carter, Santa Fe County District Court, March Term 1858, Criminal, (NMSRC), Case 25, Exp. 3.

384 The Territory of New Mexico to the Sheriff of the County of Santa Fe, March 18, 1858 in Territory vs. Carter, Santa Fe County District Court, March Term 1858, Criminal,New Mexico NMSRC, Case 25, Exp. 3.

385 Sheriff's Fee in Territory vs. Carter, Santa Fe County District Court, March Term 1858, Criminal, NMSRC, Case 25, Exp. 3.

386 *Ibid.*

387 "The Defendant also introduces the Record of the District Court of the United States, *Ibid.*

388 He meant to write the 2nd of February, not the 7th.

Declaration be issued to them and that they pay the costs of this Declaration. Said days proceedings was signed.[389]

Judge Benedict added that Anastasio Sandoval was the foreman of the Grand Jury "who found the bill of indictment in said court"[390] against Carter.

Protesting his indictment on grounds that the grand jury foreman was not a U.S. citizen,[391] Carter basically charged that his rights had been violated because he had not been properly accused by a jury of his peers as was the custom. At his arraignment, the court heard Carter's plea "that the territory of New Mexico ought not further prosecute the said indictment against him, because he saith that Anastasio Sandoval, one of the grand jurors who found said indictment, was not at the time of finding said indictment a citizen of the United States, but was...a citizen of the Republic of Mexico, etc. He prayed 'judgment' that he be discharged and dismissed from the premises in said indictment specified."[392] The attorney-general moved that the "issue...be tried by jury." Sandoval was from an old New Mexico family and a relative of Rafael Chacón.[393]

On September 13, 1858, the case was heard, and the jury foreman Gaspar Ortiz y Silva issued the verdict first in Spanish, then in English: "We the jury unanimously certify and sign that we find the accused guilty and impose a fine on him of 60 dollars.[394] Carter's lawyer quickly

---

389 *Ibid.*
390 *Ibid.*
391 *Carter v. Territory* (1859), 1 N.M. 317.
392 Statement signed by George W. Carter *Territory vs. Carter*, Santa Fe County District Court, March Term 1858, Criminal, NMSRC, Case 25, Exp. 3. See also, *Carter v. Territory* (1859), 1 N.M. 319.
393 Rafael Chacón wrote that Anastasio Sandoval "was a relative of mine." Meketa, *Legacy of Honor: The Life of Rafael Chacón*, p. 311.
394 "Nosotros los Jurados Sertificamos y firmamos unánimemente que el acusado lo [h]allamos con culpa y le ymponemos $60 de multa, Septiembre 13 de 1858." Signed by Gaspar Ortis y Silba, Presidente, in *Territory vs. Carter*, Santa Fe County District Court, March Term 1858, Criminal, NMSRC, Case 25, Exp. 3.

issued a plea of abatement and asked the court to rule on the original issue of Sandoval's citizenship.

In the ensuing case revolving around the issue of Sandoval's citizenship, the certified jury members were Bautista Mestas, Juan Romero, Antonio Rivera, Antonio Trujillo, Jesús María de Herrera, Camilo García, Pablo Gonsales, Alejandro Mora, Geronimo Martín, José Salaz, Marcial Prado, and Manuel Aragon. Jury Foreman Jesús María de Herrera read the verdict in Spanish: "Nosotros los del jurado [h]emos opinado unánimemente que Anastasio Sandoval es ciudadano de los Estados Unidos." The verdict was quickly translated "We, the jury, find the issue for the territory in this, that Anastasio Sandoval is a citizen of the United States."[395] Carter's assault case was then continued into the 1859 term.

At his arraignment in the new term, Carter pleaded not guilty to his indictment. In that trial, Carter was found guilty and the original fine of sixty dollars was upheld. Carter's lawyer then moved for a new trial on grounds that "the jury found against the law and the evidence in the trial of the issue upon the plea in abatement, and also upon the final issue of not guilty."[396] The motion was overruled, but the court allowed an appeal, and granted Carter a stay of execution of the sentence.

Apparently, the court preferred to give Carter the benefit of the doubt because

> Such shrinking, however, would be unworthy of the independence and dignity of an intelligent tribunal of justice. We may take judicial notice of the public and notorious acts which constituted a portion of the history of New Mexico during the past thirteen years, and in the midst of these the question of the

---

395 Signed Verdict by Jesus María de Herrera, Presidente in *Territory vs. Carter*, Santa Fe County District Court, March Term 1858, Criminal, NMSRC, Santa Fe, Case 25, Exp. 3. See also *Carter v. Territory* (1859), 1 N.M. 319.
396 *Carter v. Territory* (1859), 1 N.M. 319.

retention of the character of Mexican citizenship has been exciting and disturbing. It is so now, and this fact imposes, in the investigation of this question on its legal merits, the greater labor and care.[397]

The case was reopened to allow the introduction of evidence to prove that Anastasio Sandoval, the grand jury foreman, had in fact retained the character of a Mexican citizen as stipulated in Article 8 of the Treaty of Guadalupe Hidalgo, and had "thereby established his Mexican citizenship and disqualification to serve as a juror."[398] It appeared that the court went through an extraordinary length to serve justice and satisfy Carter's plea.

The court, indeed, undertook an exceptional position to demonstrate to Carter that he had been tried by a jury of his peers. In the best interests of justice, nevertheless, the ensuing arguments labored to indict or, at least, accuse, New Mexican Hispanics of being disloyal to the United States, and that Governor Washington had acted in the best interests of territorial security to weed out disloyal Mexicans.[399] Using the 1849 Taos Rebellion as the prime example to question the loyalty of New Mexican Hispanics, the argument was put forth that

It was now after the peace confirming the conquest and its consequences and engendered among a people foreign in language, laws, customs, and religion, with the pride of kindred and race peculiar to all Spanish races, in the midst of those who had lately, as the Mexican cabinet council said, 'risen against the government and the American name and blood in the country,' and when risen, whose steps and deeds were marked with murder, robbery, and fiendish atrocity in the village of Taos, and who, as the counsel assert, through 'their plans

---

397 *Ibid.* 320.
398 *Ibid.* 320.
399 *Ibid.* 325 and 337.

were discovered and disconcerted, their conspiracies frustrated, did not cease to conspire.[400]

The Taos Rebellion seemed to have spawned a scepter of distrust and disloyalty that followed New Mexican Hispanics in all their undertakings in society inclusive of their role in the Civil War, the Spanish-American War of 1898 and New Mexico's struggle for statehood culminating in 1912.[401]

The court argued that it was necessary to establish certain legal tests that would determine those persons of Mexican allegiance. In subdued but inflammatory language, the judge stated that it was the "imperious duty of Washington to allay the increasing excitement and tranquilize the inhabitants....He was the power to call the excited Mexicans to pause, to consult more calmly and wisely their true interest, and let reason and judgment assume the control of passions and prejudices in the selection to be made between Mexico and the United States."[402]

Returning to the issue at hand, that is, Sandoval's citizenship, the court attempted to ferret out the salient facts revolving around Sandoval's right to serve as foreman of the grand jury that indicted Carter. The court stated,

> it must be borne in mind that the whole effort of the defense was to prove that Sandoval's Mexican citizenship resulted from his having elected to retain it under the treaty. If he was a resident of this territory, as was apparent at the time of the ratification of the treaty, and was so remained, and did not elect in favor of Mexico, then, with this explanation, neither one nor a hundred declarations of intention in the district court would prove him a Mexican citizen, in fact and law. With

400 *Ibid.* 338.
401 Richard Melzer, "Governor Migel Otero's War: Statehood and New Mexican Loyalty in the Spanish American War," *Colonial Latin American Historical Review* [*CLAHR*](Winter 1999), 8:87.
402 *Carter v. Territory* (1859), 1 N.M. 339.

such residence, the presumptions would be in favor of his citizenship to the United States, nor should he lose it or be deprived of it without the clearest proof. He may not have known his rights, or mistaken them, and had a fancy to make them doubly secure. The date at which he did that act, as it seems jointly with fifteen others, does not appear, but it is shown by the record that it was some time during the judicial administration of Chief Justice Deavenport. Sandoval was not defending his own rights of citizenship on the trial, and it is but a reasonable inference that he had perfected his naturalization, even if such in law be needed. The evidence was wholly insufficient to authorize the jury to find in the defendant's favor. They found rightly for the territory.[403]

As the judge's gavel came down, it made a resounding sound, for Carter's conviction was upheld. The price, of course, was the revelation that some nineteenth century Anglo-Americans in New Mexico harbored an intense disdain and distrust of Hispanics and would continue to question their loyalty to the United States. That distrust would hamper Anglo-Hispanic relations, and would affect the ability of Hispanics to progress in all aspects of American life.

What the Territorial Court did not consider is that between 1849 and 1850, local authorities in Territorial New Mexico did everything they could to discourage the out-migration of Mexicans because of the cost of moving them as well as financially disposing of or administering their property within the ceded territory. During that time, 900 New Mexicans had petitioned the Mexican government to move to Chihuahua.[404] Hoping to convince Mexicans to remain

---

403 *Ibid.* 345.
404 Martín González de la Vara, "El traslado de familias de Nuevo México al norte de Chihuahua y la conformación de una región fronteriza, 1848-1854," *Frontera Norte* Vol. 6, Núm. 11 Enero-Junio de 1994, p. 15.

within the territory, authorities argued that the move would result in great inconveniences, suffering and misery. Additionally, their move would take place without the protection of either government against Apache raiders because New Mexicans would be living in isolated areas. Despite Governor Washington's proclamation, Territorial officials "pressured Mexicans not to sign the lists."[405]

Ironically, while the Territorial Court had argued that Mexicans had a choice, officials in the territorial administration sought to convince them not to leave. Notwithstanding the provisions of the Treaty of Guadalupe Hidalgo and Governor Washington's proclamation, the effort to curb their out-migration demonstrated yet another force in keeping New Mexicans within the territory.[406]

The historical conundrum over citizenship rights, as they existed in the post Treaty years of the late nineteenth and early twentieth centuries, made Hispanics wary about how they would be treated in the courts as well as in the territorial political arenas whenever they would present their land grant petitions for approval. In many cases, the land grant issues would be decided in the District Courts where Hispanics would lose their claims to their lands unless they persisted to the higher courts, or made their pleas to the Surveyor General, the Court of Private Land Claims, or Congress, where they cast their lots. Some fared better than others. Even today, the struggle for land grant rights continues.

---

405 *Ibid.*, 6:13.
406 *Ibid.*, 6:15.

Chapter XI
Epilogue

> If your history is not respected, neither will you be
> in education, employment, the workplace, housing,
> justice, law, medicine, banking, the arts or any other
> institution in our society.
>
> — Joseph P. Sánchez

Colorado's Hispanic heritage is longstanding. It is, indeed, a part of our national heritage that is shared with Spain, Mexico and Native American tribes in the region. None really supersedes the other, for they are all a part of making America what it is today. They are all a part of our national story and heritage. The historical process allows for the good and bad, relatively speaking, of the causes and effects, on a multi-factor analytic level, which, in part, explains where we, as a people, are today. The Native Americans have their own story to tell, for while their history is contained within their cultures and beliefs, they lived in a world that was paralleled by the fast moving changes brought about by Spanish, Mexican, and Anglo-American expansions into areas where they lived. Somewhere in the tangled workings of history, their destiny tied into that of the United States.

The history of Hispanic Colorado has taken many turns. Little is known or understood about New Mexico's history prior to the U.S.-

Mexico War of 1846 regarding the development of the area. That history, as reflected in other histories about Spain's settlement of the Americas, is readily seen as if Hispanic came to plunder the area for "God, Glory and Gold," a formula that was created by historians in the nineteenth century that fed into anti-Spanish propaganda fostered by England and other "have-not nations" in the sixteenth century who envied Spain's success.[407] Based on the historical mindset about Spain, which is attributed to the "Black Legend," inadvertent intrepretations of Spanish Colonial history are sometimes made. For example, a current error-filled statement about Colorado's Hispanic history and heritage is advertised on the internet for the world to see by the Zapata Ranch, a Nature Conservancy Preserve in the San Luis Valley.[408] The disparagement of the Hispanic people and

---

407 Joseph P. Sánchez, *Comparative Colonialism, the Spanish Black Legend, and Spain's Legacy in the United States Perspectives on U.S. Latino Heritage and our National Story* (Denver: Government Printing Office), 2013, p. 7 .

408 The Zapata Ranch: A Nature Conservancy Preserve, advertisement, filled with factual errors reads "SAN LUIS VALLEY. Early European explorers, mistaking the plains bison for water buffalo, tried to domesticate the animals. One of the earliest recorded histories of the San Luis Valley includes an account of one such incident. The tale involves Spaniards who entered the Valley around 1599 in search of gold, meat and religious conquest. Upon hearing of the bison in the north, a small party of Spaniards was sent to domesticate the animals. On the East Side of the Valley, The [sic] Ute, who gave an elaborate demonstration of bison hunting, greeted the party. With little knowledge of the temperament of bison, the would-be Vaqueros stampeded a herd of 500 bison. Many of their horses were killed, and the idea of domestication was abandoned.

With winter approaching, the initial friendliness between the Native Americans and the Spaniards deteriorated rapidly. The Spanish needed food and shelter, so they commandeered the Native Americans' corn and enslaved them. For nearly a century the Spaniards enslaved the native peoples. When the slaves finally rebelled, they drove the Spaniards down from the mountains, across the sand dunes, and into makeshift rafts on the Río Grande River.[sic] Francisco Torres, a Catholic missionary had been mortally wounded in the uprising. Too weak to make it into the raft, his dying vision was the mountain peaks tinged blood red by the setting sun. As he lay dying in great pain, he cried out, "Sangre de Cristo!" (Meaning blood of Christ) giving the mountains surrounding the ranch their name." See http://www.zranch. org/index.cfm?id=78c59282-b953-4aa0-bf4ec2b2e24c4d76&history-of-the-ranch. html. Last used on 23 May 2015

culture in the area prevails in the minds of those who believe that Spain was the evil empire and cast as "the citadel of darkness,"[409] in comparison to the "benevolent" English colonies in North America, whose settlers came to do good in a world that does evil. As a consequence, the history of Hispanics in North America is not respected. This in part, contributed to the nineteenth century relationships between Anglo-Americans and Hispanics when it came to property and citizenship rights.

In many ways, within the historical process, Hispanics, in their struggle for property and citizenship rights,through the territorial, state, and federal courts influenced the modern definition of democracy. For sure, with each historical step, the definition of democracy had been expanded by the Treaty of Guadalupe Hidalgo (1848) and its aftermath from the way it was considered in 1789. Certainly, by 1868, with the promulgation of the 13th Amendment the definition of democracy had moved a long way from slavery and pointed to promises that would be made in the 14th Amendment in 1868. By the beginning of the twentieth century, womens' right to vote would touch a cord with other such rights by the 1960s. Thus, democracy is ever changing. Hispanics have contributed to America's national story in many ways.

Today, the U.S. federal government has responded to the preservation of Hispanic heritage in the San Luis Valley and other places in southern Colorado. The Trujillo National Historic Landmark focuses on that very important chapter of the Hispanic heritage and settlement in Colorado. Not only does the Trujillo Homestead commemorate the Hispanic settlement of the area, it celebrates the genealogical history

---

409 In *Pioneers of France in the New World* (1881), Francis Parkman wrote eloquently but falsely, for example: "The monk, the inquisitor and the Jesuit were lords of Spain – sovereigns of her sovereign, for they formed the dark and narrow mind of that tyrannical recluse. They had formed the minds of her people, quenched in blood every spark of rising heresy, and given over a noble nation to a bigotry blind...as the doom of fate. Linked with pride, ambition, avarice, every passion of a rich, strong nature, potent for good and ill, it made the Spaniard of that day a scourge as dire as ever fell on man...Spain was the citadel of darkness..." in Sánchez, Comparative Colonialism, p. 22.

of the Trujillos, Luceros, and other Hispanics who lived in similar settlements. The Sangre de Cristo National Heritage Area commemorates the Hispanic settlement pattern in the area and tells about the Hispanic and Anglo-American agricultural communities and ranches within the original Sangre de Cristo Land Grant. Bent's Old Fort National Historic Site is an another important part of southern Colorado's history as it pertains to its Hispanic heritage and immigration from the United States during the Mexican Territorial Period. Significantly, the Old Spanish Trail National Historic Trail exemplifies the history of New Mexican Hispanics blazing the original routes aimed at establishing a trade route to California, which was achieved in 1829 by Antonio Armijo and his men. Old Spanish Trail in many ways represents early Spanish exploration, trade, migration, and settlement of southern Colorado and Utah. As an iconic event, Old Spanish Trail National Historic Trail catapults Hispanic heritage onto our national story for it represents exploration, pioneering, trade and immigration not only among Hispanics but of Anglo-Americans as a part of western expansion of the United States in the nineteenth century.

Sometimes the preservation of heritage and the conservation of the land is bitter-sweet. Millions of acres that were once considered to be a part of the land grant heritage of Hispanics are tied to state and federal lands. Lands managed by federal agencies, for example, are tied to national interests and are done so in the name of preservation of public lands. In southern Colorado, some of them are a part of the history of the land grants and Hispanic Heritage. They include, for example, the Río Grande National Forest, the Uncompahgre National Forest, Gunnison National Forest, Uncompahgre National Forest and Grand Mesa National Forest as well as Northern Río Grande National Heritage Area, Great Sand Dunes National Monument and Black Canyon of the Gunnison National Monument managed by the National Park Service, inclusive of other agencies that, in many ways, preserve the history and place names made by New Mexican Hispanics since the sixteenth century as well as the Hispanic heritage that forms our national patrimony.

230

Early Hispanic Colorado, 1678-1900 narrates a part of the history, heritage and preservation of our national patrimony as a part of the American story, for much of the Hispanic heritage in southern Colorado is tied to the land and its history. In the best spirit of telling how our nation came to be, it was forged by Hispanic, Anglo-American and Native American peoples, who share a common history with Mexico and Spain.

Appendix A

Mexican National Government Decree of August 18th, 1824[410]

Article

1. The Mexican Nation offers to foreigners who may come to establish themselves in its territory, security in their persons and in their property; *provided* they submit to the laws of the country.

2. The object of this law is those lands of the Nation, which not being private property nor belonging to any corporation or town, can be colonized.

3. For this purpose the Congresses of the States shall enact, as soon as possible, laws or regulations for the colonization of their respective demarcations, in strict conformity with the Constitutive Act, the general Constitution and the rules established in this law.

4. The Territories* comprised within twenty leagues of the boundaries of any foreign nation, or within ten litoral leagues, can not be colonized without the previous approval of the supreme general executive power.

---

410 Comp. Laws, Vol., I, page 712, No. 416 in Matthew G. Reynolds, *Spanish and Mexican Land Laws: New Spain and Mexico.* Buxton & Skinner Stationery Co. St. Louis, Missouri, 1895, pp. 121-122.

5.   If, for the defense or security of the Nation, the Government of the Federation should see fit to use any portion of these lands to construct warehouses, arsenals or other public buildings, it may do so with the approval of the General Congress, and in its recess, with that of the Council of Government.

6.   Prior to four years after the publication of this law, no tax whatever shall be levied on the entry of the persons of foreigners who may come to establish themselves for the first time in the Nation.

7.   Prior to the year 1840, the General Congress shall not prohibit the entry of foreigners to colonize, unless imperious circumstances force it to do so with respect to the individuals of some particular nation.

8.   The government, without prejudice to the purpose of this law, shall take such precautionary measures as it may consider convenient for the security of the Federation, with respect to foreigners who may come to colonize.

9.   In the distribution of lands, preference shall be given to Mexican citizens, and no distinction shall be made between them, except that only to which their individual merits and services to the country entitle them, or in equality of circumstances, residence in the place to which belong the lands to be distributed.

10.   Soldiers who, in accordance with the offer of March 27th, 1821, are entitled to lands, shall be attended to in the States, upon presentation of the warrants the Supreme Executive power shall issue them for the purpose.

11.   If, by the decrees of capitalization, according to the probabilities of life the supreme executive power should consider it advisable to alienate any portions of land in favor of any employees whatever, military or civil, of the Federation, it may do so from the public lands in the territories.

12.   It shall not be allowed that more than one square league of one hundred varas** of irrigable land, four of temporal*** land, and six of range land, be united as a property in a single hand.

13. New Settlers shall not dispose of their property in mortmain.

14. This law guarantees the contracts contractors may make with the families they bring at their own expense; provided they are not contrary to the laws.

15. No one who acquires property on lands by virtue of this law can retain them, if domiciled and residing outside of the territory of the Republic.

16. The government, under the principles established in this law, shall proceed to the colonization of the Territories of th Republic.

*Reynolds: "The word 'territorio,' in this article, evidently means 'land.'"

** Reynolds: "This is an error. A square league of land contains twenty-five million square varas."

***Reynolds: "The term, 'tem-por-al' accented on the last syllable, is applied to lands that are not irrigated, but depend on the seasons to produce a crop."

Appendix B
Regulations for the Colonization of the Territories
November 21st, 1828[411]
General Provisions

Regulations for the colonization of the Territories of the Republic.

It being provided in Article 14 of the general Colonization Law of the 18th of August, 1824, that the government, under the principles established in said law, proceed to the colonization of the Territories of the Republic, and it being opportune to give to said article the most punctual and exact compliance, to enact some general provisions to facilitate its execution in the cases that may arise, the President has been pleased to adopt the following articles:

1. The Political Chiefs of the Territories are authorized, under the law of the General Congress of the 18th of August, 1824, and under the conditions that will hereafter be stated, to grant the public lands of their respective Territories to the contractors, families or private persons, Mexicans or foreigners, who may apply for them, for the purpose of cultivating them and living upon them.

2. Every applicant for land, whether contractor, head of family or private person, shall apply to the Political Chief of the respective Territory, with an application in which is given his name, country, profession, the number, nature, religion and other circumstances of the families or persons whom he desires to colonize, and shall also mark as distinctly as possible and describe on a map the land he applies for.

3. The Political Chief shall proceed immediately to obtain the necessary information as to whether or not the conditions required

411 Code of Colonization, Mexico, 1893, Page 237, No. 71 in Matthew G. Reynolds, *Spanish and Mexican Land Laws: New Spain and Mexico*. Buxton & Skinner Stationery Co. St. Louis, Missouri, 1895, pp. 141-142.

by said law of the 18th of August are found in the application, both as regards the land and the applicant, either that this latter be attended to simply or that he be preferred, and shall at the same time hear the respective municipal authority as to whether any objection or not is found to the grant.

4.   In view of all of which the Political Chief shall grant or not said application, in strict conformity with the law applicable to the matter, especially with that of the 18th of August, 1824, already cited.

5.   The grants made to private persons or families shall not be held to be definitely valid without the previous consent of the Territorial Deputation, for which purpose the respective proceedings shall be forwarded to it.

6.   When the political Chief shall not obtain the approval of the Territorial Deputation, he shall report to the Supreme Government, forwarding the proceedings in the matter for its consideration.

7.   Grants made to contractors for the colonization of many families shall not be held to be definitely valid until the approval of the Supreme Government is obtained, to which a report of the Supreme Government is obtained to which a report shall be made and the proceedings forwarded, together with the statement that may appear proper to the Territorial Deputation.

8.   The grant asked for being definitely made, a document signed by the Political Chief shall be issued to serve as a title to the party in entire conformity with the provisions of the laws, in virtue of which the possession shall be given.

9.   The corresponding entries of all the applications presented and grants made shall be made of the lands that shall be granted and a detailed report shall be forwarded to the Supreme Government every quarter.

10. No stipulation shall be admitted for a new settlement unless the contractor obligates himself to furnish at least twelve families as settlers.

11. The Political Chief shall set a reasonable time for the settler, within which he must necessarily cultivate or occupy the land in the terms and with the number of families which he has stipulated, in the intelligence that if he does not do so, the grant of the land shall be void, but the Political Chief may, nevertheless, re-evaluate it in proportion to the part in which the party in interest has complied.

12. Every new settler, after he has cultivated or occupied the land under his stipulation, shall be careful to so show to the municipal authority, in order to consolidate and secure his right to the property to enable him to freely dispose thereof, after the proper record has been made.

13. The aggregation of many families in the settlement, in its formation, internal government and police, shall follow the rules established in existing laws for the other settlements of the Republic, special care being taken in new settlements that they be constructed with the regularity possible.

14. The minimum of irrigable land that may be given for colonization by a single person shall be two hundred varas in a square; the minimum of grazing land shall be one thousand two hundred varas.

15. The land that may be given for a building lot shall be one hundred varas.

16. The vacant tracts that may exist between colonized lands may be distributed between adjoining holders, who have cultivated their own lands with application and have not received the full extent of land the law allows, or the children of said holders who apply for them to consolidate the properties of their families, bearing in mind therefor the morality and industriousness of the parties in interest.

17. In the territories where there are missions the lands occupied by them cannot be colonized at present, and until it is decided whether they should be considered as the property of the settlements of the Neophytes, Catechumens and Mexican settlers.

Bibliography

DOCUMENTARY SOURCES:

Albuquerque, New Mexico. University of New Mexico Microfilm. Francisco Trebol Nabarro, governador ynterino y comandante general de este reyno de Nuevo Mexico por el Señor Comandante General Caballero de Croix, Bando, 13 September 1778, Spanish Archives of New Mexico (SANM), II, Microfilm Roll 10, frame 1055.

Proceeding (fragment) in a suit against [settlers of Abiquiú] for having traded with the Utes without permission, 3 February 1783, SANM, II, Microfilm Roll 11, frame 520.

Proceedings against Salvador Salazar, Santiago Lucero and Francisco Valverde, 22 April to 9 May 1785, SANM, II, Microfilm Roll 11, frame 853; Proceso contra Vicente Serna y los demas que expreza por infraciones del comercio del pais de los Yutas gente relados en la conformidad que refiere #920, 31 March to 29 April 1785, SANM, II, Microfilm Roll 11, frame 837.

Proceso contra Marcelino Mansanares y demas que espresa por infracciones del comercio en el pais de los Yutas, y sentenciados como se refiere, 10 April 1785, SANM, II, Microfilm Roll 11, frame 845.

Proceedings against Cristóbal Lovato, et al, Río Arriba, 2 August to 2 September 1797, SANM, II, Microfilm Roll 14, frame 112.

Father José Vela Prada, Custos, to Governor Real Alencaster, Abiquiú, 18 August 1805, SANM, II, Microfilm Roll 15, frame 780.

Governor Real Alencaster to Comandante-General Salcedo, 1 September 1805, SANM, II, Microfilm Roll 15, frame 810.

Proceedings against Miguel Tenorio, et al, Río Arriba 6 September 1813, SANM, II, Microfilm Roll 12, frame 783; Ritch Papers.

Orders from Albino Pérez, 16 October 1835, Roll 2, frame 153; Mexican Archives of New Mexico (MANM) Benjamin Read Papers, Roll 24, frame 807; Ritch Papers.

Depositions and certificates testifying to the loyalty of Donaciano Vigil in the fight with the insurrectionists in August 1837, MANM, Roll 24, frame 169.

Madrid, Spain. Archivo del Servicio Histórico Militar. Diarios de reconocimientos de una parte de la América Septentrional española, 1766. Juan María Antonio Rivera's Journals of June 1765 and November 1765 are contained therein.

Madrid, Spain. Real Academia de la Historia. Colección Muñoz, 9/4873. Capitulo 11, Del Principio de la Cristianidad de esta Pimería Progressos y Contradicciones que ha tenido, y estado que al presente tiene.

Madrid, Spain. Real Academia de la Historia. Colección Muñoz. Carta del Padre Fr. Carlos Delgado al Reverendo Padre Comisario General, Fr. Pedro Navarrette, Misión de la Isleta, Junio 18 de 1744.

Madrid, Spain. Real Academia de la Historia. Colección Muñoz. Dictamen del Padre [Alonso de] Posada, Año de 1686.

Sevilla, Spain, El Virey de Nueva España Conde del Venadito continua dando cuenta de las novedades ocurridas en las costas y Provincias internas de aquel Reyno, 30 de Noviembre de 1818, Archivo General de Indias, Sección Estado, Legajo 33.

Sevilla, Spain, Plan de la tierra que se anduvo y descubrió en la campaña que hizo contra los comanches el teniente coronel Don Juan Bautista de Anza, governador y comandatee propietario de est provincia de Nuevo México y la victoria que consiguió de los enemigos, AGI, Mexico 577. Also, Albuquerque, Spanish Colonial Research Center, SCRC-ITEM 176. NEW MEXICO

Upper Río Grande & Southern Colorado,Plan of the campaign of Don Juan Bautista de Anza against the Comanches, 1779

Mexico City. Archivo General de la Nación. Sección Historia, Tomo 395, pt. 6, folio 1, numero 161. Diario y derrotero de lo caminando visto, y observando en el discurso de la visita general de presidios situados en las Provincias Internas de Nueva España que de orden de su Magestad executó D. Pedro de Rivera, Brigadier de los Reales Ejércitos, 1736; Archivo Historico de la Nación. Ramo de las Provincias Internas, tomo 47, folio 263. Juan Bautista de Anza, Hoja de Servicios, 1767.

Santa Fe, New Mexico. New Mexico State Archives and Record Center. Spanish Archives of New Mexico. Francisco Cuervo y Valdés, Bando, Santa Fe, 5 August 1705, #118.

Juan Ignacio Flores Mogollon, Bando, Santa Fe, 16 December 1712, #185; *Alcalde mayor* of Taos, Bando, 9 September 1725, #339.

Juan Domingo Bustamante, Bando, Santa Fe, 17 September 1725, #340; Francisco Marín del Valle, Bando, 26 November 1754, #530.

Proceso contra Juan Baldes, genízaro, May 1762, #548; The Prince Papers: Contemporary New Mexicans.

J.M. Chávez #4. "A Famous Centenarian, General José María Chaves of New Mexico. An official under three flags;" Prince Papers.

J.M. Chávez #14. Rosa Chávez to Governor Prince, Abiquiú, New Mexico, 5 December 1902; Prince Papers. Contemporary New Mexicans.

J.M. Chávez #14. Rosa Chávez to Governor Prince, 24 August 1902; Prince Papers, J.M. Chávez #14. "On the Road."

Santa Fe, New Mexico. Archives of the Archdiocese of Santa Fe. General List of Patentes, Patentes 1. Patente de Custos Zavaleta, Santa Fe, 2 July 1700.

Santander, Spain. Archivo Diocesano. Libro de Bautizados, Parroquia Santa María de Treceño, Año 1736 al 1781.

Government Publications:

Old Spanish Historic Trail Feasibility Study and Environmental Assessment, United States Department of the Interior, July 2001.

Sánchez, Joseph P., *Comparative Colonialism, the Spanish Black Legend, and Spain's Legacy in the United States Perspectives on U.S. Latino Heritage and our National Story* (Denver: Government Printing Office), 2013.

Sánchez, Joseph P., Jerry Gurulé, and Mario Milliones, translators, *El Tratado de Guadalupe Hidalgo: Hallazgos y Opciones Posibles Con Respecto a Los Reclamos de Larga Duración de Mercedes de Tierras Communitarias en Nuevo Mexico.* GAO, June 2004.

Treaty of Guadalupe Hidalgo: Findings and Possible Options Regarding Longstanding Community Land Grant Claims in New Mexico. A Report to Congressional Requesters by the United States General Accounting Office (GAO-04-60), June 2004.

BOOKS:

Adams, Eleanor B., ed. *Bishop Tamaron's Visitation to New Mexico, 1760.* Albuquerque: Historical Society of New Mexico, 1954.

_____; and Fray Angelico Chávez, O.F.M., trans. and ed. *The Missions of New Mexico, 1776: A Description by Fray Francisco Atanasio Domínguez with other contemporary documents.* Albuquerque: University of New Mexico Press, 1956.

Bancroft, Hubert Howe. *History of California.* Vol. 3. San Francisco: A.L. Bancroft & Company, Publishers, 1885.

Bolton, Herbert E. *Outpost of Empire: The Story of the Founding of San Francisco.* New York: Alfred A. Knopf, 1931.

_____. *Pageant in the Wilderness: The Story of the Escalante Expedition to the Interior Basin, 1776.* Salt Lake City: Utah State Historical Society, 1950.

_____, ed., *Spanish Exploration in the Southwest, 1542-1706.* New York, Charles Scribner's Sons, 1908.

Brayer, Herbert O., *William Blackmore: The Spanish-Mexican Land Grants of New Mexico and Colorado, 1863-1878* (Denver, 1949), 59-62.

Briggs, Walter. *Without Noise of Arms: The 1776 Domínguez-Escalante Search for a Route from Santa Fe to Monterey.* Flagstaff: Northland Press, 1976.

Burrus, S.J., Ernest J. *Kino and Manje, Explorers of Sonora and Arizona: Their Vision of the Future: A Study of their Expeditions and Plans.* Rome: Jesuit Historica Institute, 1971.

C. de Baca, Vincent, ed. *La Gente: Hispanio History and Life in Colorado.* Niwot: The University Press of Colorado and Colorado Historical Society, 1998.

Carroll, Bailey H.; and Villasana Haggard, J., trans. and eds. *Three New Mexico Chronicles: The* Exposición *of Don Pedro Bautista Pino, 1812; the* Ojeada *of Lic. Antonio Barreiro, 1832; and the additions by Don José Agustín de Escudero, 1849.* Albuquerque: The Quivira Society, 1942.

Carter, Harvey L. "Mariano Medina." In Leroy R. Hafen, *Mountain Men and the Fur Trade of the Far West.* Vol. 8. Glendale: The Arthur R. Clark Company, 1971.

Chapman, Charles Edward. *Founding of Spanish California: The Northwestward Expansion of New Spain.* New York: Macmillan, 1916.

Chávez, Fray Angelico, trans. and Ted J. Warner, editor. *The Domínguez-Escalante Journal: Their Expedition through Colorado, Utah, Arizona, and New Mexico in 1776.* Provo: Brigham University Press, 1977.

Coues, Elliott, trans. and ed. *On the Trail of a Spanish Pioneer: The Diary and Itinerary of Francisco Garcés (Missionary Priest) in His Travels through Sonora, Arizona, and California, 1775-1776.* 3 Vols. New York: Francis P. Harper, 1900.

Covey, Cyclone, trans. *Cabeza de Vaca's Adventures in the Unknown Interior of America.* Albuquerque: University of New Mexico Press, 1961.

Ebright, Malcom. *Land Grant and Lawsuits in Northern New Mexico.* Albuquerque: University of New Mexico, 1994.

Fisher, Lillian Estelle, ed. *Franciscan Explorations in California by Herbert I. Priestly.* Glendale: The Arthur H. Clark Company, 1946.

Forrestal, Peter P., trans. and Cyprian J. Jynch, ed. *Benavides' Memorial of 1630 by Alonso de Benavides.* Washington, D.C.: Academy of American Franciscan History, 1954.

Franke, Louis Gerber, *J. Frank Torres, Crusader and Judge: An Oral History.* Foreward by Marc Simmons. Santa Fe: Sunstone Press, 2007.

Geiger, O.F.M., Maynard. *Franciscan Missionaries in Hispanic California, 1769-1848.* San Marino: The Huntington Library, 1969.

Gregg, Josiah. *Commerce of the Prairies.* Vol. I. Chicago: Press.

Hafen, Leroy R. "Louis Vasquez." In Leroy R. Hafen, *Mountain Men and the Fur Trade of the Far West.* Vol. 2. Glendale: The Arthur H. Clark Company, 1971.

_____; and Ann Hafen. W. *Old Spanish Trail, Santa Fé to Los Angeles: With extracts from contemporary records and including diaries of Antonio Armijo and Orville Pratt.* Glendale: The Arthur H. Clark Company, 1954.

Hallenbach, Cleve. *Alvar Núñez Cabeza de Vaca: The Journey of the First European to Cross the Continent of North America, 1534-1536.* Glendale: 1939.

Hammond, George P. and Agapito Rey, trans. *Narratives of the Coronado Expedition, 1540-1542.* Albuquerque: University of New Mexico Press, 1940.

_____, trans. *The Rediscovery of New Mexico, 1580-1594.* Albuquerque: University of New Mexico Press, 1966.

Hamalainen, Pekka. *Comanche Empire.* New Haven: Yale University Press, 2008.

Himmerich y Valencia, Robert, *The Domínguez-Escalante Journal: Their Expedition through Colorado, Utah, Arizona, and New Mexico in 1776.* Salt Lake City: University of Utah Press, Reprinted 1995.

Hodge, Frederick Webb, George P.Hammond, and Agapito Rey, trans. *Fray Alonso de Benavides' Revised Memorial of 1634.* Albuquerque: University of New Mexico Press, 1945.

Hordes, Stanley M. "A Sixteenth-century Spanish Campsite in the Tiguex Province: A Historian's Perspective," in Bradley J. Vierra, General Editor, *Current Research on the Late Prehistory and Early History of New Mexico.* Albuquerque: New Mexico Archaeological Council, 1992.

Jiménez Nuñez, Alfredo. *El Gran Norte de Mexico: Una frontera imperial en la Nueva España (1540-1820)* Madrid: Editorial Tébar, 2006,

John, Elizabeth A.H. *Storms Brewed in Other Men's Worlds.* College Station: Texas A & M Press, 1975.

Jones, Jr., Oakah L. *Pueblo Warriors & Spanish Conquest.* Norman: University of Oklahoma Press, 1966.

Keleher, William A. *Turmoil in New Mexico, 1846-1868* (Santa Fe: Rydel Press, 1952.

Lecompte, Janet. "Antoine Francois ('Baronet') Vasquez." In Leroy Hafen, *Mountain Men and the Fur Trade of the Far West.* Vol. 7. Glendale: The Arthur H. Clark Company, 1969.

_____. "Marcelino Baca." In Leroy Hafen, *Mountain Men and the Fur Trade of the Far West.* Vol. 3. Glendale: The Arthur H. Clark Company, 1966.

López Tushar, Olibama, *The People of El Valle.* Pueblo: El Escritorio, 1975, reprinted in 1992.

Meketa, Jacqueline Dorgan, editor, *Legacy of Honor: The Life of Rafael Chacón, A Nineteenth-Century New Mexican.* Albuquerque: University of New Mexico Press, 2000.

Milich, Alicia Ronstadt, trans. *Relaciones by Zarate Salmerón.* Albuquerque: Horn & Wallace Publishers, Inc., 1966.

Navarro García, Luis. *José de Galvez y la Comandancia General de las Provincias Internas.* Sevilla: Publicaciones de la Escuela de Estudios Hispano-Americanos de Sevilla, 1964.

Oglesby, Richard E. "Manuel Lisa." in Leroy Hafen, *Mountain Men and the Fur Trade of the Far West.* Vol. 5. Glendale: The Arthur H. Clark Company, 1966.

Priestly, Herbert I., ed. *A Historical, Political and Natural Description of California by Pedro Fages, Soldier of Spain.* Berkeley: University of California Press, 1937.

Reynolds, Matthew G., *Spanish and Mexican Land Laws: New Spain and Mexico.* St. Louis: Buxton & Skinner Stationery Co., 1895.

Russell, Carl P. *Firearms, Traps & Tools of the Mountain Men.* New York: Alfred A. Knopf, 1967.

Salazar de Valdez, Olivama and Dolores Valdez de Pong. *Life in Los Sauces.* Monte Vista: Adobe Village Press, 2005.

Sánchez, Joseph P. *The Río Abajo Frontier, 1540-1692: A History of Early New Mexico*. Albuquerque: Albuquerque Museum History Monogaph Series, 1987, revised second edition 1996.

_____. *Spanish Bluecoats: The Catalonian Volunteers in Northwestern New Spain, 1767-1810*. Albuquerque: University of New Mexico Press, 1990.

_____. "Twelve Days in August: The Pueblo Revolt in Santa Fe." *In Santa Fe: History of an Ancient City*, edited by David Grant Noble. Santa Fe: School of American Research Press, 1989.

Simmons, Marc. *The Little Lion of the Southwest: A Life of Manuel Antonio Chaves*. Chicago: The Swallow Press, Inc., 1973.

_____. *Spanish Government in New Mexico*. Albuquerque: University of New Mexico Press, 1968.

Swadesh, Frances Leon, *Los Primeros Pobladores: Hispanic Americans of the Ute Frontier*. Notre Dame: University of Notre Dame Press, 1974.

Thomas, Alfred Barnaby. *After Coronado: Spanish Exploration Northeast of New Mexico, 1696-1727*. Norman: University of Oklahoma Press, 1935.

_____. *Alonso de Posada Report, 1686: A Description of the Area of the Present Southwestern United States in the Seventeenth Century*. Pensacola: Perdido Bay Press, 1982.

_____, trans. and ed. *Forgotten Frontiers: A Study of the Spanish Indian Policy of Don Juan Bautista de Anza, Governor of New Mexico, 1777-1787*. Norman: University of Oklahoma Press, 1932.

_____. *The Plains Indians and New Mexico, 1751-1778*. Albuquerque: University of New Mexico Press, 1940.

Vierra, Bradley J. "A Sixteenth-century Spanish Campsite in the Tiguex Province: An Archaeologist's Perspective," in Bradley J. Vierra, gen. ed., *Current Research on the Late Prehistory and Early History of New Mexico*. Albuquerque: New Mexico Archaeological Council, 1992.

Warner, Ted J. ed., and Fray Angelico Chávez, trans. *The Domínguez-*

Escalante Journal: Their Expedition through Colorado, Utah, Arizona, and New Mexico in 1776. Salt Lake City: University of Utah Press, reprint 1995.

ARTICLES:

Adams, Eleanor B. "Fray Francisco Atanasio Domínguez and Fray Silvestre Vélez de Escalante." *Utah Historical Quarterly* 44.

Auerbach, Herbert S., trans. "Father Escalante's Journal, 1776-1777: Newly Translated with Related Documents and Original Maps." *Utah Historical Quarterly* 2:1-142.

Bloom, Lansing B. "New Mexico Under Mexican Administration." *Old Santa Fe* II.

Bolton, Herbert E. "In the South San Joaquín Ahead of Garcés." *California Historical Quarterly.*

Burrus, S.J., Ernest J. "Quivira and Teguayo in *The Correspondence of Bandelier and Shea with Collet, 1882-1889.*" *Manuscripta* 11:67-83.

Cutter, Donald C. "Prelude to a Pageant in the Wilderness." *The Western Historical Quarterly* 8:4-14.

Hafen, Leroy. "Armijo's Journal." *The Huntington Library Quarterly* 11:87-101.

Hill, Joseph J. "Spanish and Mexican Exploration and Trade Northwest from New Mexico into the Great Basin." *Utah Historical Quarterly* 3:4-23.

Lawrence, Eleanor. "Mexican Trade Between Sant Fe and Los Angeles, 1830-1848." *California Historical Society Quarterly* 10:27-39.

Olsen, Michael L. and Harry C. Myers, "The Diary of Pedro Ignacio Gallego wherein 400 Soldiers following the Trail of Comanches met William Becknell on His First Trip to Santa Fe," *Wagon Tracks*, Volume 7 November 1992, Number 1.

Richie, Eleanor. "General Mano Mocha of the Utes and Spanish Policy in Indian Relations." *The Colorado Magazine* 9:150-157.

Sánchez, Joseph P. "Año Desgraciado, 1837: The Overthrow of New Mexico's *Jefe político*, Albino Pérez." *Atisbos: Journal of Chicano*

Research. Stanford University, Summer-Fall, 1978:180-191.

Snow, William J. "Utah Indians and Spanish Slave Trade." *Utah Historical Quarterly* 2:68-90.

Taylor, Morris F., "The Two Land Grants of Gervacio Nolan," *New Mexico Historical Review,* April 1972, 47:151-84.

Thomas, Alfred B., translator, "Diary which Second Lieutenant don José María Arce made and copy of other documents, 1818." in "Documents Bearing upon the Northern Frontier of New Mexico 1818-1819, " *New Mexico Historical Review*, 1929, Vol. 4: 157-164.

Tyler, Lyman S. "The Myth of the Lake of Copala and Land of Teguayo." *Utah State Historical Society.* Vol. 20.

Index

Z

About the Author...

Dr. Joseph P. Sánchez retired from the National Park Service in January 2014 after 35 years of service, having also served as superintendent of Petroglyph National Monument (2003-2014). He is also the founder and director of the Spanish Colonial Research Center at the University of New Mexico (1986 to present)and founding editor of the *Colonial Latin American Historical Review (CLAHR)*. Prior to his career with the National Park Service, Dr. Sánchez was a professor of Colonial Latin American history at the University of Arizona, Tucson, where he was also director of the Mexican-American Studies and Research Center. He has taught at the University of New Mexico, Santa Ana College in Southern California and at the Universidad Autónoma de Guadalajara in Mexico.

Dr. Sánchez has presented papers at professional conferences in the United States, Canada, Sweden, Italy, Spain, and Mexico. Throughout his career, he has researched archives in Spain, Mexico, France, Italy, and England, and has published several studies on the Spanish frontiers in California, Arizona, New Mexico, Colorado, Utah, Texas, and Alaska. He has directed and conducted research for a number of studies by the United States Congress which resulted in the designation of several historical roads, including "Camino Real de Tierra Adentro" that runs from Mexico City to Santa Fe, designated a National Historic Trail; "Camino de los Tejas" that runs from Saltillo to San Antonio, Texas, designated a National Historic Trail; and "Old Spanish Trail" that runs from Santa Fe to Los Angeles via southern Utah, also designated a National Historic Trail.

In 2000 he was awarded the Medalla de Acero al Mérito Histórico Capitán Alonso de León by the Sociedad Nuevoleonesa de Historia, Geografia y Estadistica, Monterrey, Mexico. In 2005, he was inducted into the knighthood of the *Orden de Isabel la Católica* by King don Juan Carlos of Spain. From 2006 to 2012, he served on the History Commission of the Instituto Panamericano de Geografía e Historia, headquartered in Mexico City and affiliated with the Organization of American States in Washington, D.C. From 2010 to 2011, the Secretary of the Interior and the Director of the National Park Service named him to serve as chair of the American Latino Heritage Theme Analysis Task Force, charged with determining how Latino themes can be integrated into our national narrative.

CPSIA information can be obtained at www.ICGtesting.com
Printed in the USA
LVOW06s0831170815

450395LV00002B/2/P

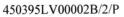